Children's Well-Being: Indicators and Research

Volume 17

This series focuses on the subject of measurements and indicators of children's well being and their usage, within multiple domains and in diverse cultures. More specifically, the series seeks to present measures and data resources, analysis of data, exploration of theoretical issues, and information about the status of children, as well as the implementation of this information in policy and practice. By doing so it aims to explore how child indicators can be used to improve the development and the well being of children.

With an international perspective the series will provide a unique applied perspective, by bringing in a variety of analytical models, varied perspectives, and a variety of social policy regimes.

Children's Well-Being: Indicators and Research will be unique and exclusive in the field of measures and indicators of children's lives and will be a source of high quality, policy impact and rigorous scientific papers.

More information about this series at http://www.springer.com/series/8162

Sabine Andresen • Susann Fegter
Klaus Hurrelmann • Ulrich Schneekloth
Editors

Well-being, Poverty and Justice from a Child's Perspective

3rd World Vision Children Study

Springer

Editors
Sabine Andresen
Department of Education, Institute of Social Pedagogy and Adult Education
Goethe University Frankfurt
Frankfurt am Main, Germany

Susann Fegter
Department of Humanities, Institute of Educational Sciences
Technische Universität Berlin
Berlin, Germany

Klaus Hurrelmann
Hertie School of Governance
Berlin, Germany

Ulrich Schneekloth
Kantar Public
München, Germany

Translated by Jonathan Harrow

ISSN 1879-5196 ISSN 1879-520X (electronic)
Children's Well-Being: Indicators and Research
ISBN 978-3-319-57573-5 ISBN 978-3-319-57574-2 (eBook)
DOI 10.1007/978-3-319-57574-2

Library of Congress Control Number: 2017944443

Printed on acid-free paper

This Springer imprint is published by Springer Nature
The registered company is Springer International Publishing AG
The registered company address is: Gewerbestrasse 11, 6330 Cham, Switzerland

Foreword from World Vision Deutschland e.V.

Once again, the researchers carrying out the Third World Vision Child Study have entered uncharted territory and opened up previously untapped areas for childhood studies. This particularly includes the focus on "justice"—a topic that research in this field is beginning to address only recently. The first two World Vision Child Studies (2007 and 2010) already showed how closely children associate well-being with justice. Even younger children reveal a marked sense of justice. However, they also link justice closely to equal opportunity and equality of treatment—as the present study also shows (see Chap. 2).

The Third World Vision Child Study focuses once again on the *subjective well-being of children* and thereby the world they experience. Well-being is more than just safeguarding *children's rights* and being guided by the *best interests of the child* as understood in legal terms. It is a multidimensional concept containing both *objective* and *subjective* criteria. By asking 6- to 11-year-old children to give their own *subjective* appraisals of their well-being, the child study confirms once again that children are able to give competent and authentic accounts of their own life situation; they are the specialists on their own lives. In addition, the study grants children in Germany a voice that deserves to be heard—not only by parents and teachers but also by academics and politicians. Children need child-oriented surroundings and a child-oriented society.

As the results of the *quantitative* and *qualitative* surveys in this study show, child well-being has much to do with participation in society and how far children are able to participate and to develop their capabilities. The Second World Vision Child Study (2010) already placed great value on the concept of *self-efficacy*, showing how this gains in strength the more children are able to codetermine the environment in which they live. However, the precondition of codetermination is for parents (and other persons involved in rearing and educating children) to take children seriously, to listen to them attentively and honestly, and to devote enough time to them. Here, the study shows once again that when parents have to go to work, this does not necessarily impede the quality of the time and care they devote to their children.

Well-being also involves a fine balance between care and freedom. The children tell us that too many regulations and prohibitions can constrain their well-being. However, the granting of freedom to children can only develop its full potential when they also have the chance to use the existing possibilities to shape their own lives. Here is where we so clearly see that we are living in a four-fifths society in Germany—one in which most children are growing up comparatively contentedly, but one-fifth are living in precarious circumstances and have only very limited possibilities of participating in society.

Poverty and the risks of poverty, the Third World Vision Child Study reveals once again, remain an urgent social problem in Germany. However, child poverty is a multifaceted phenomenon: It is characterized by the constrained financial possibilities of the parents, by their ability or inability to get by with the money available to them, and, above all, by limited participation in social and cultural activities.

The risks that can lead to child poverty include unemployment, single parenthood, a migration background, fear of failure, and parents who lack an educational background and educational aspirations—or a combination of these factors. However, how do children perceive their own poverty? How do they deal with it? How do they cope with poverty and the other constraints to their well-being? When asked, most children place themselves in the middle between poor and rich and indicate that they are fully aware of their responsibility for their own lives. However, whereas some children seem to have an almost fatalistic outlook and simply accept their fate of having limited opportunities, others display an amazing resistance to everyday strains and obstacles. The secret of this *resilience has yet to be worked out in full.*

The World Vision Child Study starts off by reviewing the situation of children in Germany. However, it also aims to go beyond just a review: It should grant the children a voice, give parents and teachers new findings to work with, and point to fields in which policymakers can actively strive to create a society that is friendlier to children. To underline clearly what policymakers need to address, the authors of the study have once again devoted a special chapter to this topic under the heading "Policy for Children" (see Chap. 9). Because poverty and disadvantage affect all areas of life, the challenge for policymakers is to counter the growing social divisions in our society. Poverty is always relative, because exclusion and limited participation are generally perceived to be more painful than mere financial constraints.

When a children's charity such as World Vision, which has predominantly taken up the fight against global poverty, once again addresses the subjective well-being of children in Germany, this is in no way a sign of inconsistency. First of all, in our developmental work throughout the world, the principle of child well-being has become increasingly the decisive criterion for measuring the efficacy of our programs, and, second, the poverty that we have committed ourselves to fight does not respect national borders. The gap between poor and rich no longer runs along the divide between north and south but right through the middle of all societies, and that includes Germany.

At this point, we wish to thank Sabine Andresen, Klaus Hurrelmann, Ulrich Schneekloth, and their research team for their comprehensive and painstaking research along with their competent and careful analyses. We also particularly wish to thank the children and their parents who first made this survey possible. Our wish is that policymakers and the society will hear the voices of these children and strive to create more child-oriented conditions. Indeed, it is only when we can offer children a promising future that this will also come about to the benefit of us all.

World Vision Institute for Research and Innovation
Friedrichsdorf, Germany

Hartmut Kopf
Kurt Bangert

Summary

When asked about their well-being, the great majority of children in Germany give positive or even very positive answers. This reflects the security and care they experience within their own families and the active ways in which their parents attend to their needs. One central aspect in the eyes of the 6- to 11-year-old children in our study is to have their opinions taken seriously and not to be ignored. Other essential aspects for their well-being are their circle of friends, being able to organize their leisure time by themselves, and having a variety of leisure-time pursuits. These are the areas in which children absorb important (informal) learning incentives that extend and substantially supplement the formal education processes they experience at school.

One finding that also stands out in this new 2013 World Vision Child Study is that the social origins of children continue to be a recurring theme in their life situations and the accompanying chances for them to participate in society. The results of the latest 2013 Child Study indicate that it is above all those children coming from the lowest social class[1] who are being broadly left behind. These children are unable to participate adequately in the wide range of services and opportunities available in Germany. Instead, social risks accumulate in their daily lives, and, as a consequence, they are denied their chances of development, capabilities, and thereby life perspectives.

[1] In this study, social class is used in a similar way to socioeconomic status. Our use of this term will be explained in detail in Sects. 1.3 and 3.5.

The Focus on Justice

Equality and Reciprocity as Benchmarks in the Sense of Justice

One of the focuses in this Third World Vision Child Study is on the topic of justice. Children orient themselves strongly toward their need for equality and equality of treatment when they express their sense of justice. This includes not only personal fairness when dealing with others but also being sure that there are equal chances for everybody to join in. This is why they think that goods and opportunities of access should be shared out among themselves. Depending on the situation they are in, children initially favor the principle of equal distribution (equality) in their daily lives, although, generally speaking, only when this is simultaneously accompanied by respect for the principle of reciprocity. If this is not the case, for example, when a few children do not stick to the rules or do not make any contribution themselves, then they also evaluate this as unjust and intolerable. The sense of justice developed by children in this age range has a clearly recognizable altruistic dimension and serves not only their own interests but also the well-being of others. It is interesting to see how the views of children and their desire for justice link up with the debate on social justice. Even in the "grown-up" world, the final concern is "that we share with each other and don't leave anybody just standing there" (girl aged 7 years).

High Level of Satisfaction with Life but with Some "Fine Differences"

More than 90% of the children give positive or even very positive reports on their personal life satisfaction. Indeed, satisfaction even seems to be showing a slight increase. In contrast, 28% of the children from the lowest social class give ratings ranging from negative to neutral and trail notably behind this positive appraisal.

Children Judge Their Own Family and Their Personal Surroundings to Be Just and Germany as Well—Though with Some Reservations

About 90% of children rate the social interaction within their own family and circle of friends as being just, and almost 80% consider social interaction at school to be just as well. Almost 50% consider Germany as a whole to be just, but only 16% think that the world is just. Slightly more than one-quarter of the children were unable to give any answer to these last two questions.

Not Only Lower-Class Children but Also Children with a Migration Background, Children from Single-Parent Families, and Children from Large Families with a Lot of Children Feel Disadvantaged

A total of 44% of the children report disadvantages in daily life—10% frequently and 34% occasionally. Children with the lowest social origins report these by far the most frequently at 68%. Disproportionally frequently, 51% of children with a migration background report personally experiencing disadvantages in their daily lives. The same applies to 51% of the children growing up in single-parent families and 50% of the children from large families with a lot of children.

The latter matches the views of parents: Here as well, it is 51% of single parents who report having difficulties in reconciling family and profession (38% just about okay, 13% less well). Likewise, 32% of parents with three or more children (23% just about okay, 9% less well) report being confronted with difficulties more frequently than average (26% just about okay, 6% less well).

Family and Background

Diversity of Family Lifestyles and the Mothers' Wish to Have a Job

Today's children are growing up in a variety of different kinds of family. Recent years reveal an increasing trend toward more children (in our age range from 6 to 11 years) having two working parents: For 35% of the children (2010, 30%; 2007, 25%), either one parent works full-time, while the other works part-time, or both work part-time. In contrast, at currently 32% (2010, 40%; 2007, 42%), the "classic" single-earner family is in decline. For 13% of the children, both parents work full--time (2010 and 2007, 10%); 12% in single-parent families have a parent in full- or part-time work (2010, 12%; 2007, 10%); 4% have unemployed parents (2010, 5%; 2007, 8%), and, as in the first two surveys, 4% have a parent who is studying, training, or looking after the home without participating on the labor market.

Mothers who work part-time report being most satisfied with their working hours (74% are positive, 8% would like to work more, and 18% would like to work less). However, the majority of mothers who work full-time are also satisfied with their working hours (59% are positive, 35% would like to work less, and 6% would like to work more). The majority of unemployed mothers would also prefer to work part-time (55% prefer part-time, 31% prefer full-time, and 14% say that things are fine the way they are).

Both Children and Parents Consider That Going to Work Is Compatible with Reliable Care for Children

As a trend, children continue to complain most frequently about a lack of care and attention ("Both parents do not have enough time or one parent does not have enough time; the other parent, sometimes yes and sometimes no") when they have either a working single parent (2013, 32%; 2010, 31%; 2007, 35%) or a parent who is unemployed or not working for other reasons (2013, 29%; 2010, 30%; 2007, 29%). However, the proportion of children who lack care and attention when both parents are employed either part- or full-time has remained constant at 8%.

Parents' estimates do not differ from those of their children. Reconciling family and work is most difficult for working single parents (49% just about okay or less well) and also for parents who are unemployed or not employed for other reasons (46% just about okay or less well). Relatively speaking, compatibility is considered to work best in families in which both parents go to work either full- or part-time (27% just about okay or less well).

Experiencing Poverty and Participation Risks Continues to Be an Everyday Reality for Significant Numbers of Children

Eighteen percent of children report personally experiencing poverty: They report experiencing one of the nine indicators of poverty tapped in our survey in their daily lives. Here as well, however, the more frequently that both parents are employed, the lower the risk of poverty.

According to the social class (origins) index developed specially for our child studies, 29% of the children belong to the middle class, 30% to the upper middle class, and 16% to the upper class. This leaves 16% in the lower middle class and 9% in the lower class. Trends indicate that the proportion in the lower middle class is declining slightly (2010, 18%; 2007, 19%), whereas the proportion in the upper classes is rising slightly. The reason for this is above all the improvements in the educational status of parents over time. In contrast, the proportion of children from the lowest and thereby least educated class remains constant at 9%.

The background to this slight general improvement with regard to the risks of poverty and exclusion is naturally the comparatively favorable economic situation and the proportionally low unemployment throughout Northern Europe. This makes it all the more discouraging when looking at the trend since our first child study to see that there have been hardly any changes in the life situation and the poor chances of participation among those children with the lowest social origins. The life conditions of a portion of the children from the lower middle class also continue to be precarious. As a result, it has to be assumed that roughly one-fifth of all children continue to be constrained in their developmental possibilities because of their social origins and are in need of the support of society.

Only 15% of the parents of lower-class children and also a disproportionately low 22% of the parents of lower middle-class children report that their children used to attend a day nursery (middle class, 25%; upper middle class, 31%; upper class, 27%). Earlier attendance of a preschool (kindergarten) is also reported for only 78% of lower-class children. In contrast, more than 90% of children in the lower middle class, as in the other classes, attended a preschool. For the 6- to 11-year-old children in our survey, this information was gathered retrospectively in the parent questionnaire. Nonetheless, it still underlines the importance of a quantitatively adequate, reliable, and simultaneously high-quality institutional care service.

Migration Background

A total of 34% of the children (aged 6–11 years) have a migration background. The majority of these children also have German citizenship and were born in Germany. A migration background is found in 59% of children from the lower class and also a slightly disproportionally high proportion of 41% of children in the lower middle class. Hence, children with a migration background continue to come disproportionately frequently from families of origin with little education. The lower the education in the class of origin, then the likelier it is that the children from migrant families will not speak German at home. Our results showed that 33% of the children with a migration background speak predominantly their parents' mother tongue at home (2010, 33%; 2007, 35%), and here, it is 43% of the children from the lower classes of origin compared to 26% from the upper classes of origin.

School

Hardly Any Changes in the Relation Between Origins and Educational Position of Children

Compared to most other nations, children's academic performance is shaped more strongly by social origins in Germany. Hence, which grade 6- to 11-year-old children attend in school and which type of school they attend are unequally distributed according to social origins. Slightly more than every fifth child surveyed from the lower class is attending a fifth- or sixth-grade class compared to every third upper--class child. Two-thirds of the 6- to 11-year-old children surveyed, and therefore the majority, are still attending elementary school, but the one-third that have already left elementary school are distributed very unequally across the different kinds of secondary school. Whereas the majority of lower-class children are attending the

Hauptschule,[2] the upper-class children are particularly frequently attending a *Gymnasium*. Compared to the last two surveys in 2007 and 2010, this has hardly changed.

Decline in Those Wishing to Complete Their Secondary Education with "Abitur"

Regarding the aspired school-leaving qualifications, the number wishing to complete their secondary education with the university entrance qualification, the *Abitur*, has declined over the years—and this applies to all social classes of origin. Moreover, the ideas about which secondary school-leaving qualification can be attained seem to have become less clear over time, as shown by the increased proportion of "don't know/don't care" responses.

Markedly More Children Attend All-Day Schools

Since the first survey in 2007, the proportion of children attending an all-day school or class has grown markedly. Among the 8- to 11-year-old children, it has almost doubled from 13% in 2007 to 23% in 2013. However, the analyses show that even today, whether a family has a realistic chance of deciding freely in favor of a place in an all-day school depends decisively on where that family lives. In Eastern Germany, almost twice as many children report attending an all-day school in 2013 compared to children in Western Germany (39% vs. 21%).

It Is Particularly Lower-Class Children Who Report Above-- Average Well-Being When They Attend an All-Day School

According to their own reports, the number of lower-class children taking advantage of all-day school provisions is above average at 31%, whereas only one in every five upper-class children spends the whole day at school. In all, we can determine an increasing number of all-day students in all social origin groups in the World Vision Child Studies since 2007. A total of 61% of all-day students are

[2]All children attend elementary school together until the end of fourth grade. On the secondary level (mostly from fifth grade onward), the school system follows three tracks: *Hauptschule*, *Realschule*, and *Gymnasium*. The Gymnasium leads to the highest school-leaving certificate, the *Abitur*. Some of the German states (or Länder) have merged the *Hauptschule* and *Realschule* together. There are also integrated comprehensive schools.

satisfied with this type of school. However, this is the case for only 41% of lower--class children.

Continuing Need to Extend Child Participation at School

Child participation at school differs in its degree and frequency. A total of 40% of all 6- to 11-year-old children do not feel that they have any say in the seven areas we asked them about and feel that they are unable to often have their say in any of these areas. Boys have this impression far more frequently than girls (44% vs. 35%) and, at 57%, 6- to 7-year-old children much more than 10- to 12-year-olds. We already asked about some areas of child participation in the first child study in 2007, and there have been hardly any changes since then.

Justice, Satisfaction, and School

A very large majority of the children surveyed judge their school to be "very fair" (22%) or "quite fair" (56%). Negative reports of "rather unfair" (1%) and "very unfair" (3%) are very rare. However, the sense of justice relates closely to the degree of participation possibilities in the school.

The children's sense of justice also reveals a close relation to general satisfaction with school. Students who find their school to be rather or very unfair are less satisfied with their school in general and vice versa.

A total of 79% of the children talk about their school positively. Compared to 2010, this satisfaction score has increased by 9% and is particularly strong in elementary school children.

Leisure Time

The Use of Computer Games and Game Consoles Remains Constant

From 40% to 50% of 6- to 11-year-old computer users play games on their computer or game console several times a week; about 15% report playing every day, and 30% "not very often" spend their free time playing with computers and game consoles. The trend over the last 6 years indicates that the frequency of use within different age groups has remained broadly stable.

Girls as "All-Rounders," Boys as Media Consumers

As reported already in the last study, girls belong more than three times as often (38%) to the group of all-rounders than boys (12%). Vice versa, boys spend at least three times more of their leisure time (39%) as media consumers than girls (13%). Whereas the latter tend more toward the creative-musical field and have a stronger interest in theater, ballet, and dance as well as reading, their male peers continue to engage particularly frequently in passive media-related activities such as watching television or playing computer games.

Television, Computers, and Reading: Deviating Trends in Different Leisure-Time Groups

Since the First World Vision Child Study, the frequency of television consumption has declined somewhat across all 8- to 11-year-old children. Whereas in 2007, 56% reported watching television very often, this applied to only 48% in 2010 and 49% in 2013. Nonetheless, a more marked decline can be seen above all in the all--rounders from 24% in 2007 to 12% in 2013. In the group of media consumers, television is one of the most frequent leisure-time pursuits for 80–90% of these children. And whereas the reported amount of viewing has declined in all-rounders, it has increased in media consumers.

The use of computer and video games proves to be largely constant across all three child studies (25–30%). However, it differs across various leisure types. Among the all-rounders, the proportion of frequent players has sunk from an already low starting level of 10% in 2007 to 2% in 2013, whereas about 60% of each group of media consumers report playing computer games very frequently.

The proportion of children who read books frequently has declined slightly as a whole. This finding applies to all three leisure types. Currently, 31% of children read very often (2010, 37%; 2007, 34%). However, in the group of media consumers, only 8% read very often in 2013 compared to 61% in the group of all-rounders.

Club Memberships: As Before, Insufficient Integration of Lower-Class Children

According to parents' reports, the proportion of children who belong to at least one club or organized group as well as other provisions (e.g., music school or cultural center) is very high in the upper and upper middle class where it ranges from approximately 80% to over 90%. Middle-class memberships are also constant. Approximately three-quarters of the children from this social class and roughly two-thirds of children from the lower middle class possess at least one membership. In contrast, the proportion of children from the lower class who are members of a club or organized group has remained below 50% in all three child studies and is also subject to strong fluctuations.

The trend indicates a conspicuous decline in memberships of clubs, groups, or musical and cultural provisions among 6- to 7-year-olds. This applies particularly to children from the lower classes. In general, children from the lowest social class still continue to be able to participate to a markedly lesser extent in institutionally organized leisure-time activities, and, at this stage, no change in this trend can be ascertained.

Older Children Are on the Internet, but Access Continues to Be Determined by Social Class

In all, 4% of 6- to 7-year-olds, 11% of 8- to 9-year-olds, and then already 36% of 10- to 11-year-olds report being regularly online every week. Looking at the trend, the proportion of both 6- to 7-year-olds and 8- to 9-year-olds has remained stable and has not grown since 2007. What has increased, in contrast, is Internet use among 10- to 11-year-olds: from 29% in 2007 to 32% in 2010 and 36% in 2013. As a rule, the children are online only from time to time during the week. Just a small minority is online daily or for several hours at a time.

The earlier child studies already showed that children from lower social classes somewhat less frequently have access to the Internet than children from higher classes. The current study also confirms this finding. As a result, a smaller percentage of lower-class children report being regularly on the Internet each week (proportion of Internet use in 10- to 11-year-old children: lower class, 23%; lower middle class, 37%; middle class, 39%; upper middle class, 36%; upper class, 36%). In contrast, however, this class effect disappears when we look only at children who have access to the Internet.

Mobile Phones: Increasingly More Widespread Among Children in General, but Girls Remain in the Lead

The trend toward increasingly more children in this age range having a mobile phone already reported in 2010 has continued in 2013. In 2007, only 17% of 8- to 9-year-olds and 56% of 10- to 11-year-olds had a mobile telephone; in 2010, this rose to 27% and 66%, respectively, and, in the current study, to 31% of 8- to 9-year--olds and 72% of 10- to 11-year-olds. However, even when the proportion of those with a mobile telephone is increasing, boys have not caught up with girls. At 56%, 8- to 11-year-old girls continue to more frequently have their own mobile telephone than boys at 49% (across all age groups together, 42% of the girls and 37% of the boys have a mobile telephone). Another finding that has remained constant since 2007 is that children in single-parent households more frequently have their own mobile telephone (62%) than children in other families (50%).

Satisfaction with Own Leisure Time Continues to Increase

In 2013, only 8% of children give a negative to neutral evaluation of how satisfied they are with the organization of their leisure time; 33% evaluate this as positive and 59% as very positive. This is a slight increase in the very high satisfaction reports in 2010. As before, judgments on satisfaction reveal a clear influence of social origins, with children from the lower class less frequently reporting a very positive judgment and more frequently giving a negative to neutral or a positive judgment than their peers from higher classes. Nonetheless, in this group as well, there is at least a slightly positive trend. Whereas in 2010, 28% of the children with lower-class origins still judged the organization of their leisure time to be negative to neutral, in 2013, this proportion is markedly lower at 17%.

Friends

Less Frequent Personal Contacts During Leisure Time, but the Size of the Circle of Friends Remains Constant

Compared to the two previous child studies, there has been a marked decline in the frequency of personal meetings with friends during leisure time. In both 2010 and 2007, 68% of the children surveyed reported meeting their friends very often, whereas in 2013, this is only 53%. However, this has no effect on the size of the circle of friends. In all three child studies, approximately 40% of 8- to 11-year-olds report having a large circle of friends containing 10 or more peers. Roughly one--half of the children have between four and nine friends, whereas slightly more than 10% report having only a small circle of friends or none at all.

The Size of Circle of Friends Depends on the Leisure Type

Across all three child studies, we can see that media consumers have fewer friends than normal leisure-time users or all-rounders. Only about one-third of this group report having 10 or more friends compared to roughly 35–40% in the other two groups. In line with this, all three child studies show that among 8- to 11-year-old media consumers, the proportion that have only a small circle of friends containing three or less children is higher (17–21%) than that among normal leisure-time users (12–14%) or all-rounders (7–11%).

School and "Outside" Continue to Be by Far the Most Frequent Locations in Which Children Meet Their Friends

Children aged 6–11 years most frequently meet their friends at school (78% just about every day during the week) or outside (17% just about every day and 50% several times a week). Online, 3% of all children meet their friends just about every day (among the 10- to 11-year-olds, 6%), and a further 6% meet their friends online several times a week (among the 10- to 11-year-olds, 14%). In comparison, 2% of all children meet their friends just about every day in a club and a further 41% several times a week there.

Contact with Friends Over the Internet: Chat Lines Are Losing Their Popularity—In Favor of Social Networks

Among the 8- to 11-year-olds in the survey, the use of chat lines has lost its popularity since 2007. Probably the reason for this decline is not that children are less interested in using the Internet for social contacts but the increasing popularity of other social networks such as Facebook. These are already used by a total of 15% of the oldest respondents (10- to 11-year-olds).

Being Well Regarded by One's Circle of Friends

The majority of children see themselves as being well regarded in their circle of friends, and this positive impression has increased since 2007. In the first child study, 43% of the 8- to 11-year-olds reported that their opinion was quite well regarded in their circle of friends. In 2010, this rose to 45% of 8- to 11-year-olds, and in 2013, it is now 53%.

Codetermination and One's Own Opinion

Opportunities for Self-Determination in Daily Life: Still Limited for Lower-Class Children

Children have different opportunities to shape their daily lives for themselves. The most possibilities of codetermination are given to them in the family and have to do with their leisure time and their circle of friends. Here—depending on age—almost 90% of children themselves decide which friends they meet and what they do in their leisure time. On the other hand, two out of every three children are told when to do their homework by their parents, and every second child cannot decide for her or his self how many other children she or he may bring back home.

Children from the lower class have the least possibilities of self-determination in daily life. Only three out of every four children, and thereby far fewer than the average, can themselves decide which friends they want to meet, and also only two out of every three children report that they themselves can decide what to do in their leisure time. Another restriction to the possibilities of self-determination is deficits in care. Having parents with little time for their children is accompanied, from the child's perspective, by stricter rules and regulations in daily life. Independent of this, children with a migration background—regardless of gender—report being subject to comparatively stricter regulation. The same applies, though to a markedly lesser extent, to children from families with lots of children.

Some of these limitations relate to a lack of household resources. On the other hand, (class-specific) differences in child-rearing styles also manifest here.

Children with Lower Possibilities of Self-Determination in Daily Life Perceive Less Codetermination at School

Possibilities of self-determination in daily life and codetermination at school go hand in hand. On the one hand, this naturally relates to the children's age. However, the class of origin also functions as a selection mechanism here. Children who attend one of the two higher secondary schools, a *Gymnasium* or a *Realschule*, are offered far more possibilities of codetermination both in daily family life and at school. Here as well, the class of origin controls daily life and the children's scope of action.

Remarkably, the relation between class of origin and experience of codetermination can already be traced in elementary school children, though to a lesser degree. The social class effect here has two causes: first, the social homogeneity in the residential zone within which children are assigned to a specific elementary school and, second, the role of personality characteristics. Self-confident and "self-efficacious" children will tend to demand more codetermination than children coming from milieus offering them hardly any possibilities of codetermination.

Personal Opinions Are Taken Slightly More Seriously in the Family and Circle of Friends and Slightly Less Seriously at School and in Institutions

As a trend, children's reports indicate an increase in how far their personal opinions are taken seriously in the family and also in the circle of friends. Currently, 60% report that their mothers take their personal opinions rather more seriously (2010, 57%; 2007, 56%). Among fathers, 49% value the opinions of their children rather more seriously (2010, 48%; 2007, 47). About one-quarter of the children replied with "sometimes one, sometimes the other" and about 10% (9% for the mother and 13% for the father) with "generally less"; the rest gave no reports on this. Regarding the circle of friends, a rise to 51% of the children reported that their opinions were taken more seriously (2010, 42%; 2007, 43%).

In contrast, only 29% of the children still reported that their class teachers tended to take the children's opinion more seriously. In 2010, this was 32% and, in 2007, 26%. Findings are similar for children attending a care institution such as a daycare center. According to the children's reports, 33% take the children's opinion more seriously (2010, 36%; 2007, 24%).

Once again, effects of class of origin emerge here. A total of 16% of lower-class children report that their mothers do not take them seriously, and even 31% give explicitly negative reports on their fathers. It is also notable that 19% of the children with a migration background compared to 10% of the native German children evaluate being taken seriously by their fathers negatively, whereas there are no significant differences regarding reports on the mothers. Here as well, this underlines the significance of the parental child-rearing style.

World Vision Child Study 2013

The Third World Vision Child Study surveyed a nationally representative sample of 2535 children aged 6–11 years. The children were assessed personally through oral surveys in their homes. These surveys took an average of 35 min. At the same time, one parent was also asked to provide supplementary information on the origins and social situation of the family. The qualitative part of the study was based on 12 interviews with children in this age range lasting between 1.5 and 3 h. Detailed accounts of the children interviewed in the qualitative part are presented as individual portraits.

Contents

Chapter 1
How Children See Well-Being, Poverty, and Justice: The Focus of the Third World Vision Child Study

Sabine Andresen, Susann Fegter, and Klaus Hurrelmann

1.1 The World Vision Child Studies and International Childhood Research

The World Vision Child Studies have just one basic philosophy: to give a voice to children in Germany. These studies view children as the experts on the world they live in: on their feelings, opinions, and experiences. Of course, it goes without saying that mothers and fathers, brothers and sisters, grandparents, childcare workers, sports coaches, and teachers are all experts as well, and they can tell us a lot of what they know about children and childhood. However, it is now widely accepted that the adult perspective on childhood and adult knowledge about children should not be taken to be all-powerful and that it is important to view the children themselves as informants and interpreters of childhood and being a child.

The First World Vision Child Study in 2007 presented and substantiated this theoretical and methodological approach in some detail (Andresen and Hurrelmann 2007). One of the findings emphasized in 2007 has had a notable impact both in Germany and abroad: the notable gaps the study revealed in what we know about middle childhood, that is, children between the ages of 6 and 11 years. The World

S. Andresen (✉)
Department of Education, Institute of Social Pedagogy and Adult Education,
Goethe University Frankfurt, Frankfurt am Main, Germany
e-mail: S.Andresen@em.uni-frankfurt.de

S. Fegter
Department of Humanities, Institute of Educational Sciences,
Technische Universität Berlin, Berlin, Germany
e-mail: fegter@tu-berlin.de

K. Hurrelmann
Hertie School of Governance, Berlin, Germany
e-mail: hurrelmann@hertie-school.org

S. Andresen et al. (eds.), *Well-being, Poverty and Justice from a Child's Perspective*, Children's Well-Being: Indicators and Research 17,
DOI 10.1007/978-3-319-57574-2_1

Vision Child Studies have contributed to closing these gaps. Together with other studies in Germany, above all, the Kinder-Panel and the AID:A Studie (both from the German Youth Institute), the KIGGS childhood health study (Robert Koch Institute), and the Robert Bosch Stiftung's (2012) study on child well-being, we now have a range of well-designed surveys addressing this age group.

What is the state of international childhood studies in 2013 and how does the Third World Vision Child Study relate to this research? These are the questions we want to address in this introductory chapter. We shall start by positioning our approach within national and international research on child well-being. Although we have been looking at child well-being continuously ever since our First Study, there have been further developments in this field since the Second Study in 2010. These are presented in Sect. 1.2 and continue the theoretical discussion to be found in the Second Study (Andresen et al. 2010).

A further important topic is the situation of children living in poverty. The First World Vision Child Study in 2007 highlighted the effects of child poverty in Germany. Our findings attracted a lot of public attention and led many people to ask how the children themselves experience it. When we started to plan the Second Study, such reactions encouraged us to focus more strongly on how children living in Germany actually perceive poverty themselves. In the Third Study presented here, we also deal intensively with the social differences that children experience in Germany and take a closer look at the effects of poverty from the children's perspective. This is another field in which there have been advances in the discussion in research, politics, and education since 2010. In Sect. 1.3, we shall discuss recent poverty research in detail.

It is particularly children from families with a migration background along with those whose parents have low educational qualifications who are subject to poverty. Therefore, in Sect. 1.4, we shall consider what has now become an established statistical concept in Germany: a migration background. This concept, which offers an improved way of distinguishing the diverse experiences of migration to be found in the population of Germany, is also important when surveying children. Many a child who is assigned a migration background has been born in Germany and often has German nationality. Nonetheless, it is assumed that, for example, the experiences of parents or grandparents as immigrants can have specific effects on their child born in Germany. We examine these relationships while also considering the international discussion on these topics. This should make poverty and migration visible as possible experiences of children and as a part of their family history.

The Third World Vision Child Study also broadens the range of the two previous studies and examines the children's sense of justice. What children require for a good and thereby a just life is certainly something they frequently think about themselves. In our previous studies, we noticed that whenever we asked children about their values or to tell us what a good life means for children regardless of where they are growing up, their answers always addressed the core of the debates to be found in justice theory. Children want to have their say here, and they have something to say. In the Third Study, we explicitly address the topic of justice and report on the children's sense of justice and how they judge injustice and inequality. This opens up a new field of research in both national and international childhood studies. Section 1.5 reports on how we position our study within interdisciplinary research on justice and the justice discussion that is frequently philosophical in nature. In the final Sect. 1.6, we present some comments on our methodological approach.

1.2 Well-Being as a Concept in Childhood Studies and its Application in the Third World Vision Child Study

Like the past two studies in 2007 and 2010, the present study addresses the concept of well-being. Although it also integrates new discussions and findings in this field, our basic understanding remains unchanged: Once again, we are interested in finding out about not only the subjective appraisals of our respondents but also their specific social framing conditions. Having now carried out three studies in a row, we are also in a position to compare the well-being and satisfaction of children in Germany across time. One finding we can report straight away: In 2013, just as in the two prior studies, overall well-being continues to be mostly very high. Nonetheless, those children who are exposed to poverty frequently belong to the group whose well-being is limited.

The concept of well-being does not just link up to academic issues but also to political and educational practice. In general, one can define well-being by saying that it stands for a comprehensive understanding of the qualities of a child's life situation, welfare, and participation in society. Hence, well-being goes far beyond the "best interests of the child." This latter concept focuses predominantly on protecting children, whereas well-being also includes children's rights and thereby their participation in society along with their capabilities. This shifts attention to children as subjects with their own rights. As such, children do, of course, depend on the care, protection, and education provided by adults, but they also have their own autonomous status. A further trend revealed by the present study illustrates this clearly: In 2013, as in the previous studies, one major aspect that continues to contribute to the well-being of children is a measured balance between care and freedom in everyday life (Andresen et al. 2012).

In general, research on child well-being is embedded in a tradition of striving to make societies more child-friendly.

1.2.1 Dimensions and Indicators: The Study Design

Generally, well-being is conceived as a multidimensional concept (Minkkinen 2013). This means that it is composed of several dimensions such as material resources, education, health, and relationships. Whereas the dimensions define and systematically frame the concept of well-being as a whole, the single indicators assigned to each dimension serve to specify and measure well-being. For example, one possible indicator for education is the proportion of 15-year-olds attending the highest level of secondary school in a nation. Hence, this refers to the objective framing conditions of childhood in a nation and it considers who profits in what way from, for example, the given educational provisions.

Only recently, two well-being researchers in the United States, William O'Hare and Florencia Gutierrez (2012), collected and examined all available studies so far that have applied an index of well-being. Their overview reveals the growing interest in constructing dimensions and indicators of child well-being. Nonetheless, the authors also showed that the concept is used in a broad range of ways. Indeed, just about every research team has put together its own different set of dimensions and indicators.

One reason for this heterogeneity is the political interest in obtaining practical facts and statements. Important actors here are not only the major international organizations such as the United Nations and its subsidiary organization UNICEF, the World Health Organization (WHO), and the Organization for Economic Cooperation and Development (OECD) but also national foundations. They frequently work with comprehensive instruments to measure well-being. For example, since 2007, UNICEF has been carrying out regular studies of the well-being of children in 29 wealthy industrialized nations. In addition, UNICEF's annual report on the State of the World's Children also addresses aspects of well-being in all regions of the world. In 2013, for instance, it focused on children with disabilities (UNICEF 2013). Very recently, UNICEF presented new data on well-being in wealthy societies in its Report Card 11. These findings were based on an analysis of overall satisfaction in 11-, 13-, and 15-year-old children in studies carried out by the "Health Behaviour in School-aged Children" (HBSC) team.

The approach taken in the UNICEF study on the well-being of children in wealthy countries has had many imitators. These have formulated dimensions of well-being and developed indicators to measure it. Nowadays, many researchers are also focusing on the dimension of subjective well-being, because results have shown the need to pay attention to not only objective social framing conditions but also the way they are perceived subjectively—especially when studying children.

1.2.2 Subjective Well-Being: The Children's Own Evaluations

One major advance has been the intensive work on determining the role of the important dimension of subjective well-being and how it should be measured. This has also drawn on established psychological research into, for example, the "quality of life." There are now many studies addressing the assessment of subjective well-being. The UNICEF studies also work with this dimension, and they have analyzed it in depth in their latest Report Card 11. This uses an index to assess subjective well-being as broadly as possible. The index covers overall life satisfaction, close relationships with parents and peers, general well-being at school, and subjective health reports. In the near future, there will certainly be a need for further studies, including international comparisons, in order to further clarify the state of subjective well-being in children (Bradshaw et al. 2013).

In this context, we should also mention the qualitative studies on the subjective ideas of children, because we also drew on these in the Second World Vision Child Study. One example of this is the research carried out in Australia by Tobia Fattore and his colleagues (Fattore et al. 2012). This research team asked children to report which areas of life they considered to be most important for well-being. They identified three areas: self, agency, and security. Self-refers essentially to the children's self-esteem, that is, their appraisal of themselves as good and valuable personalities. Agency assesses how far children feel that they have control over their own lives and the self-efficacy of their actions. Finally, security describes their feeling of being secure and in good hands in their relationships with their parents and other adults while nonetheless having sufficient scope when it comes to doing what they themselves want to do.

1.2.3 Developing and Testing Comprehensive Composite Indices

A further discussion should be mentioned here: whether it is possible to develop a composite index that will be broadly valid for all children regardless of where they are growing up. Likewise, efforts are being made to develop an index to assess disadvantage, as we shall show in the next section. Up to now, the international discussion reveals that, despite the many calls for such a comprehensive composite domain-driven index (O'Hare and Gutierrez 2012), there are still numerous hurdles when it comes to developing and methodologically testing such an instrument. Perhaps one will be available for the Fourth World Vision Child Study. The advantage would be the possibility of integrating all indicators into a composite evaluation by combining information from various areas. This would include and give appropriate weight to all the aforementioned indicators assessing all dimensions of well-being.

A more comprehensive instrument would make it possible to measure the quality of life of children in a society with just one indicator. Such a composite index would be of enormous political significance for both international comparisons and regional comparisons within one nation. For example, South Korea has recently published a study that uses one index to report on the situation in all the provinces in the nation. Policymakers now have precise statements on which problems are to be found in which regions and which intervention strategies may be applicable. The field of social reporting also reveals a search for such an index. For example, the 14th Youth Report commissioned by the German parliament (Deutscher Bundestag 2013) has been able to work out national differences in the childhood life phase on the basis of just a few single dimensions.

In the United States, a Child Development Index (CDI) has been derived from the Human Development Index (HDI) used by the United Nations. The annual results published by a foundation receive a great deal of attention. They permit a comparison between the different levels of well-being in the various federal states. As a comprehensive index, the CDI can also be used for longitudinal observations of, for example, how the well-being of children in families with different social origins has changed over the last 20 years (Hernandez and Marotz 2012).

1.2.4 The Concept of Well-Being in the 2013 World Vision Child Study

Whereas the first study in 2007 already defined well-being in terms of three dimensions, namely, satisfaction with the freedom granted by parents, satisfaction with the number of friends along with the quality of friendships, and general well-being at school, we applied a more complex framework in 2010. We developed a broader concept based on the idea of the "good life" and what is necessary to lead such a good life in the sense developed by the American social philosopher Martha Nussbaum in her Capability Approach (Andresen et al. 2010; Fegter and Richter 2013). The Capability Approach addresses the possibilities of self-realization and the action scopes of individuals in the greatest range of different social contexts. We have drawn on this approach for the World Vision Child Studies because it addresses the abilities to act and possibilities of acting in a self-determined way, and because we also know that this is a major concern for 6- to 11-year-old children. The questionnaire reveals our use of the Capability Approach in items asking children about their self-efficacy—as a central foundation of capability. At the end of the individual interviews, we also asked the children to name five things that every child needs in order to have a good life—regardless of where that child is growing up. As the 2010 Study showed, this theoretical framework for well-being proved to be extremely informative. For example, we were able to confirm a close relationship between high self-efficacy and experiencing that one's opinion is taken into account when decisions are made in the parental home, at school, and among friends.

When conceptualizing child well-being in 2013, we have not only built on our two earlier studies but also integrated the national and international discussion sketched above. Because satisfaction can be a rather vague and everyday term in German, we asked the children to tell us how satisfied they were with every single different life domain in turn. The following dimensions form the concept of well-being in our study:

- Care from one parent/both parents measured in terms of the amount of time they devote to their children
- Freedoms in daily life measured in terms of how satisfied children are with the freedoms their parents grant them

- Recognition and participation measured in terms of who, in their experience, respects their opinion and how far they are involved in making everyday decisions
- General satisfaction with institutions measured in terms of satisfaction with school and with daycare institutions
- Leisure measured in terms of satisfaction with leisure-time opportunities
- Friendships with other children measured in terms of satisfaction with the circle of friends
- Subjective well-being measured in terms of overall satisfaction with life

As in the previous World Vision Child Studies, the majority of children in our survey reported being very satisfied in each of the life domains. However, this exceptionally high level of satisfaction might possibly be due to the way we surveyed the children, suggesting a need to reconsider our methods. Another possibility is that children simply accept the position of adults in the power hierarchy, and are quick to express their satisfaction for this reason alone. In that case, we need to take a more critical look at the theoretical approach in childhood studies.

1.3 The Challenge of Child Poverty: Applying International Discussions to the World Vision Child Study

What is well-being like for children living in poverty? Research on child well-being is focusing increasingly on this issue. It needs to clarify how strongly poverty and social disadvantage impact on well-being, what can be done to counter this, and how child poverty needs to be defined and measured. As we shall show here, there have been major new international studies in this field since 2010 along with systematic analyses of how child poverty needs to be measured and evaluated. Nonetheless, we still know very little about what the children themselves experience. Up to now, studies on how children in poverty themselves see their world are very rare in both national and international childhood research. However, such studies are essential if we are to understand which strategies children use to counter precarious life conditions, how they themselves perceive their situation, and what phenomena they have to deal with in their daily lives.

The last World Vision Study in 2010 addressed perceptions and experiences of poverty in individual child portraits. However, none of the children we interviewed in 2010 were themselves living in poverty; and the same applies to the children in the Third Study. In the 2010 interviews, we gave children photographs to look at. These depicted typical scenarios for relatively poor, relatively affluent, and very affluent living conditions. On the basis of the children's responses to these photographs in 2010, we were able to show that most children were quite capable of classifying "being poor." Some referred to families they knew or children at their school whom they perceived to be disadvantaged. We noticed that when discussing this topic, children preferred to position themselves and their own families as being located in the middle between poor and rich, and they generally associated wealth with the need to be socially responsible.

For children, responsibility seems to be an important topic in the context of poverty. It also plays an important role in the few studies carried out with children who actually are poor. For example, poor children know exactly what the things they desire cost, but they frequently do not ask their parents for them. They know the prices and they know how much money per month their family has at its disposal. Poor children also adopt responsibility for their parents when, for example, they look after younger siblings and thereby try to ease the burdens on their mothers (and fathers). Or they adopt responsibility for the emotional well-being of their parents by worrying about them (Andresen et al. 2013; Meiland et al. 2013a, b). There is a great need to find out about the daily lives of children living in poverty because adults such as childcare workers or teachers need to be aware of the precarious living conditions of these children in each and every location in which they interact with them.

1.3.1 International Discussions and Comparative Data

Both the major international comparative studies and the studies of child poverty in Germany have contributed to a better understanding of the topic. We draw on all these studies in our own work and we shall examine them in more detail here. One intensive discussion centers on the fundamental question of how to measure poverty in adults, youths, and children and how to interpret statistical data. One established measure of poverty—also used in childhood studies—is oriented toward median income. In the European Union (EU), anybody earning less than 60% of the median disposable income in a given nation is considered to be at risk of poverty. Having less than 50% of median income at one's disposal is viewed as severe poverty; less than 40%, as very severe poverty.

Report Card 10, published by UNICEF (2012) under the title *Measuring child poverty*, has had a major impact on research. It assesses child poverty with a deprivation index and contrasts this index with findings based on the relative poverty concept using the median disposable household income. The approach is in line with the aforementioned efforts to establish a composite index of well-being. This assumes, on the one hand, that child poverty can be assessed in relation to child development and children's needs independently from the comparative wealth of a society, but, on the other hand, that it still has to be related to a nation's median income.

What goes into this deprivation index? It assesses whether a child has appropriate and at least partially new clothing; all-weather shoes; regular daily meals including fresh fruit, fresh vegetables, and meat (or a vegetarian equivalent); access to books; regular leisure activities in the sense of nonformal education; and outdoor leisure equipment such as a bicycle or roller skates. However, the index also includes the opportunity to celebrate special occasions such as birthdays and the opportunity to sometimes invite friends home. Because these are aspects that also characterize children's lives in Germany, we also include some of them in our study (see Chap. 3).

If two or more of the above indicators that are considered to be relevant for an average child's life, for what we could call "normal childhood," are lacking, then a child's situation is considered to be deprived. Based on these findings, the international UNICEF research team has classified the European nations into different groups with deprivation rates ranging from low to high.

One important finding from this international comparison, which is also confirmed in the World Vision Child Studies, is the particular risk of poverty facing children in single-parent families and in families with unemployed parents or parents with low education. This is also in line with the present findings. In Germany, children in large families with more than two siblings also face a significantly higher risk of poverty.

1.3.2 Child Poverty in Germany: Statistics and Trends

Germany currently reveals new trends in exposure to the risk of poverty. Most available statistics are based on the concept of relative income poverty, and, as pointed out above, children whose families have less than 60% of median disposable household income at their disposal are taken to be at risk of poverty. In exact figures for 2011, this threshold stood at 880 Euro per month for a single-person household, 1848 Euro for a two-person household with two children under the age of 14 years and 1144 Euro for a single parent with one child (Tophoven et al. 2015). Twenty percent of children under the age of 15 live in households with less than 60% of median disposable household income and 24.2% are considered to be at risk of poverty and/or currently receiving welfare payments (SGB-II Bezug) (Tophoven et al. 2015).

If we then go on to look at poverty trends over the last 20 years, poverty risk rates reveal major fluctuations. For a long time, children and adolescents faced a higher risk of poverty than the general population in Germany. For children up to the age of 10 years, the rate has now dropped to the same level as the general population. This contrasts strongly with the group of 11- to 20-year-olds who continue to face a disproportionally high risk (Deutscher Bundestag 2013). Our latest figures in the Third World Vision Child Study confirm this trend. However, when we look at children up to the age of 10 years with a migration background, we can see that they continue to reveal a comparatively high poverty risk of 15.1% (Deutscher Bundestag 2013).

1.3.3 *Child Poverty from a Longitudinal Perspective: The AWO-ISS Studies*

As well as asking how child poverty rates change over the years, it is particularly important to know how being exposed to poverty in the early years influences a child's later life. Thanks to national and international monitoring, we can observe trends in poverty over a longer period of time—as in the latest Youth Report of the German Federal Government (Deutscher Bundestag 2013). It is particularly important to know which groups experience poverty at an early age, for how long, and how permanently. One highly relevant piece of research for this is the AWO-ISS study that presented its latest findings from the fourth wave of measurement in 2012. The AWO-ISS is a longitudinal study of child and youth poverty that takes a multidimensional, child-related, and resource-oriented approach. It has now been tracking 900 children over a period of 15 years by comparing the living conditions of children from low-income families with children from more affluent families in a range of different areas of life. It has identified three groups of children who are living in poverty:

- Poor children who experience no social, cultural, health-related, or material constraints despite growing up in a low-income family ("poor, but with well-being")
- Poor children who experience constraints in a few areas and therefore have to be considered disadvantaged ("poor, disadvantaged")
- Poor children who experience massive deprivations or disadvantages in various areas ("poor, multiply deprived")

The longitudinal perspective also reveals the large proportion of children who were exposed to poverty as young children and have continued to have repeated experiences of poverty as they grow up (AWO-ISS 2012). In adolescence, these children have an increased risk of multiple deprivations and disadvantages in all areas of life as well as low well-being. In contrast, poverty experienced in early childhood that is then permanently overcome seems to have no negative consequences.

The trend across all three of our studies reveals, on the one hand, a slight drop in the poverty rate, but, on the other hand, a decline in membership of clubs and associations among children living in poverty since 2010 (see Chap. 6).

1.3.4 *Poverty and Coping*

One important issue, on which we can make only marginal statements in our study, is coping with experiences of poverty. Back in 2000, Antje Richter already worked out two different forms of coping in a study of child poverty in rural elementary school children: problem-avoidant and problem-solving coping. These two forms revealed marked gender-specific differences: Whereas both girls and boys were equally capable of realizing they had a problem, it was girls who more frequently applied the strategy of seeking social support to overcome it. Moreover, international resilience studies have shown that boys react more strongly to family poverty in early childhood, preschool age, and the first years of school by exhibiting externalizing problem behavior and impaired academic ability (Ittel and Scheithauer 2007; Luthar 1999). In contrast, the new AWO ISS study (2012) has found no gender-specific effects in 10-year-olds living in poverty. Although nonpoor girls tend to have fewer problems than nonpoor boys, this effect disappears under poverty conditions. In other words, girls living in poverty are just as disadvantaged as boys living in poverty. The current discussion on resilience as an ability to resist stress and negative external influences reveals one very interesting finding in this context: Resilient children tend to exhibit less gender-typical behavior and therefore possess a broader repertoire of behaviors with which to counter everyday stress (see Zander 2013).

1.3.5 Child Poverty as Experienced Constraint: The Approach Taken by the World Vision Child Studies

Poverty is a major topic in all three World Vision Child Studies. Our concept of poverty is multidimensional. In other words, we do not view poverty as being just a question of financial want, but take various areas of a child's life into account such as the family or leisure. This links up with the question whether research needs a specific child poverty concept and how such a concept may differ from that of youth or adult poverty. The question has emerged from concerns about whether children are particularly helpless when it comes to the causes of their poverty and whether the negative consequences of poverty have a stronger and more long-lasting effect on children than on adults; in other words, whether children represent a particularly vulnerable group.

Our study takes the perspective of the actors seriously; it tries to examine the everyday experiences of children and to relate these to social conditions. In addition, we understand child poverty as a limitation of chances to participate in society and to engage in self-realization.

The concept of child poverty in the World Vision Child Studies is based on the following dimensions:

- Limited financial options in the family measured by the children's subjective assessments of whether the family is short of money or has enough for all necessities such as warm clothing or school books.
- Limited participation in social and cultural life measured by the children's subjective assessments of various experiences such as not being able to go away on vacation, go to the movies, or learn to play a musical instrument.

- In addition, parents' subjective assessments of how well they manage the money at their disposal. These were entered into what we called a class index that divided all children into five groups with different social origins. The parents' level of education, type of accommodation (owned or rented property), and reports on the number of books in the household are also major components of this index.

Both our own research and other studies have emphasized the extent to which poverty is associated with shame and shaming. Children often feel stigmatized together with their parents. Although the German government has launched nonformal education and participation grants for poor children, not all local authorities and institutions have developed good ways of implementing them. This sociopolitical measure is known as the *Bildungs- und Teilhabepaket* [education and participation packet] is based on the assumption that parents will spend funds allocated to children in other ways so that they will fail to reach the children concerned. Therefore, parents may, or may have to, apply to receive school materials, private lessons, excursions, or 10 Euro for a club membership for their children. However, the great bureaucratic effort involved in this means that much of the funding allocated to this measure also fails to reach the children. Moreover, children are ashamed to be identified as "aid recipients" for free meals at schools or daycare centers. The research itself can also contribute to generating shame: Language, for example, can have a powerful effect. In this context, although we apply the term "lower class" in our World Vision Child Studies, we wish to emphasize that we use it exclusively to label low socioeconomic status. We distance ourselves emphatically from stigmatizing uses of the term such as "lower class culture." The primary purpose of such discourses is to stigmatize the behavior of people living in precarious circumstances and to ignore the conditions in which they live. The children are very much aware of these public discussions and the attributions of blame that frequently accompany them. This is something that any study of well-being in children should acknowledge and reflect on critically.

1.4 Migration as a Social Phenomenon in Childhood Studies

Unconsidered use of the term "with a migration background" can also be stigmatizing. This is despite the fact that recent findings such as the latest child migration report of the German Youth Institute from 2013 show that there are only a few cases in which migration alone predicts, for example, enrolment in daycare facilities for children, school-leaving qualifications, or learning potentials. Nonetheless, how to appropriately integrate children with different experiences of migration remains one of the challenges facing childhood studies (Hunner-Kreisel and Stephan 2013). One starting point and concern in the 2013 World Vision Child Study is to determine in which cases migration can or cannot serve as an explanatory factor.

1.4.1 Migration as a Concept

Migration is an international phenomenon and one that is of just as much significance for children and their families as it is for the society to which they migrate. Looking at Germany, more than one in four of all young people living in the country has a migration history with, for example, one parent having moved to Germany from another country (Deutscher Bundestag, 2013). In 2005, the microcensus of non-Germans was redesigned on the basis of a migration concept. The resulting statistics reveal the great diversity of migration histories in Germany. Since this reform, persons with a migration background are defined in official statistics as "all persons who have migrated to the current territory of the Federal Republic of Germany since 1949 as well as all foreigners born in Germany and all those born as Germans in Germany who have at least one parent who migrated to Germany or was born as a foreigner in Germany" (Statistisches Bundesamt 2011a, p. 6, translated). Following this conceptual reformulation, the detailed assessment of nationality, potential naturalization, and the migration experience of the persons surveyed and their parents permits a more differentiated view of the structure of the population of the Federal Republic of Germany (see Statistisches Bundesamt 2009, pp. 5–6). According to the reported methods used in the 14th Youth Report (Deutscher Bundestag 2013, p. 84), this distinguishes between Germans without a migration background and persons with a migration background. This second group is differentiated further, first into people who have migrated themselves (1st generation) with German or non-German nationality, and second, into persons who have been born in Germany (2nd and 3rd generation).

1.4.2 Children in Germany with a Migration Background

Which findings can we draw on for our Third World Vision Child Study or which are relevant for childhood studies? Migration is frequently discussed in relation to education and inequality. Despite a general shift toward higher participation in education, marked differences still persist: For example, 37% of migrants complete only basic secondary school (*Hauptschulabschluss*) compared to 20% of nonmigrants.

Further differences in where people live and the risk of poverty are also certainly relevant for the daily lives of children. First, the majority of children attributed with a migration background live in large cities (Statistisches Bundesamt 2011b, p. 14). Second, children with a migration background more frequently live in socially precarious situations than children without a migration background. This is due to a concentration of structural risk factors such as income poverty, unemployment, and parents with a low level of education (Autorengruppe Bildungsberichterstattung 2012). Children from families of Turkish origin are particularly at risk or exposed to multiple risks here.

A final aspect that is also relevant for childhood studies is that the proportion of people with a migration background is higher in younger age groups than in the general population. Indeed, the younger the children, the higher the proportion with a migration background. However, the children themselves mostly have no personal history of migration but were born in Germany. Accordingly, children in German cities meet other children with a wide range of different backgrounds when they attend a Kindergarten or school, join a youth club, or go to the playground.

1.4.3 Using the Migration Concept in the World Vision Child Study

The data from the Federal Statistical Office reveal the heterogeneity of migration contexts and experiences. As in the previous studies, we also looked into the concept of migration background when planning the Third World Vision Child Study. For the sample recruited for the quantitative part of the study, we decided to orient our research toward the concept of migration background on the basis of the microcensus. For the qualitative interviews, we decided to trace the children's individual histories; and, this time, to purposefully select 7 children with a migration background within the sample of 12 children interviewed. Only the German version of this book contains a chapter with the results of this qualitative part of the study. This should cast light on the histories of the children, their families, and their daily lives, and allow us to work out not only their resources but also their possible disadvantages with the help of the children's narratives. Combining these portraits with the analysis in the qualitative part provides us with an even more detailed approach.

1.5 Justice: A Previously Neglected Topic in International Childhood Studies

The concept of well-being and the analysis of poverty go hand in hand with ideas about the "good life," a "good childhood," and just conditions. Children themselves do not just relate well-being to justice but also the differences between poor and rich. Based on what we learned in our previous studies, critical discussions on family policy, and the available options for children to participate or make complaints, we decided to focus particularly on justice in the Third Study. Although justice has not been an explicit topic in recent childhood studies, we consider that it is time for this to change. Many of the current challenges facing society relate to intergenerational justice and social justice, and there is a need to clarify how the concept of childhood on the one side and the experiences, feelings, and perceptions of children on the other side relate to classic or contemporary ideas on justice.

In the World Vision Child Study, we are particularly interested in the sense of justice among 6- to 11-year-olds. We have developed our questionnaire and our interview guidelines with this in mind. We started off with everyday observations showing that children in this age group discuss fairness but also injustice in a range of different contexts. In interviews with children, we found that, for example, promises that are given, kept, or broken play an important role; and that conflicts with other children can also be traced back to ideas on justice. Moreover, sanctions or punishments for breaking the rules also relate to justice. In the parental home and at school, children additionally get to know different reward systems, and it is certainly worth examining whether they perceive these to be just or unjust.

1.5.1 Preparing the Topic for the Third World Vision Child Study

Proceeding from these everyday observations and with reference to the fundamental scientific interest and objectives of the World Vision Child Studies, we see an urgent need for childhood studies to pay more attention to justice. However, up to now, there has been a lack of research in this field apart from studies in developmental psychology and the classic studies on moral development such as those carried out by Jean Piaget. In our approach, we started by examining justice theory and exploring its potential for issues in childhood studies. We then examined relevant empirical research and considered how we could apply the knowledge accumulated there to our study. In particular, after examining empirical research starting initially with developmental psychology and then moving on to recent experiments in economics, we decided not to look for evidence of different concepts of justice but to ask the children directly about their own sense of justice. This also links up with philosophical discussions on the significance of the sense of injustice compared to more abstract concepts of justice that require a great deal of cognitive reflection and a distancing of oneself from one's own interests.

This roughly sketches the focus of our study. Our aim is to understand what children between the ages of 6 and 11 years consider to be just or unjust. Earlier interviews have already revealed that justice or fairness is of great concern to children and that they discuss it in completely different ways—sometimes, more abstractly and philosophically; other times, very concretely and in everyday terms. We have tried to operationalize "justice" as closely as possible to the world of this age group. We have done this by also focusing on selected positions in justice theory. What do 6-year-olds and what do 10-year-olds perceive as being just or unjust in the family, in interaction with peers, and at school? What do they think about specific situations and relationships? How do they judge the standards set by society and how do these influence their daily lives? Finally, we are interested in what indications can be derived from the findings for the concrete implementation of children's rights in all areas of their lives.

1.5.2 Important Philosophical Approaches for Childhood Studies

The issue of just behavior and a just organization of society is as old as philosophy itself. Systematic ideas on just behavior and relations entered Western thought particularly in classical philosophy through the work of Socrates, Plato, and Aristotle. One major aspect here is understanding justice as a virtue and therefore as a personality trait in the sense of personal integrity. The Platonic dialogues conceive justice as the highest virtue following wisdom, courage, and moderation. What is important here is the human striving toward a just order.

In Aristotelian philosophy, justice serves not only as a general moral concept but also for the appraisal of specific situations in interpersonal relations. Therefore, put very simply, Aristotle points out that justice regulates essential aspects of human coexistence and he tells us how it does this. Basically, these topics have lost none of their relevance today; and not least for children, because they continue to be concerned with the distribution of goods or positions, how to behave, and how to solve conflicts. Accordingly, justice theories are concerned just as much with distribution and compensation or exchange as with procedures for setting up and regulating a just human coexistence.

One way of introducing such procedures is, for example, for partners to enter contracts based on reasonable and transparent rules that have to be honored as far as possible. However, being in any way able to make a contract already calls for a lot of preconditions, and these are mostly not possible for a child to fulfill. Adults then act on the child's behalf. However, the questions whether a good is distributed justly or unjustly, whether an exchange is disadvantageous for one of the parties, and whether reward and punishment follow a just logic arise in the everyday experiences of children. It is these that correspond to their sense of justice—as our findings reported in Chaps. 2 and 7 clearly show.

1.5.3 Fairness as an Orientation in Childhood Studies

The justice theory proposed by the American scholar John Rawls has had a major impact on the recent history of philosophy. In his book *A Theory of Justice* (1971), he explains how justice in the sense of fairness has to be fundamental for social institutions. Nonetheless, it should not restrict the freedom of individuals. In an obituary for Rawls who died in 2002, the German philosopher Winfried Hinsch expressed this fundamental idea as follows: "Justice as fairness is the central theme in Rawls' theory. A society is just when the institutions on which it is based are guided by basic principles that its citizens would personally impose on themselves—given fair conditions of freedom and equality" (Hinsch 2002, translated). Rawls put his ideas into concrete terms by formulating a model of the "original position". This is a hypothetical or even experimental situation in which the members of a society come together behind a "veil of ignorance" with the goal of jointly determining the highest principles of justice for their society. Because of the veil, none of them know who they and the others are in real life and what they can achieve in the future. In this way, the veil prevents the decisions that citizens make in this original position from being influenced by individual interests and socially given balances of power. Rawls was convinced that this was the way to guarantee and ensure fairness.

In order to pursue justice, according to Rawls, it is necessary for all persons to possess basic goods such as fundamental rights, social privileges, resources, and the social preconditions for self-respect. Simply leafing through any daily newspaper shows us how crucial it is to guarantee such basic goods and how important this is particularly for children—examples in Germany being the current call for a guaranteed child allowance independent of parents, or the implementation of basic rights such as being able to point to injustice through an established complaints system in sport clubs or schools.

1.5.4 Justice and Inequality

Rawls was also interested in the social inequality that always goes hand in hand with justice theories—a topic with a strong impact on children and therefore also on childhood studies. Here he makes an interesting proposal: He suggests that social inequality can be justified only after two conditions have been met: First, fair access to positions and goods has to be ensured, that is, equality of opportunity; and second, the greatest advantages have to be given to those least favored in a society. Hence, he proposes a universal justice oriented toward strong principles.

In his book *The Idea of Justice*, the economist Amartya Sen (2010), however, asks whether a more pragmatic theory of justice oriented toward situational ideas might be more appropriate than one oriented toward universalistic principles, especially when making decisions on and dealing with social conflicts. He explains what he means in an allegory over "three children and a flute:"

> You have to decide which of three children—Anne, Bob, and Carla—should get a flute about which they are quarreling. Anne claims the flute saying that she is the only one of the three who knows how to play it (the others do not deny this), and that it would be quite unjust to deny the flute to the only one who can actually play it. If that was all you knew, the reason for giving the flute to the first child would be strong. (p. 13)

But that is not everything that Sen tells us about in his allegory because Bob points out that he should be given the flute, because unlike the other two, he has nothing to play with, no pretty things with which to occupy himself. This is because Bob is poor and the two girls concede this. Carla, in contrast, also claims the flute because

> She has been working diligently for many months to make the flute . . . and just when she had finished her work, "just then," she complains, "these expropriators came along to try to grab the flute away from me." (p. 13)

In our qualitative interviews, we read this allegory out loud to the children and ask them to tell us how they would decide. As Sen suspected, very different criteria and deliberations are applied and all of them have something in their favor. Sen uses this allegory to work out how theorists in different schools of social justice can find good reasons for reaching their decision: Economic egalitarians, who find material inequality unjust and wish to overcome it, would favor Bob who has no possessions; utilitarians would probably want to give the flute to Anne, the only musician in the group; and libertarians, who emphasize productivity, would have to favor Clara because she made the flute.

This rough sketch of ideas in justice theory should particularly emphasize what childhood studies can borrow from it. Our attempts to express this empirically and the results obtained from the Third Study reveal a great deal of potential in interrelating theories of childhood and theories of justice.

1.5.5 Justice in the Piagetian Tradition

What does empirical research have to tell us about justice in children; or, to put it better, about the development of an orientation toward justice in children? How important is it for children to feel that they are treated fairly, and do they develop a sense of injustice? Here we can link up with the work and insights of moral psychology and particularly with the studies of Jean Piaget and their continuation in the work of Lawrence Kohlberg. Piaget was interested in children's legal awareness and how they deal with rules in groups. His observations of games of marbles and the derivation of central developmental stages were a milestone in the discussion on the development of a moral awareness in children and hence a development oriented toward just arrangements. One of Piaget's interests was in when and how children switch from obeying adults to orienting themselves toward the rules of, for example, the peer group and toward their desire for cooperation. "What is decisive is the development of the concept of justice. Whereas for the younger child, what is just means almost exactly the same as the will of adults, the ideas of equality and reciprocity already assert themselves toward the end of early childhood" (Piaget 1999, p. 158, translated from German). Piaget emphasized that the shaping of the environment and the behavior of adults play a decisive role in this developmental process. As a result, he called for teachers to actively involve even the youngest students in their classes.

Recent childhood studies have tended to distance themselves from assumptions in developmental psychology in order to view children as actors in the construction of their reality and to find out about their co-constructions. Nonetheless, it is worth taking a new look at the work of Piaget and examining its potential for justice and well-being. This is the reason for mentioning these works here—especially because both the quantitative and qualitative parts of our study show clear age differences in the appraisal of justice.

1.5.6 Justice in Recent Empirical Research with Children

For many years, anthropologists, social anthropologists, and evolutionists have been studying how human beings build up trust, why they keep or break promises, and how cooperations can emerge between not only groups of persons who know each other but also groups of strangers. These questions are also related to fundamental issues in economics or social theory such as whether competition impedes the striving for justice and tends to encourage the egoistic behavior. What is interesting is that we only tend to see a willingness to share in societies once conditions of exchange and trade have become established. Such findings point to the significance of economics. Recent empirical research such as the work of the Zurich economist Ernst Fehr offers much food for thought regarding questions in justice and childhood theory. Fehr and his team not only draw on findings from evolutionary research into the social behavior of primates and findings on the theory of mind but are also interested in genetically determined characteristics that contribute to the development of preferences for justice in human beings. Fehr poses the fundamental question whether human beings have a more egoistic or more altruistic orientation and how and under which conditions altruism develops.

On the basis of experimental studies in various regions of the world and with all age groups—including very young children—Fehr has worked out that recognition is the main motor driving just judgments and behavior. This introduces an important element into the discussion within childhood studies: recognition as a need in interactions between children and adults, but also between peers, and as an aspect of well-being.

A further essential element in the work of Fehr, however, is research on the sense of injustice or the rejection of injustice or inequality. This does not mean that inequality is rejected in general. Whether inequality, according to Fehr, is rejected because of the sense of justice depends decisively on the circumstances in which it has emerged, that is, on the context. This reveals links to Rawls' theory of justice. However, what can economists tell us about children and their rejection of injustice?

On the basis of various experimental games with children, Fehr and his colleagues have determined that "inequality aversion" develops between the ages of 3 and 8 years and is age-dependent: the younger children are, the stronger their selfish orientation toward their own interests (Fehr et al. 2008). However, they develop preferences in the sense of parochialism, that is, a social togetherness. Fehr has also shown that children prefer to favor their own group, be it in preschool, school, or a club. The World Vision Child Studies do not observe the behavior and practices of children and they do not engage in experimental research. Nonetheless, the economist's approach reveals much knowledge potential for our research in which we are asking the children to tell us about their evaluations, their understanding, and the reasons they give for the decisions they favor.

1.5.7 Justice as a Topic in the Third World Vision Child Study

Until now, hardly any orientation toward justice theory has found its way into recent childhood studies. The Third World Vision Child Study is also unable to build on a sound basis in justice theory because it is entering new territory here. However, in a first step, we draw on earlier findings on the good life from the perspective of children. In the Third Study, justice also serves as a strong link between the qualitative and quantitative assessments. For our in-depth interviews, we developed case scenarios that we presented to the children. Alongside the allegory of the three children and the flute, these contain concrete cases taken from the everyday world of today's children that address just distribution, rewards for achievements, keeping or breaking promises, punishments, and finally the topics of codetermination and justice.

We have also developed new justice-theory-oriented items for the questionnaire. Moreover, the results deliver interesting findings on the age dependence of the sense of justice. Our initial concern is to find out how far the children consider things to be just in the proximal environment of their family and school, then more broadly in Germany, and finally in the world as a whole. However, when looking at the sense and perception of injustice, it is also important to find out which persons the children consider being particularly exposed to injustice. Therefore, we finally ask the children to evaluate specific cases addressing the provision and distribution of goods.

Detailed results on this can be found in the following Chap. 2. They encourage us to carry out more systematic work on this topic.

1.6 The Design of the Third World Vision Child Study

Any comparison of the instruments used in each of the three studies will initially reveal the same body of items. However, a closer inspection uncovers modified or new items and scales. Both sticking to a constant set of items and setting new accents are important to us. Comparable items are needed to document change, but new ones are necessary to introduce focal topics and further develop our questionnaires and our interview techniques. This also brings us into line with international advances in this field.

The Third World Vision Child Study also tackles new developments and challenges in international childhood studies. We are studying well-being, the experience of poverty, and the sense of justice among children in Germany and gaining new knowledge about the main areas of life of children between the ages of 6 and 11 years. With the Third Study and the same body of questionnaire items in 2013, we can perform numerous comparisons with the two prior studies. With our representative sample, we can uncover differences between boys and girls, between urban and rural districts, and also differences due to contexts codetermined by migration.

References

Andresen, S., & Hurrelmann, K. (2007). Was bedeutet es, heute ein Kind zu sein? Die World Vision Kinderstudie als Beitrag zur Kinder- und Kindheitsforschung. In World Vision Deutschland. (Hrsg.) *Kinder in Deutschland 2007. 1. World Vision Kinderstudie* (S. 35–64). Frankfurt a. M.: Fischer.

Andresen, S., Hurrelmann, K., & Fegter, S. (2010). Wie geht es unseren Kindern? Wohlbefinden und Lebensbedingungen der Kinder in Deutschland. In World Vision Deutschland. (Hrsg.) *Kinder in Deutschland 2010. 2. World Vision Kinderstudie* (S. 35–59). Frankfurt a. M.: Fischer.

Andresen, S., Hurrelmann, K., & Schneekloth, U. (2012). Care and freedom. Theoretical and empirical aspects of children's well-being. *Child Indicators Research, 5*, 437–448.

Andresen, S., Mailand, S., Milanovic, D., & Blume, J. (2013). Erfahrungen und Erleben von Armut aus der Sicht von Kindern: »Ich würde meiner Familie was schenken und dafür sorgen, dass sie nicht so viel in Schwierigkeiten sind.« Unsere Jugend 65. Jg. (S. 123–129).

Autorengruppe Bildungsberichterstattung. (2012). *Bildung in Deutschland 2012*. Ein indikatorengestützter Bericht mit einer Analyse zu Perspektiven des Bildungswesens im demografischen Wandel. Bielefeld: W. Bertelsmann Verlag.

AWO-ISS. (2012). *Lebenssituation und Zukunftschancen von (armen) Kindern und Jugendlichen*. AWO-Verlag.

Bradshaw, J., Martorano, B., Natali, L., & de Neubourg, C. (2013) *Children's subjective well-being in rich countries* (Working Paper). UNICEF Office of Research, Florence.

Deutscher Bundestag. (2013). Der 14. Kinder- und Jugendbericht. Bericht über die Lebenssituation junger Menschen und die Leistungen und Bestrebungen der Kinder- und Jugendhilfe Iin Deutschland. Deutscher Bundestag, Drucksache 17/12200. http://dip21.bundestag.de/dip21/btd/17/122/1712200.pdf (Stand: 24.06.2013).

Fattore, T., Mason, J., & Watson, E. (2012): Locating the child centrally as subject in research: Towards a child interpretation of well-being. *Child Indicators Research, 5*(3), S. 423–435.

Fegter, S., & Richter, M. (2013). The capability approach as a framework for research on children's well-being. In A. Ben-Arieh, F. Casas, I. Frones, & J. Korbin (Eds.), *Handbook of child well-being: theory, indicators, measures and policies*. Dordrecht/Heidelberg/ London/New York: Springer. Chapter No. 151.

Fehr, E., Bernhard, H., & Rockenbach, B. (2008). Egalitarianism in young children. In *Nature* (Vol. 454, pp. 1079–1083).

Hernandez, D. J., & Marotz, K. G. (2012). Disparities in child well-being across income groups: Trends in the U.S. from 1985 to 2008. *Child Indicators Research, 5*(1) S. 93–121.

Hinsch, W. (2002). *Gerechtfertigte Ungleichheiten: Grundsätze sozialer Gerechtigkeit*. Berlin: Walter de Gruyter.

Hunner-Kreisel, C., & Stephan, M. (Hrsg.). (2013). *Neue Zeiten, neue Räume: Kindheit und Familie im Kontext von (Trans-)Migration und sozialem Wandel*. Wiesbaden: Verlag für Sozialwissenschaften.

Ittel, A., & Scheithauer, H. (2007). Geschlecht als »Stärke« oder »Risiko«? Überlegungen zur geschlechterspezifischen Resilienz. In Opp, G., & Fingerle, M. (Hrsg.). *Was Kinder stärkt. Erziehung zwischen Risiko und Resilienz* (S. 98–115). München/Basel: Reinhardt.

Luthar, S. S. (1999). *Poverty and children's adjustment*. Thousand Oaks: Sage.

Meiland, S., Andresen, S., Milanovic, D., & Blume, J. (2013a) Denkst du, die Kinder sind hier arm? Sichtweisen und Erfahrungen von Kindern in prekären Lebenslagen. In Fisher, D., Gathen, J., Höhmann, K., Klaffke, T., Rademacker, H. (Hrsg.). *Friedrich Jahresheft XXXI 2013a, Schule und Armut* (S. 16–18). Oldenburg: Friedrich Verlag.

Meiland, S., Andresen, S., Milanovic, D., & Blume, J. (2013b). *Erfahrungen und Erleben von Armut aus der Sicht von Kindern: »Ich würde meiner Familie was schenken und dafür sorgen, dass sie nicht so viel in Schwierigkeiten sind.«* Unsere Jugend 65. Jg. (S. 123–129).

Minkkinen, J. (2013). The structural model of child well-being. *Child Indicators Research, 6*(3), 547–558.

O'Hare, W. P., & Gutierrez, F. (2012). The use of domains in constructing a comprehensive composite index of child well-being. *Child Indicators Research, 5*, 609–629.
Piaget, J. (1999). *Über Pädagogik*. Beltz: Weinheim.
Rawls, J. (1971). *A theory of justice*. Harvard University Press.
Robert Bosch Stiftung. (2012). *Starke Kinder – starke Familie. Wohlbefinden von Kindern in Städten und Gemeinden*. Stuttgart: Robert Bosch Stiftung.
Sen, A. (2010). *Die Idee der Gerechtigkeit*. München: C. H. Beck Verlag.
Statistisches Bundesamt. (2009). *Bevölkerung und Erwerbstätigkeit-Einbürgerung 2008* (Fachserie 1 Reihe 2.1). Wiesbaden.
Statistisches Bundesamt. (2011a). *Bevölkerung und Erwerbstätigkeit. Bevölkerung mit Migrationshintergrund-Ergebnisse des Mikrozensus 2010* (Fachserie 1 Reihe 2.2). Wiesbaden.
Statistisches Bundesamt. (2011b). Pressemitteilung Nr. 345 vom 20. September 2011b: Knapp die Hälfte der Großstadtkinder aus Familien mit Migrationshintergrund. Wiesbaden.
Tophoven, S., Wenzig, C., & Lietzmann, T. (2015). Kinder- und Familienarmut: Lebensumstände von Kindern in der Grundsicherung. Institut für Arbeitsmarkt- und Berufsforschung für die Bertelsmann Stiftung.
UNICEF. (2012). *Measuring child poverty*. New league tables of child poverty in the world's rich countries. Report Card 10, Innocenti Research Centre, online unter. www.unicef-irc.org/publications/pdf/rc10_eng.pdf (Stand: 14.07.2013).
UNICEF. (2013). The state of the world's children 2013: Children with disabilities. online: http://www.unicef.org/sowc2013/files/SWCR2013_ENG_Lo_res_24_Apr_2013.pdf (Stand: 14.07.2013).
Zander, M. (2013). Resilienz – Gender – Prekäre Lebenslagen. Wie kann eine gendersensible Resilienzförderung aussehen? *Betrifft Mädchen, 3*/2013.

Chapter 2
What's Fair and What's Unfair: The Different Faces of Justice

Ulrich Schneekloth and Sabine Andresen

Questions of fairness and justice are of much concern to children. In their world, these are important and sometimes even existential challenges. This does not just apply to everyday life in the family, in the circle of friends, at school, and during leisure, but also to more general problems in our society that they perceive as the "adult world." This also confronts them with the question of what role children have to play in this world.

Classical developmental psychology oriented toward the work of Jean Piaget and Lawrence Kohlberg reveals a broad consensus that children overcome their early childhood egocentrism during the transition from early to middle childhood. Increasingly, they develop the ability to recognize and emulate social rules and thereby to comply with them (Piaget 1932/1983, 1937/1975; Kohlberg 1964, 1974; see Oerter and Montada 2002, for a German-language overview). When these observations and experiments were carried out in either the 1930s or the late 1950s, it was assumed that it is only from the age of roughly 9 years onward that children develop the ability to grasp social rules as (potentially changeable) shared agreements and to view themselves as members of a community for which they have to adopt responsibility (the so-called conventional stage according to Kohlberg; see Trautner 1991). Younger children between the approximate ages of 4 and 8 years, in contrast, were assumed to see social rules as indisputable givens that they comply with through either a fixation on authority or fear of punishment (the preconventional stage; see Trautner 1991).

U. Schneekloth (✉)
Kantar Public, München, Germany
e-mail: ulrich.schneekloth@kantarpublic.com

S. Andresen
Department of Education, Institute of Social Pedagogy and Adult Education, Goethe University Frankfurt, Frankfurt am Main, Germany
e-mail: S.Andresen@em.uni-frankfurt.de

S. Andresen et al. (eds.), *Well-being, Poverty and Justice from a Child's Perspective*, Children's Well-Being: Indicators and Research 17,
DOI 10.1007/978-3-319-57574-2_2

However, more recent studies on (early) childhood development have shown that even at the age of 3 years, children already reveal a sense of justice oriented toward the principle of reciprocity in their mutual play. For example, Hamann et al. (2011) have shown that children distribute rewards relatively fairly, that is, more or less equally, in return for acts that have been performed collaboratively. Recent experimental studies have also shown that children between the ages of 3 and 8 years increasingly reveal a willingness to also consider the well-being of others, particularly when these others belong to their own proximal surroundings (neighborhood, preschool, school). From roughly the age of 7 years onward, they reveal a clearly recognizable altruism in the sense of a marked orientation toward the well-being of others (Fehr et al. 2008). These studies suggest that children in this age range do not judge justice abstractly or in principle, but always in relation to everyday situations and to familiar individuals or groups. In this context, children develop their own idea of justice that they then apply to different situations in their daily lives.

According to the findings from these experimental studies, the 6- to 11-year-old children in the Third World Vision Child Study of 2013 are located exactly in that age window during which they develop their own understanding of justice in relation to the well-being of others. What is decisive here is the child's own environment, that is, how fair and, where applicable, how cooperative children experience life to be in their own family, in their circle of friends, or at their school. Moreover, in this Child Study, we are also interested in how children perceive their social environment and how fairly they think people are treated in Germany as a whole. In the last Child Study in 2010, we already showed that 6- to 8-year-old children are capable of describing their life situation very clearly and comprehensibly, and they are also able to report how they evaluate certain general problems in Germany. The more they have to experience social problems directly in their daily lives, for example, through poverty or perceived exclusion, the clearer and more unequivocal their answers. The fact that 6- to 7-year-olds differ somewhat in the breadth of their experience and their understanding compared to somewhat older children does not contradict this statement. Not all the children could answer the questions we posed in our quantitative assessment equally well. Therefore, when we asked for general evaluations of social problems, and we could see that particularly 6- to 7-year-old children were unable to give their own answers, we dropped such questions from the further course of the interviews. In addition, all children had the basic right not to answer such evaluative questions if they chose not to.[1]

In this chapter, we want to present the children's views on how fairly children are treated and how fair our society is in general. We developed our instruments in the quantitative and qualitative parts of the study on the basis of the theoretical ideas presented in Chap. 1 and the unstructured questions posed during our preparatory

[1]A typical example is when children are told that there are no "right" and no "wrong" answers here, but still reply by asking "I don't know. Do you know?" Another example is when children do not want to answer because they are clearly unable to relate the question to their world. In such cases, interviewers were instructed to use the "don't know" response category. Any related follow-up questions were then simply skipped for 6- to 7-year-old children.

pretest survey. We are guided by two principle ideas: first, to classify the children's perception of situations, conflicts, and socially determined inequalities as being fair or unfair; and second, to relate this to the children's well-being and social living conditions. Our underlying assumption is that there is a relation between well-being and the idea of justice, and that the social context in which children are growing up plays a very significant role in this relation. Hence, we test possible links between the ideas of justice and social origin. In the following, we shall refer primarily to the results of our quantitative survey. However, these are also integrated with the findings from the portraits in the qualitative part of our study, because this enables us to present and interpret 6- to 11-year-old children's ideas of justice in depth (see Chap. 8, on the qualitative part of the study in general). The open and unstructured questions on justice in our pretest already gave us many very informative ideas. We should like to illustrate the breadth of ideas children have by reporting those of a 6-year-old girl. When asked simply what she understands by justice, what comes to her mind are the categories of freedom (being allowed to say everything), a just way of dealing with the mistakes people make (not getting into trouble straight away), and an open and inclusive community of all children:

> That people are allowed to say what they want, that people don't get into trouble straight away when they sometimes do something wrong, that all children should be allowed to play together regardless of whether they come from somewhere else or whether they are poor. (6-year-old girl)

2.1 Well-Being and Life Satisfaction

This focus on the idea of justice and the sense of injustice links up systematically with a central theme in all three Child Studies: our interest in child well-being.

One major issue in empirical research on justice is to ask people what they feel to be just and unjust in a society and on which ideas of justice they base these feelings. There can be no denying that these specific ideas and evaluations are closely related to subjective well-being and the societal framing conditions that contribute to well-being (see Liebig and Lengfeld 2002, for an overview). This also suggests using the personal well-being of children in Germany as a starting point for asking them what they think about justice in the nation. At the end of our representative survey, we ask children "And, finally, how happy are you with your life in general?" The children can answer this item on a 5-point smiley scale.[2]

In all, the 6- to 11-year-olds in our survey report an even slightly higher satisfaction with their own lives compared to the Second World Vision Child Study in 2010 (Fig. 2.1). In this the Third Child Study, 59% of the children give very positive and

[2] The question was formulated in line with the life satisfaction surveys frequently used in German empirical social research. However, surveys of the general population generally use an 11-point scale (from 0 to 10).

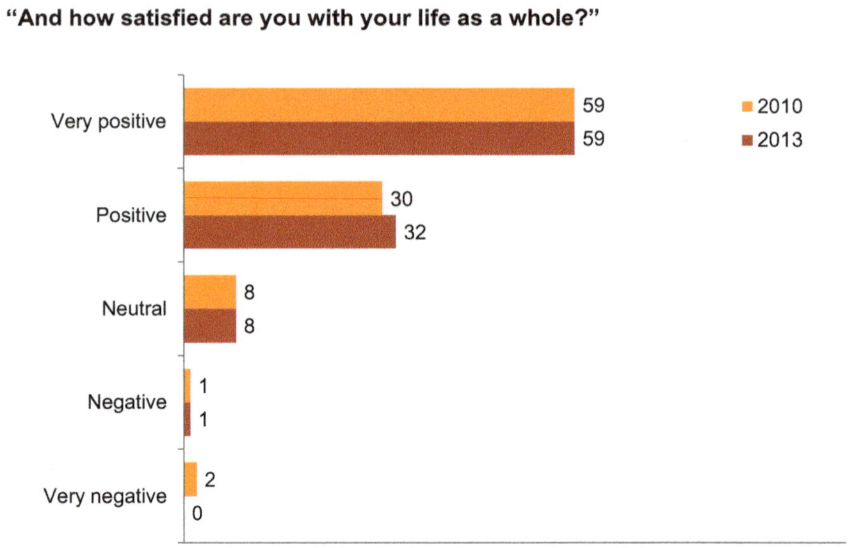

Fig. 2.1 One's own well-being
Children in Germany aged 6–11 years (%)

a further 32% give positive answers. No more than 8% give a neutral answer, and only 1% report an explicitly negative life satisfaction.

Naturally, at this point, it is always necessary to bear in mind that children in particular will always tend to give positive answers when asked about their overall life satisfaction, and that neutral or negative answers will usually be the exception.[3] This makes it all the more remarkable that only 72% of the children with the lowest social origins, the so-called lower class, give positive answers, whereas 28% (compared to 26% in 2010) give neutral or explicitly negative answers (on the demarcation of the social classes in the Child Study, see Chap. 3 and Appendix 2). No other social class articulates such a conspicuously different and also negative evaluation of the personal situation (Table 2.1).

As our analyses in the Second World Vision Child Study in 2010 have already shown, the lack of life satisfaction in children is due to a combination of household risk factors (parental poverty and/or unemployment, growing up in a single-parent family) and what is frequently in consequence a deficit in care and attention from parents coupled with the children's own feeling of having no chance in life or of

[3]This is also the case in the most recent UNICEF study "Child Well-Being in Rich Countries" UNICEF, 2013). It cites findings from the "Health Behavior in School-Aged Children 2009/10" (HBSC-Studie 2011) study of life satisfaction in 11-, 13-, and 15-year-olds. Here as well, 84% of respondents gave positive answers. Among 11-year-olds, this even reached 86%, which is almost equal to the 89% measured in the Second World Vision Child Study in 2010.

Table 2.1 Life satisfaction of children with different social origins
Children in Germany aged 6–11 years

Proportion of children (very positive or positive),[a] per column in %	2010	2013
Upper class	92	95
Upper middle class	90	95
Middle class	91	93
Lower middle class	90	91
Lower class	70[b]	72

[a]The table reports the proportion of children who rated their own life satisfaction very positively or positively in 2010 or 2013
[b]A further 4% of lower class children gave no answer in 2010

being unable to cope with the demands they have to face (low expected self-efficacy). All these factors accumulate particularly in children from the lowest social class (Schneekloth and Pupeter 2010b, pp. 210–215).

A look at the children's ratings for important domains in their daily lives reveals small but subtle differences in the latest Child Study as well. The highest satisfaction is with the circle of friends (94% positive ratings) and leisure (91% positive). A large majority of children also rate parental care very positively (88% positive). At 84%, a slightly higher percentage of children rate the freedoms granted to them by their parents very positively or positively, although 16% rate this negatively or neutrally. A positive rating of school is found in 79% of the children; 21% give negative to neutral ratings—making this the largest negative to neutral proportion (Fig. 2.2).

Evidently, in the latest Child Study, just as in 2010, it is the relation between individual freedoms on the one side and regulations and duties on the other side that concerns children in this age range. Despite the high level of overall satisfaction, there are still differences: both in the evaluation of the various areas of daily life and also against the backdrop of origins and social class. Some individual domains also reveal age or gender effects: Younger children rate school slightly more positively than older children; and girls also tend to rate school somewhat more positively than boys. Vice versa, it is the younger children who somewhat less frequently give positive ratings on the freedoms granted to them by their parents. Girls, in contrast, give more positive ratings than boys here. However, when it comes to overall life satisfaction, we once again find no significant differences in terms of age and gender. We shall address these points in later chapters in which we shall consider them in detail. When commencing the topic of justice, it is important at this point to bear in mind the very positive view of their own lives and see this as a backdrop to the children's ideas about "justice."

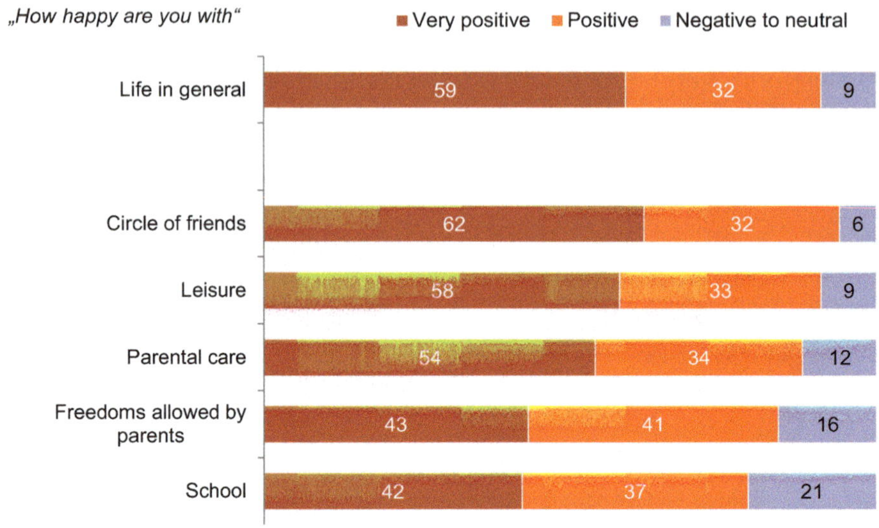

Fig. 2.2 Well-being by domains
Children in Germany aged 6–11 years (%)

2.2 Fears

Fears and anxieties are normal phenomena accompanying children throughout their development. As mid-childhood progresses, the early fears of loss or also the fantasy fears in what is called the "magical phase" give way increasingly to real fears. This only becomes critical when fears not only accumulate but also exert an influence on everyday behavior and start to become chronic. However, this is generally an exception for children in this age range.[4]

In the Child Study, we also check through a list of fears with the children. We mention problems related to daily life (such as school grades or the fear of being bullied) as well as risks related to society (such as poverty or environmental pollution) and then ask the children whether this hardly, ever, sometimes, or very often makes them afraid. A comparison of their replies with the results of the last Child Study in 2010 shows that the proportion of children who "sometimes" or "very often" are afraid of one or more of the items on our list has declined. This matches the aforementioned slight increase in overall life satisfaction. Taken as a whole, at 81%, the majority of children report sometimes being afraid in at least one of the domains surveyed.

The most frequent fear named by 46% of the children (compared to 51% in 2010) is that of poverty ("that there are more and more people who are poor in

[4] Only roughly 10% of those anxieties in children and adolescents that meet the criteria for an anxiety disorder actually become chronic (Woodward and Fergusson 2001).

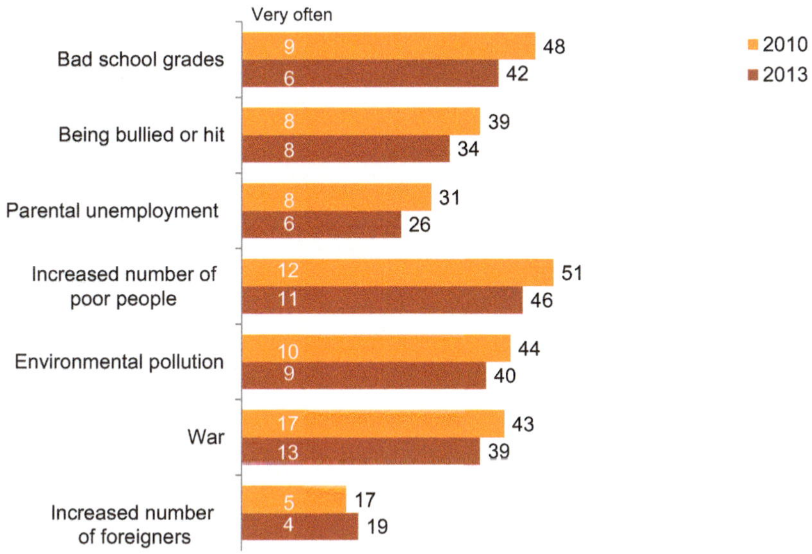

Fig. 2.3 Children sometimes have fear from Children in Germany aged 6–11 years (%)

Germany"). This is followed by the fear of having poor school grades in 42% (48% in 2010). Then 40% (44% in 2010) mention environmental pollution; 39% (43% in 2010) that there might be a war; 34% (39% in 2010) that they are afraid of being bullied or hit; 26% (31% in 2010) that they are afraid of their parents becoming unemployed; and 19% (17% in 2010) that they are afraid of "more and more foreigners" coming to Germany. In general, the children report that these topics "sometimes" made them afraid. The proportion of children who reply "very often" is more or less markedly below 10%. The only exception is fear of war with 13% (17% in 2010) reporting that they are "very often" afraid of this (see Fig. 2.3).

The older children aged 11–12 most frequently report on existing fears and anxieties. Conspicuously high at 52% are fears about poor school grades; at 55%, the fear of increasing poverty; and at 50%, the fear of increasing environmental pollution. These real anxieties reflect a growing problem awareness and confirm the increasing significance of these issues for children as they mature (see Table 2.2).

Girls tend to report more fears than boys. For example, 36% of girls report being afraid of being bullied or beaten compared to 32% of boys. Fear of growing environmental pollution is reported by 42% of girls compared to 38% of boys. This inverts for the item on the migration of more foreigners to Germany. Only 17% of the girls are afraid of this compared to 21% of the boys (see Table 2.2).

That girls report fears somewhat more frequently is not a new trend; it could already be seen in our previous Child Studies. One common explanation for this is that boys tend to be raised to be "protectors and heroes" whereas girls are raised to be "those in need of protection," and that both sexes reproduce corresponding role

Table 2.2 Things that children sometimes fear
Children in Germany aged 6–11 years

Sometimes or very often, per cell in %	All children	Girls	Boys	6-7 years	8-9 years	10-11 years
Bad school grades	42	43	40	27	42	52
Being bullied or hit	34	36	32	31	39	32
Parental unemployment	26	26	27	21	27	30
Increasing number of poor people	46	48	45	34	47	55
Environmental pollution	40	42	38	27	41	50
Outbreak of war	39	40	38	30	42	43
Increasing number of foreigners	19	17	21	15	18	23

stereotypes. However, another possible explanation is that it is still "uncool" and inappropriate for boys to admit fears, whereas it is more acceptable for girls to communicate their feelings. This makes it notably easier for girls to cope with fears together instead of denying them and/or trying to hide them behind aggressiveness (Essau 2003; Morschitzky 2009).

2.3 What Children Understand by Justice

In modern research in developmental psychology and behavioral economics, the categories *self-interest and (interpersonal) well-being* have become central benchmarks for judging moral and emotional development in early to middle childhood. This line of research assumes that children's ideas of justice are based on a concept of equality that can take different forms depending on whether they are considering equality of need or reciprocity.[5] In the eyes of children, equality can mean not only an egalitarian distribution of that which is there ("sharing") but also a redistribution of what is mine ("giving"). We already came across this finding in the Second World Vision Child Study when the children also talked about the responsibility of the rich to give to the poor.

We consider that these ideas link up with the fundamental assumptions in justice theory presented in Chap. 1, and that they relate simultaneously to the discussions on "social justice" to be found in social and welfare state theory. This perspective also results in ideas and consequences regarding how to treat each other and how to distribute the available means that differ according to the specific social relations between individuals or groups. Based on an idea proposed by Fiske (1992, as cited in Liebig and May 2009, pp. 6–7), Liebig and May distinguish four general models of social relations. Each of these specific models then has its own principles of justice.

[5] In this context, Fehr et al. (2008) talk about "inequality aversion" as the characteristic feature of (moral) development in children of this age.

Model 1 is based on close and long-term social relations as in a family or other form of shared household. The characteristic feature in this case is the *need principle*. A just distribution is oriented in principle toward that which each single individual considers that she or he needs for her or himself in a situation in which all individuals are there for each other and will share if necessary. *Model 2* is shaped by hierarchic interrelations. Here, higher ranking persons have more important roles or take on more responsibility. What is characteristic here is the *rights principle*. Those of higher rank can claim what is assigned to them and to which they have a right due to their status and function. *Model 3* is based on social relations in network structures, community associations, or cooperatives. In principle, each member initially has equal rights and equal duties. Relations are based on exchange and the characteristic feature is the *equivalence principle*. Everybody gives back roughly what they have received. *Model 4* is characteristic for relations among strangers who interact with each other on the basis of relations of economic exchange based on market principles in which each person strives to attain the greatest advantage for the self. What is characteristic in this case is the *achievement principle* as a benchmark for just interaction.

From this perspective, Liebig and May (2009) propose that conflicts regarding which of the various principles of justice should be applied to what extent and at which time are based on different interpretations of how the relations and social interactions of individuals are to be shaped in each subdomain of society.

If society is understood as more of a loose assembly of individuals or groups of individuals who are competing with each other, the primary benchmark is the achievement principle and the orientation toward individual returns based on performance. If, in contrast, society is viewed (also) as a closer community of shared responsibility, the principle of need gains central importance as a just approach, either as a corrective and principle of compensation or also as a normative principle for creating equal opportunity.

Whereas in the 1960s and 1970s, the debate on social justice centered primarily on questions of (re)distribution of income or wealth, the perspective has now shifted toward the attainment of equal opportunity and participation in society (Leisering 2004, as cited in Liebig and May 2009). This is also exactly the goal of the Capability Approach underlying our Child Study that aims to enable individuals to do and to be what they have reason to value (Sen 2010).

2.3.1 The Children's Frames of Reference and Perspectives

The issue of how to achieve social justice is particularly central for modern democratic societies with their aspirations to civil freedoms, basic social rights, and chances of participation. It is correspondingly important to look at the socialization of children in relation to these problems or, from our perspective, how they socialize themselves in relation to them over the course of their development.

One of the methodological challenges facing childhood studies is to take sufficient account of how children themselves relate to these in part complex concepts and what they associate with them. This issue naturally also emerges with regard to how children see the concept of social justice. However, up to now, empirical surveys reveal hardly any systematic approach to this that we can build on directly.[6] Typical instruments used in surveys as indicators measuring justice tap, for example, "subjective well-being/personal distributive justice" with questions asking whether one considers that one has "either more or less than one's fair share compared to others" (ALLBUS: Datenreport 2011), or asking about economic justice in Germany ("Are the economic conditions here in Germany—by which I mean what people own and how much they earn—basically fair or unfair" (Allensbach 2013)? Six- to 11-year-old children cannot answer such questions as they stand. The instruments used in psychological youth research such as the Personal Belief in a Just World Scale (Dalbert 1983; Dalbert et al. 1987) also seem to be of only limited use with children of this age.

Therefore, the first step in our pilot study was to ask selected children directly what they personally associate with justice. We also used the qualitative part of the study, which we commenced in advance of the representative survey, to assess children's ideas on the topic of justice in more detail and to use this as a basis for appropriately designing and evaluating the fully standardized items in the representative survey.[7]

We categorized the often extensive and detailed answers and used these results to critically reexamine our questionnaire. It should be pointed out that we view this categorization of children's ideas on justice as a heuristic framework and not as a strict classification of justice theories. Nonetheless, these "categories of ideas on justice" allow us not only to analyze our quantitative and qualitative results in relation to the specific frames of reference of the children but also to gain interesting starting points for further research. We used the following categories to systematize and assign the data on the topic of justice generated in the pilot study (see also Table 2.3):

- Interactional justice (*equal treatment in* personal relations)
- Procedural justice (*equal rights* and *equal access* for all)
- Need-related justice (*compensation* and well-being)
- Egalitarian justice (*equal distribution*)

In their answers, the children interpreted and evaluated justice within the context of their situational ideas of equality. However, their unstructured responses could not always be assigned exclusively to one category. Justice as fairness—in the (egalitarian) sense that "all are treated equally" frequently also has a self-serving aspect

[6] Here, we are referring to empirical surveys and not experimental studies in which children's behavior is observed in, for example, a play experiment.

[7] This approach is known as "triangulation" in social science research. It combines qualitative and quantitative methods systematically in order to exploit their different strengths and create useful synergies.

Table 2.3 Frames and categorizations of open answers
Pilot study, 95 children aged 6–11 years

Frame	Number[a]	Examples of unstructured responses[b]
"Interactional justice" – equal treatment in personal relations	40	"Justice is when everybody is treated equally"
		"Everybody should be nice to everybody – and adults should be as just to others as they are to themselves"
"Procedural justice" – equal rights and equal access for all	28	"That you share with each other and don't just leave anybody out"
		"That everybody is treated in the same way and everybody has the same opportunities"
"Need-related justice" – equality, well-being, redistribution	21	"When everybody has a job, a home, enough to eat, and still has money left over to afford something nice"
		"That all people, whether rich or poor, get the same things, are able to travel, get toys, and have enough to eat"
"Egalitarian justice" – equal distribution	16	*"When everybody has the same amount"*
		"When I am eating sweets with my friend and my friend gets more, that is unjust. It would be better to share things exactly"

[a]Multiple categorizations possible
[b]See the list of all open answers in Appendix 3

(if everybody else can do it, I want to be able to do it myself), but it can simultaneously also express the wish and the need for all to have equal chances and participation (everybody should take part).

One interesting finding is that achievement-related justice does not seem to play any role in the children's unstructured responses, even though it is such a central aspect. In the present context, this may also be because the open questioning of what the children understand by justice was prepared and framed by the fully standardized questions in the pilot test interview. These examined how fair the children considered things to be in their environment by asking them to appraise the way specific groups are treated in Germany (children and adolescents, the aged, the handicapped, foreigners, poor people). Hence, the frames of reference that the children applied when answering the unstructured question on what they understand by justice had been primed in advance in the sense of ensuring the well-being of others. As the results on the qualitative part of the study show, the achievement aspect is also taken into account, for example, when justice is linked to the children's demands for mutuality and reciprocity.

Table 2.4 I find that very fair or quite fair
Children in Germany aged 6–11 years

Very fair or quite fair, per line in %	All children	Girls	Boys	6–7 years	8–9 years	10–11 years
Some families have very little money; others have a great deal of it	23	21	26	20	24	25
Rich parents should pay more money for a daycare center trip than poor parents	61	57	65	56	62	64
Mostly it is adults who decide on, for example, building a playground	31	33	29	31	30	31
Non-German children should speak only German at class breaks, too	41	39	42	43	36	43

2.4 Categories and Aspects of Justice

To enable children to appraise justice with the closest possible reference to their daily lives and experiences, we used everyday questions or little scenarios in both the questionnaire and the qualitative interviews. The children should judge the single scenarios according to what they consider just. The representative part of the Child Study draws on the categorization of the unstructured answers from the pilot study. This targeted egalitarian, need-related, procedural, and interactional justice. Table 2.4 presents a general overview of the results. It reports the percentages of children per age group and gender who answered *very fair* or *quite fair*.

Some families have very little money; others have a great deal of it. Do you think that is very fair, quite fair, rather unfair, or very unfair?

The first question refers to *egalitarian ideas about justice* using the example of differences in the distribution of income (and wealth). Two out of three children find the unequal distribution to be unfair (23% very unfair, 43% rather unfair), and accordingly, only a minority consider it to be fair. The differences between age groups actually tend to be slight because, at 14%, younger children somewhat more frequently give no reply.

Differentiated according to gender, girls at 67% consider it to be slightly more unfair than boys at 65%. However, a larger difference in the appraisals is found when replies are differentiated according to the children's social background. At 81%, lower-class children find the financial inequality between families to be markedly more unfair than the other classes. The unfairness appraisals of upper-class children are slightly above the average at 69% (Fig. 2.4).

Our findings link up with Fehr et al.'s (2008) experimental studies by also revealing an inequality aversion. In the eyes of these children, the need for equality means "unequal is unjust" (egalitarian justice). The feeling of injustice is frequently particularly marked when the causes of this inequality are viewed negatively, or when the reasons for some having more and others having less are unknown. Both can apply in this case. However, the differentiations according to the children's social class reveal an important aspect: The children's evaluations are not independent

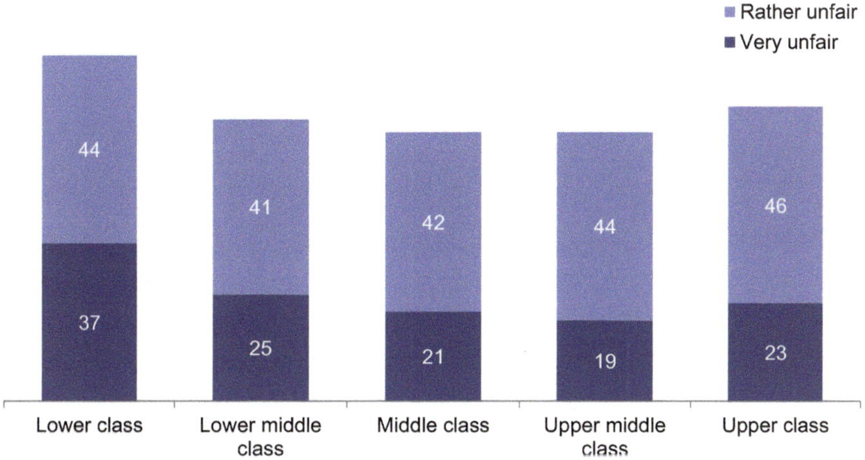

Fig. 2.4 Unequal is unfair
„Some families have very little money; others have a great deal of it
Children in Germany aged 6–11 years (%)

from their social circumstances. Evidently, unequal is not just unfair in general; for children from the lowest social class, it is quite practically oppressive and discriminatory.

> ***A group of children at the daycare center want to go on a trip together. It has been decided that rich parents should pay more money for the trip than poor parents. Do you think that is very fair, quite fair, rather unfair, or very unfair?***

Answers to the second question on need-related justice using the example that wealthier families should pay more of the costs take the opposite direction. This is judged to be fair by 61% of the children (25% very fair, 36% quite fair). Only a minority of 27% think that this is unfair. Interestingly, the appraisal that it is fair to impose the stronger and therefore unequal burden on wealthier parents increases with age (as expected, 21% of the 6- to 7-year-olds disproportionately frequently give no response). At 65%, boys agree markedly more frequently than girls at 57%. It is notable that at 69%, children from the lowest social class most frequently consider that unequal payments by poor and rich parents are fair. The lowest level of agreement at 56% is found in the middle class, whereas 64% of the children from both the higher classes think that this is fair (Fig. 2.5).

The unequal payments by parents depending on their financial resources can also be interpreted as a wish for equality, because children may well have experienced that their peers from poorer families are unable to join them on, for example, school excursions because they are too expensive. If "those who have more also contribute more," then this leads to more equal treatment, because it creates conditions in which everybody can come (participatory justice). This is joined by the idea of sharing, that those who have more are obliged to give something up and share their wealth—an idea that the children already expressed in 2010.

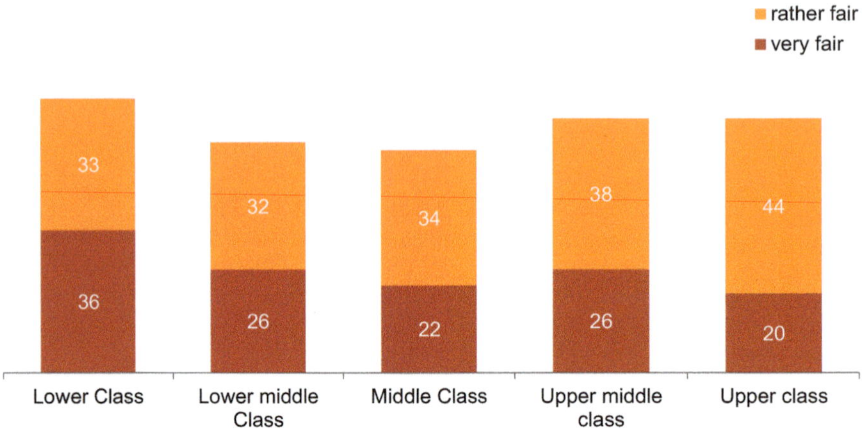

Fig. 2.5 Justice is when those who have more also contribute more
"A group of children at the daycare center want to go on a trip together. It has been decided that rich parents should pay more money for the trip than poor parents"
Children in Germany aged 6–11 years (%)

> ***Mostly it is adults—and not the children themselves—who decide where and when to build a children's playground. This is because they say that they are the ones who know best about such things. Do you think that is very fair, quite fair, rather unfair, or very unfair?***

The third question on procedural justice using the example of how frequently children are unable to contribute to decisions also receives a clear answer. A total of 62% find the lack of codetermination unfair (21% very unfair, 41% rather unfair). At 12%, younger children somewhat more frequently give no reply, so that the proportion of this group who find this unfair is slightly lower at 57%. At 64%, boys even find the lack of codetermination somewhat more frequently unfair than girls at 59%. The differences according to social origins are less clear here. Upper-class children are more self-confident, whereas the appraisals of the other children vary only slightly (Fig. 2.6).

Equality also means having equal rights. When decisions are made in Germany about things that are important for children, then "fair" means that the children have a voice here. Fairness and equal treatment also mean that children should also be informed about what is being planned and have a voice in any decision making. At this point, the children's perspective addresses the procedural principle and is less concerned with their feeling the need to or even the competence to intervene actively in the debates. Nonetheless, the view that the majority of children of this age trust in authority and are unable to question the rules of the adult world is no longer appropriate. Of course, the process of individual maturation is involved here, and it continues to be appropriate to assume that children of this age seek to adapt the views of adults. However, this does not mean that they consider it to be fair to be excluded from decisions that affect them.

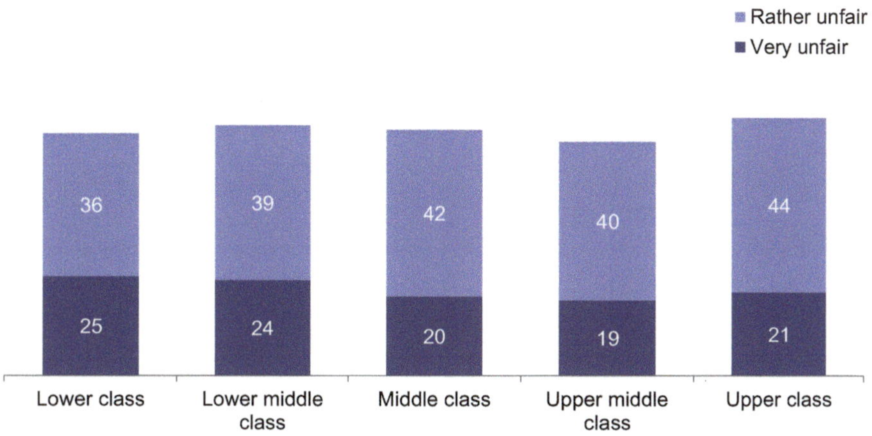

Fig. 2.6 Not being able to have a say is unjust
"Mostly it is adults and not the children themselves who decide on building playgrounds"
Children in Germany aged 6–11 years (%)

> ***What would you think if non-German children had to speak only German not just in class but also at the class breaks: Do you think that is very fair, quite fair, rather unfair, or very unfair?***

The fourth question addresses *fairness* as well as *equal treatment in personal relations (interactional justice)*. Here, we are taking up a public discourse on language. The idea of telling children with a migration background ("non-German children") what language they should speak in their daily lives also possesses a justice dimension: Justice also means that something has to be personally reasonable and acceptable if it is to be "alright."

We are aware that this question can be stigmatizing, particularly for children. On the other hand, concerns about integration and how migrants should be treated are publicly discussed topics in Germany that also frequently attract a lot of media attention. We can assume that children are also aware of this in their daily lives.

Although opinions are more divided on this issue, at 49% compared to 41%, the majority feel that it would be unfair to oblige foreign children to speak German with each other during school breaks as well as in class (19% very unfair, 30% rather unfair). Among younger children aged 6–7 years, 41% find this unfair and 43% find this fair. Sixteen percent—and thereby also more than in the other age groups—can or do not want to reply to this question. Among older children, in contrast, a clear majority of more than 50% view this as unfair. The slight deviations in the response behavior of girls compared to boys are due to the slightly higher proportion of missing reports among the former (12% compared to 9% in boys). A differentiation according to social origins reveals a clear trend: the higher the social class of origin, the stronger the rejection (Fig. 2.7).

In this context, justice seems to link up closely with the idea that it is wrong to always forbid or prescribe everything in the children's world. Fair means, in this

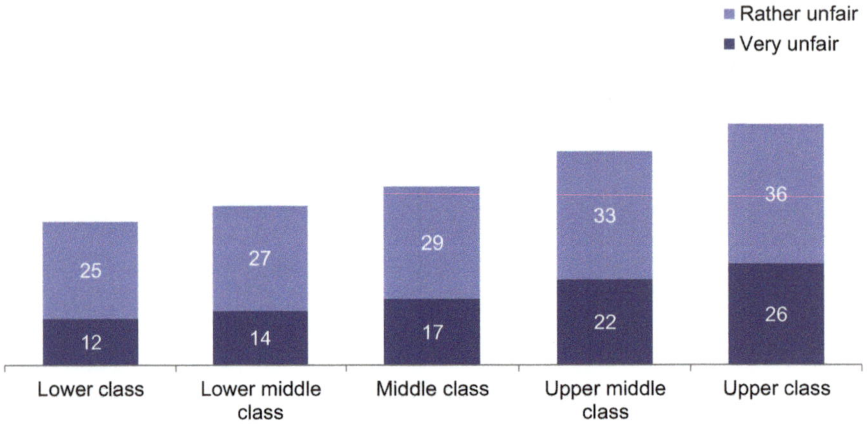

Fig. 2.7 Fair also means not always wanting to forbid or prescribe everything
"What would you think if non-German children had to speak only German not just in class but also at the class breaks"
Children in Germany aged 6–11 years (%)

case, that you can do the things you want to do. The clear class dependence in response behavior additionally indicates that being prescribed which language one can use with one's peers is clearly an unjustified disciplining for children from higher classes and therefore conceived as unequal treatment. Children from the lower classes, particularly when they are native Germans, reveal a markedly more distanced attitude here. This leads us to ask which children profit from multilingualism at school. Children who themselves have a low socioeconomic status may feel more threatened by other languages in the school yard, because they do not understand them and may feel excluded by them during school breaks. Children from higher classes have more positive experiences through travelling to distant countries and more often attend schools at which social conflicts less frequently shape daily life.

2.4.1 *Qualitative Findings*

As shown above, children's ideas of justice are shaped strongly by the characteristic need for equality in this age range. We have also adopted this finding for our qualitative interviews in which we address equal treatment, equal claims, equal rights, and equal duties.

This once again reveals that equality refers not only to participation (equal chances) but also to reciprocity (mutuality). As a result, the children are quite capable of interpreting it multidimensionally. Depending on the situation and the background, the postulate of equality can lead to different ideas of justice. We shall illustrate the different interpretations children use when judging justice by two examples taken from the qualitative interviews. We have chosen the thoughts of an 11-year-old and those of a 7-year-old. The following case report was read out loud to both children:

> *Next month, a famous circus will be coming to town. The children in a school class would really like to go to the circus and see the show. Although the class has its own savings account with money to pay for excursions, there is not enough money to pay for tickets for everybody to go to the circus. The class is discussing what they can do. The children come up with the idea of holding a garage sale. All the children should bring things they no longer need from home so that they can be put on sale.*
>
> *On the day of the garage sale, all the children bring things to be sold. Only Jana and Emil come with empty hands. Anton and Luise, in contrast, have brought a particularly large number of things. What do you think: Should all the children be able to go to the circus?*

Example 1: Adriana (A), 11 years; Interviewer (I)

"Everyone should be able to go"

I: *Should all the children still be able to go to the circus?*

A: Yes, of course.

I: *Anton and Luise have brought a lot of things.*

A: Yes, sure, then they have to share them with the others. Give something away so that the others (who haven't brought anything—ed.) then also have something to sell and can collect money to go to the circus.

I: *And what if the class has reserved a block of seats for itself alone at the circus and this means that only one-half of the children can sit in the first row and the other half have to sit further back. How should the children decide who should sit where?*

A: Oh, draw lots perhaps? Drawing lots would be a fair way to do it.

I: *So you wouldn't say that those who didn't bring anything should ...?*

A: No, no way. That would actually be completely unfair if you had had nothing to sell but still wanted to come.

I: *Um. Um ... and what if they just simply forgot? I mean, they had something at home, but simply forgot to bring it with them?*

A: Yes, then they, they should first fetch the things from the others who have brought a lot of things with them and join them in selling them. And then they can give them that later.

Adriana simply takes it for granted that all the children should go to the circus. For her, it goes without saying that those who have brought a lot have to share with those who have less. That is the only way to ensure that everybody has the same chance of also going to the circus. Spontaneously, Adriana assumes that those who have brought nothing with them simply have nothing at home that they can do without. On the other hand, from Adriana's viewpoint, reciprocity is maintained in that those children who have not brought anything with them have to compensate by fetching things that the others have brought and helping them to sell them.

Example 2: Theresa, 7 years (T)

"Then you also have to do something for it"

I: *Should all the children still be able to go to the circus?*

T: No, not the two children who didn't brought anything with them.

I: *Why not?*

T: Because that would be unfair then. Because then they come as well …and then …they have …they didn't even help at all.

[…]

I: *And tell me Theresa, what if…what I mean is could you imagine why these two did not bring anything with them?*

T: Because they didn't have anything. Or they forgot.

I: *And what if they simply didn't have anything? (Pause) Should they still not be able to go to the circus?*

T: Yes, they could help. They could split up, for example: Jana goes to him, and he goes to her.

I: *That's a good idea too. So, if, for example, they didn't have any things at home …they could help the others.*

T: Exactly, one gets one half, and the other gets the other half.

I: *Okay. But if they had had something at home and they forgot it?*

T: Well, that's not fair!

Theresa also thinks it is fair for everybody to have an equal chance of being able to go to the circus. However, unlike Adriana, it is spontaneously very important for her that everybody complies with the rule that each child has to bring something from home. If the children do not have enough things at home, then they can help the others to sell their things. However, if, in contrast, they have not complied with the rule, they have no right to go.

Both Adriana and Theresa orient themselves toward very similar principles and want everybody to be treated equally. Nonetheless, they differ in their replies to the question on treating the children fairly. They differ spontaneously in how they evaluate the motives of the children who have not brought anything with them. However, during the further course of the interview, they propose an analogue way to ensure the participation chances of those who have contributed nothing because they have hardly anything or nothing at home. From their viewpoint, this solution is also based on reciprocity.

2.5 Appraisal of Justice in Their Own Lives

Following the questions on the ideas of justice, we used the fully standardized survey to see how children more generally view justice in the family, the circle of friends, at school, in Germany, and throughout the world. They could give their answers and ratings on a four-smiley scale (very fair, quite fair, rather unfair, or very unfair). If the children either could not or did not want to give an answer, the interviewer entered them into the "don't know" category.

On the whole, just about every child gives an appraisal of justice in her or his immediate world, that is, in the family, in the circle of friends, and at school. However, 29% (and thereby 39% of the 6- to 7-year-olds, 29% of the 8- to 9-year-olds, and 21% of the 10- to 11-year-olds) are unable to or do not want to answer the question on whether things are fair in Germany. Findings are similar for the item on justice in the whole world. Here, 26% (and thereby 45% of the 6- to 7-year-olds, 25% of the 8- to 9-year-olds, but, in this case only 13% of the 10- to 11-year-olds) are unable to or do not want to answer the question.[8] In light of the intensity of development occurring particularly in middle childhood between the ages of 6 and 11 years, this low level of "don't knows" does not surprise us. Quite the opposite: From our perspective, this also reveals the aforementioned ability of children in this age range to give appraisals of "fairness" based on how they understand their personal environment and look out beyond this to Germany as well as the whole world.

A look at the answers (Fig. 2.8) reveals that, analogue to their reports on personal well-being, just about all 6- to 11-year olds (92%) describe the situation in their own family as being either very fair or quite fair. The same holds for interactions in their own circle of friends: 90% describe these as being either very fair or quite fair. This indicates that that the children have a very positive sense of justice particularly because of the personal intimacy and the major significance of these relationships. Perhaps interactional justice and procedural justice, which are linked closely to personal interactions for children and not to abstract procedures, can be experienced primarily in personal relationships. Here as well, it can be seen that promoting child well-being and granting children "justice" from the side of the parents is valued in families.

However, differences emerge when it comes to judging school. Here, 78% rate how they are treated there as being very or quite fair. At 19%, already almost every fifth child reports that school is rather or very unfair (for more on this, see the next Chap. 4 on school).

Only 47% consider that Germany is fair; 24% that it is unfair. In clear contrast, however, a mere 16% of the children believe that it is a fair world compared to 57% who consider the way the world works and the way it is to be unfair. What seems to be decisive for this appraisal is the children's association of the questions with the "Third World" and all the problems and injustices to be found there (hunger, war, and a general lack of protection of children). This information is conveyed by, for example, the media and evidently the strong impression this makes shapes their frame of reference.

In the view of a very large majority of the children, family offers a home that you can rely on and in which things are done fairly. The circle of friends offers a social environment that is independent of this. Here, you can try things out for yourself and play with others. Here as well, it is what children feel to be fair that shapes their interaction. At the same time, children do not view Germany as a whole as an

[8] Those 6- to 7-year-olds who were unable to answer the question on justice in Germany and were, therefore, no longer asked about justice in the world are also assigned to the "don't know/no answer" group here.

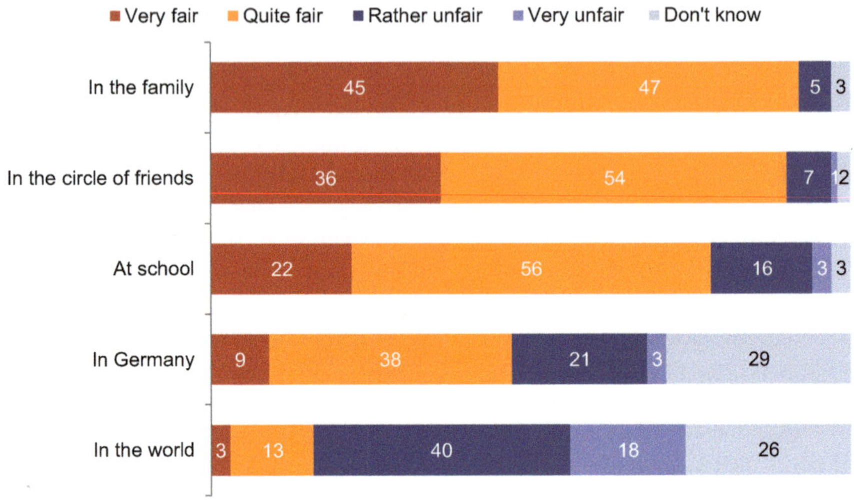

Fig. 2.8 How fair things are in general
Children in Germany aged 6–11 years (%)

"Island of the Blessed," despite the high level of satisfaction with their lives. Nonetheless, compared to the rest of the world, they do feel "privileged" as children in Germany and in a much better position than those above all in the Third World.

2.6 How Fair Is Germany?

We also studied what children think about "social justice" in Germany by asking them how fairly they consider certain groups are treated. It is easier for children to relate their idea of justice to the question of how people are handled—equal or unequal (unjust) treatment. This does not correspond directly to the usual distributive concept of empirical justice research with its orientation toward a (welfare) distribution, but is easier for children to grasp.[9] However, here as well, the challenge facing children is to perform general appraisals of the situation of certain social groups in Germany. In contrast to the (previously presented) question on general fairness in Germany, these items focus more on single groups (children and youths, the aged, the handicapped, foreigners,[10] poor people) and are therefore easier for the children to grasp in relation to their daily lives.

[9] The usual question in the Sozialstaatssurvey is "What do you think? How far has Germany achieved a fair distribution of wealth?" In contrast, personal distributive justice is tapped in, for example, ALLBUS with the question: "Compared to how other people live here in Germany, do you consider that you receive your fair share, more than your fair share, or somewhat less or somewhat more?"

[10] Instead of the term foreigner, which is based on formal nationality, research in the social sciences uses the category migration background. This places the focus on one's own origin or also the

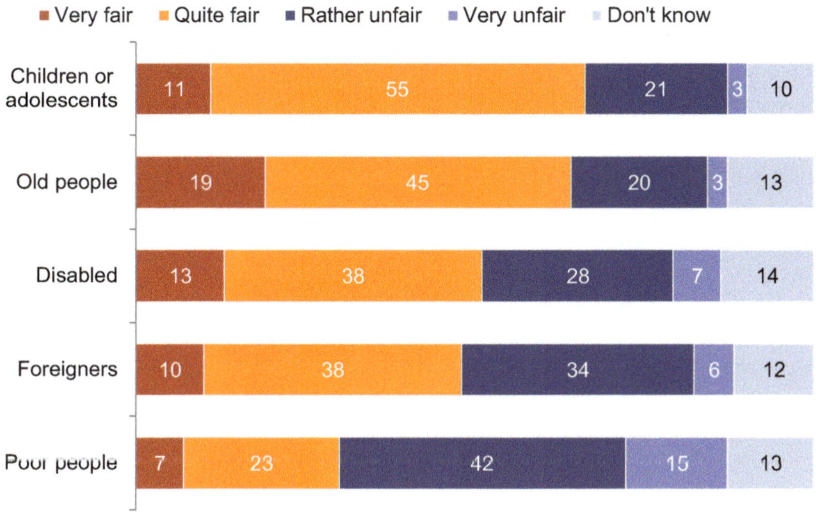

Includes only those 6-to 7-year-olds who were able to answer the question on justice in Germany

Fig. 2.9 How people treat specific social groups in Germany
Children in Germany aged 6–11 years (%)[l]

The proportion of children who are unable to answer this question lies between 10% and 15%. We already dropped these questions in advance for those of the youngest children (6- to 7-year-olds) who had been unable to answer the previous question on general fairness in Germany.[11] Considering these cases as well, the proportion of children without valid reports rises up to between 21 and 25% depending on the research question.

In the following, we shall refer only to those children who were asked the questions on "social justice" in Germany (Fig. 2.9). The majority say that children and adolescents (11% very fair, 55% quite fair) and also the aged (19% very fair, 45% quite fair) are treated fairly. Results are comparable, though slightly lower for the treatment of the disabled (13% consider this to be very fair in Germany and 38% fair) and likewise for the treatment of foreigners (10% very fair, 38% quite fair). In contrast, the majority rate the treatment of poor people in Germany negatively (30% fair and 57% rather unfair).[12]

origin of one's parents as well as the associated cultural roots and commitment. Nonetheless, "foreigner" [*Ausländer*] continues to be the usual term in everyday speech.

[11] For older children who were also unable to answer the questions, we also used the option of a "don't know" category.

[12] According to the Sozialstaatssurvey, approximately 80% of the adult population last reported in 2008 that Germany had either "rather not" or "completely not" attained a fair distribution of wealth (Glatzer 2009). According to Allensbach (2013), 69% of the over-16-year-old population reported "unfair" when answering the question: "Are the economic conditions here in Germany—by which

Appraisals of social justice in Germany vary according to age group, although this is due mostly to the different proportions of children who are unable to answer these questions. However, the main trend is a lack of any relevant differences. Differentiated according to gender, girls rate the treatment of the named groups slightly less often as being fair. As in the other questions on justice, it seems as if girls in contrast to boys somewhat more frequently emphasize injustices toward others. For example, 37% of girls compared to 32% of boys judge the treatment of the disabled to be unfair in Germany. Here as well, at 48%, the largest group of girls rate treatment in Germany as fair although this remains below the 53% of boys.

An interesting detail is that the appraisal of the treatment of foreigners hardly differs between native German children (49% as fair) and children with a migration background (46% as fair). However, this is not the case with the appraisal of the treatment of poor people: At 65%, it is by far children from the lowest social origins who most frequently consider that their treatment is unfair.

2.6.1 Forming Groups: Attitudes of Children Toward Social Justice in Germany

As to be expected, appraisals of the treatment of different groups correlate with each other. There is a strong probability that children who tend to negatively appraise the treatment of one of the groups we asked them about will appraise the other groups negatively as well.[13] Therefore, we summarized the replies of all children who could be asked about this to form a global assessment of social justice in Germany. This enabled us to distinguish between four different groups of children (Fig. 2.10).[14]

Children with a very positive view of social justice in Germany: 22% of all children.

Nearly all the children in this group consider that every social group we asked about is treated fairly (very fair or quite fair). This also applies to the treatment of poor people: 88% of these children consider this to be fair.

Children with a fairly positive view of social justice in Germany: 35%.

I mean what people own and how much they earn—basically fair or unfair?" According to the German General Social Survey (ALLBUS) in 2010, approximately 45% of the adult population considered that they received less than their fair share (ALLBUS: Datenreport 2011).

[13] This is also confirmed in a reliability and factor analysis. All five questions form the same dimension and can therefore be viewed and analyzed together.

[14] We did this by adding up the values (very fair = 1, quite fair = 2, don't know = 3, rather unfair = 4, very unfair = 5) and then grouping the children according to the central tendency. All weightings above the median indicate a negative judgment of social justice; we viewed those higher than the (statistical) standard deviation as a very negative judgment. Weightings below the median, in contrast, represent a positive appraisal of social justice in Germany, and those lower than the standard deviation as correspondingly very positive.

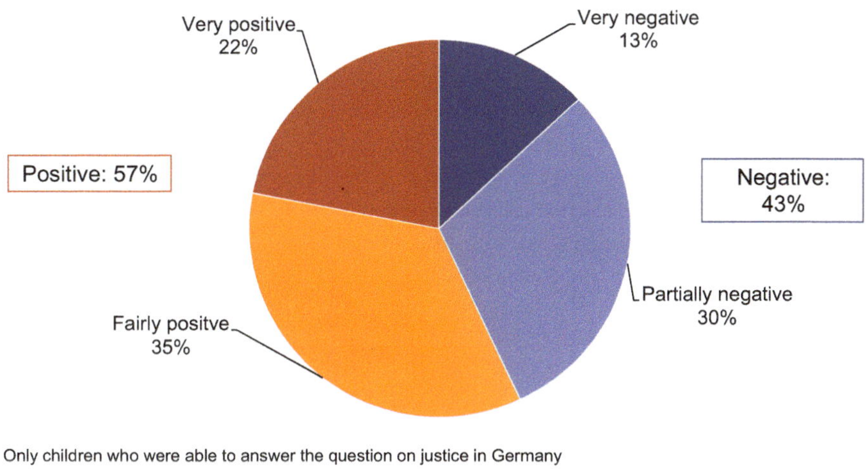

Fig. 2.10 "Social justice"
Global assessment of how are social groups treated in Germany
Children in Germany aged 6–11 years (%)

The majority of children in this group also consider that the social groups we asked about are treated fairly (fair treatment of children and adolescents: 78%, fair treatment of foreigners: 62%). However, only a minority of 27% consider that poor people are treated fairly.

Children with a partially negative view of social justice in Germany: 30%.

About one-half of the children in this group consider the treatment of children and adolescents as well as the aged to be fair. In contrast, only one in five consider the treatment of the disabled or foreigners in German to be fair, and only a small minority of 9% consider that poor people receive fair treatment.

Children with a very negative view of social justice in Germany: 13%.

The majority of children in this group consider that nearly all the social groups surveyed are treated unfairly in Germany.

Hence, in all, children's opinions on social justice in Germany vary greatly. At 57%, the majority take a positive position. Nonetheless, this still leaves 43% with a more negative view of social justice in the country. Viewed in context, at 64%, lower class children significantly more frequently have a negative perception of social justice in Germany. At 49%, the appraisal of children growing up in a one-parent family is also significantly more negative. Independent of social status, girls at 46% also significantly more frequently give more negative appraisals than boys. Younger children, in contrast, tend to view things more positively. Looked at in context, the place of residence (Eastern or Western Germany, urban or rural), in contrast, is not significant. A migration background is also, in itself, without effect. According to our multivariate statistical analysis, the existing bivariate differences are due far more to social origin (Table 2.5).

It can be seen that alongside age and gender (indicating that girls have a greater sensitivity to injustice in the treatment of disadvantaged persons), the social situation of the children shapes their view of social justice.

As a result, it is also not very surprising that the majority of children with a very positive or positive personal life satisfaction also evaluate social justice in Germany positively, whereas the majority of children with a negative to neutral evaluation of their personal life satisfaction also evaluate "social justice in Germany" negatively. Here as well, it is the social class of origin and everyday social experiences that decisively influence personal life satisfaction and the appraisal of "social justice."

2.7 Experienced Injustice in Daily Life

An important backdrop when appraising justice is also whether the children themselves feel disadvantaged in their daily lives or whether this is generally not the case. In the current 2013 World Vision Child Study, we asked about perceived disadvantages in relation to different domains (Fig. 2.11).

About one-third of the children report feeling disadvantaged (sometimes or often) because of their age. Thirty-four percent of 6- to 7-year-olds and 36% of 8- to 9-year-olds say this slightly more often than 10- to 11-year-olds at 29%. Because of their gender, 20% of girls feel disadvantaged in daily life compared to only 8% of boys. Although younger girls report this somewhat more frequently, the difference between boys and girls is retained in all age groups. Because of what they look like, 14% of children, 15% of girls, and 12% of boys feel disadvantaged; and 12% of the children report feeling disadvantaged because their parents do not have much money. We asked only children with a migration background about disadvantage due to origin. Of these children, 21% report feeling disadvantaged in daily life because their parents do not come from Germany.

Here as well, we decided to summarize different experiences of disadvantage that cannot be clearly separated from each other in order to gain a global picture. We once again formed a summary indicator and grouped children according to whether they reported disadvantage *hardly ever*, *sometimes*, or *often*.[15]

At 56%, the majority of children report being *hardly ever* disadvantaged. The second group contains 34% of the children. These report feeling *sometimes* disadvantaged. In most cases, these disadvantages are because of age (two-thirds in this group) and sometimes because of their gender or their external appearance. The third group contains 10% of the children. They report *often* being disadvantaged in

[15] We also summed the ratings here (often = 3, sometimes = 2, hardly ever/not at all = 1, don't know/no reply = 0), and grouped them according to their central tendency. Up to and including the median, there are practically no experiences of disadvantage; deviations above the median and up to the standard deviation, sometimes; and above the standard deviation, often.

Table 2.5 Relation between assessment of "social justice" and significant social variables[a]
Children in Germany aged 6–11 years

Per line in %	Positive	Negative
All children	57	43
Age groups		
6–7 years	64	**36**[b]
8–9 years	57	43
10–11 years	54	46
Gender		
Girls	54	**46**[b]
Boys	59	41
Social origin		
Lower class	36	**64**[b]
Lower middle class	56	44
Middle class	58	42
Upper middle class	61	39
Upper class	58	42
Type of family		
Single parent	51	**49**[2]

[a]Only 6- to 7-year-olds who were able to given an answer to the item on justice in Germany

The relationship was studied with a multivariate logistic regression on the criterion variable "evaluation of social justice in relation to various groups: very/quite) positive or (very/quite) negative."

Variables included: age groups, gender, East/West, urban/rural, social origin, migration background, and type of family

[b]For ease of presentation, bivariate values are presented as percentages in the table. Values that were also significant within the multivariate statistical analysis are printed in bold ($p < .05$)

daily life. Most frequently, this is because of their age (four out of five in this group), but also because of their gender or external appearance (more than two-thirds), and finally because their parents do not have enough money (more than one-half of this group).

What is decisive here is, once again, the social background and the family situation. Both significantly more frequently result in children feeling disadvantaged in daily life (Fig. 2.12). At 68%, two out of three lower-class children report disadvantage (sometimes and often combined). Findings are similar for children who have an unemployed parent (68%). Notably, 51% of children in single-parent families and 50% of children in families with three or more children tend to report being disadvantaged in daily life compared to children living in other types of family. The significance of this finding was also confirmed in a multivariate statistical analysis.[16]

[16] Here we carried out an ordinal regression on our newly formed and grouped variable "Perceived disadvantage in daily life: often, sometimes, or never." Gender, social class, form of family, unem-

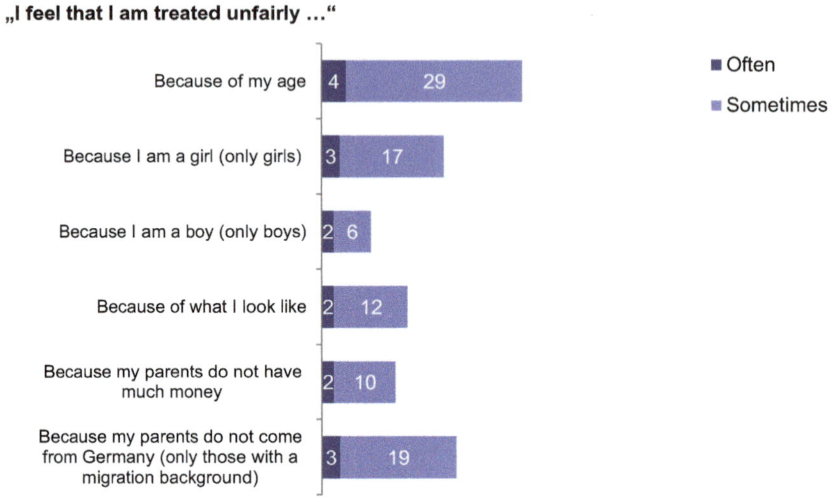

Fig. 2.11 Domains in which children feel being treated unfairly in everyday life
Children in Germany aged 6–11 years (%)

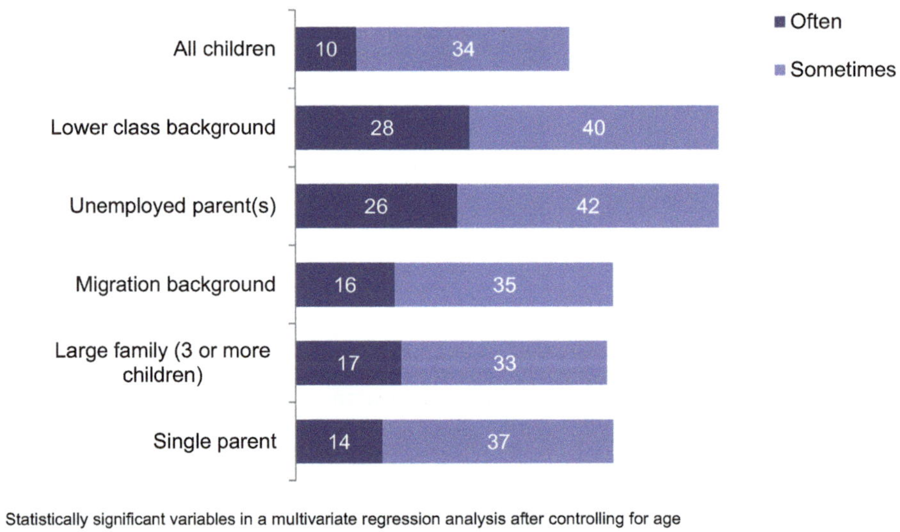

Fig. 2.12 Children who reported feeling unfair treatment
Children in Germany aged 6–11 years (%)

The same applies for children with a migration background. When asked about felt disadvantage, at 51%, children with a non-German background report significantly

ployed parent, migration background, eastern/western Germany, urban/rural were entered as dependent variables; age, as covariate.

more disadvantage in daily life independent of social origins. In contrast, gender and place of residence (Eastern or Western Germany, urban or rural) are not significant in this context.

Children who rate "social justice" in Germany more negatively also more frequently report having fears. These are also more often girls than boys and also more frequently children from the lower classes. As to be expected, the greatest fear is of increasing poverty. Only 45% of children with a more positive appraisal of "social justice" report fears of poverty compared to 59% of children with a negative appraisal. Only 16% of children with a more positive appraisal are afraid of more foreigners coming to live in Germany compared to 27% of children with a negative appraisal. When it comes to the topic of parental unemployment, in contrast, differences are much lower. A total of 26% of children with a positive appraisal are sometimes afraid of this compared to 31% of children with a negative appraisal of social justice.

Here we see once more that children growing up in socially disadvantaged families also significantly more frequently see themselves as being disadvantaged in daily life. We already managed to demonstrate the children's sensitivity toward their lack of opportunities and the disadvantages that they see in our last two Child Studies. In addition to this, and independently from poverty or unemployment in the family, children with a migration background report disadvantages in daily life. A proportion of these children accordingly experience their own roots as a stigmatization that results in exclusion. Children from "untypically" large families with three or more children also feel disadvantaged, just like children growing up in single-parent families. They are less satisfied with the justice in their families or their circles of friends. At the same time, they evidently experience a lack of compatibility in many aspects of their daily lives; that is, in this case, a persisting lack of family friendliness in our society. There are many reasons to view this sociopolitical issue more strongly than before from the perspective of the children (see also Chap. 3).

An inspection of the children's perspective on "social justice" in Germany and their own experience of disadvantages somewhat qualifies the initial reports documenting their high level of satisfaction with their lives. Children in this age range perceive and evaluate the risks in society, and when they appraise "social justice" in Germany negatively, this is accompanied by stronger fears and uncertainties. This is strengthened by everyday experiences along with their knowledge that their families are often also in a socially precarious situation. Nonetheless, it is the prevailing positive outlook that is decisive for the greatest majority of children and their trust in the family, the circle of friends, and the adult world in general. The aspects of society that children of this age associate with justice are highlighted succinctly by one of the children we surveyed.

> That everybody has enough to eat, that all live in freedom, that there is no extreme poverty, that there are not so many rich people who do not share anything (11-year-old boy)

As this chapter has shown, children demand fairness in the ways they interact with each other personally along with equal opportunities so that everybody can take part. In the modern sociopolitical discussion, this attitude is labeled "participatory justice." It focuses on ensuring and systematically extending the right of all individuals in society "to live in this world" in the sense of enabling them to determine for themselves what they rationally wish to strive toward. What is remarkable is how well the children's perspective and their desire for equality fit in with the debate on social equality. At the end of the day, the main concern in the "grown-up" world is also that "you share with the others, and don't leave anybody just standing there" (7-year-old girl).

References

Allbus: Datenreport. (2011). *Ein Sozialbericht für die Bundesrepublik Deutschland.* Bonn: Bundeszentrale für politische Bildung.

Allensbacher Institut für Demoskopie. (2013). Was ist gerecht? Gerechtigkeitsbegriff und -wahrnehmung der Bürger. Allensbacher Archiv, IfD-Umfrage 11001, Allensbach.

Dalbert, C. (1983). Die Gerechte-Welt-Skala (GWS). In Preiser, S. (Hrsg.), *Soziales Handeln im Kindes- und Jugendalter* (Dokumentation von Forschungs- und Diagnoseinstrumenten). Weinheim: Beltz, S. 139.

Dalbert, C., Montada, L., & Schmitt, M. (1987). Glaube an eine gerechte Welt als Motiv: Validierungskorrelate zweier Skalen. *Psychologische Beiträge, 29*, S. 596–615.

Essau, C. A. (2003). *Angst bei Kindern und Jugendlichen*. Stuttgart: UTB.

Fehr, E., Bernhard, H., & Rockenbach, B. (2008). Egalitarianism in young children. In *Nature* (Vol. 454, pp. 1079–1083).

Glatzer, W. (2009). Gefühlte (Un)Gerechtigkeit. *Aus Politik und Zeitgeschichte, 47*/2009, S. 15–20.

Hamann, K., Warneken, F., Greenberg, J. R., & Tomasello, M. (2011). Collaboration encourages equal sharing in children but not chimpanzees. In: Nature, doi:10.1038/nature10278. http://wkprc.eva.mpg.de/pdf/2011/Hamann_Warnek_Greenberg_Tomasello_2011.pdf (Stand: 20.08.2013).

HBSC-Team Deutschland. (2011). Studie Health Behaviour in School-aged Children – Faktenblatt »Lebenszufriedenheit von Kindern und Jugendlichen". Bielefeld: WHO Collaborating Centre for Child and Adolescent Health Promotion.

Kohlberg, L. (1964). The development of moral character and ideology. In M. L. Hoffmann (Ed.), *Review of child development research*. New York: Wiley.

Kohlberg, L. (1974). *Zur kognitiven Entwicklung des Kindes*. Frankfurt: Suhrkamp.

Liebig, S., & Lengfeld, H. (Hrsg.). (2002). *Interdisziplinäre Gerechtigkeitsforschung. Zur Verknüpfung empirischer und normativer Perspektiven*. Hamburg: Campus.

Liebig, S., & May, M. (2009). Dimensionen sozialer Gerechtigkeit. *Aus Politik und Zeitgeschichte, 47*/2009, S. 3–8.

Morschitzky, H. (2009). *Angststörungen. Diagnostik, Konzepte, Theorie, Selbsthilfe* (4. Auflage). Heidelberg: Springer.

Oerter, R., & Montada, L. (Hrsg.). (2002). *Entwicklungspsychologie* (5. vollständig überarbeitete Auflage). Weinheim: Beltz.

Piaget, J. (1932/1983). *Das moralische Urteil beim Kinde*. Stuttgart: Klett.

Piaget, J. (1937/1975). *Der Aufbau der Wirklichkeit beim Kinde*. Stuttgart: Klett.

Schneekloth, U., & Pupeter, M. (2010b). Wohlbefinden, Wertschätzung, Selbstwirksamkeit: Was Kinder für ein gutes Leben brauchen. In World Vision Deutschland. (Hrsg.), *Kinder in Deutschland 2010b. 2. World Vision Kinderstudie* (S. 187–221). Frankfurt a. M: Fischer.

Sen, A. (2010). *Die Idee der Gerechtigkeit*. München: C. H. Beck Verlag.

Trautner, H. M. (1991). *Lehrbuch der Entwicklungspsychologie* (Bd. 2: Theorien und Befunde). Göttingen: Hogrefe.
UNICEF. (2013). *Child well-being in rich countries. A comparative overview* (Innocenti Report Card 11 (UNICEF)).
Woodward, L. J., & Fergusson, D. M. (2001). Life course of young people with anxiety disorders in adolescence. *Journal of the American Academy of Child and Adolescent Psychiatry, 40*, 1086–1093.

Chapter 3
Family Backgrounds: Great Variety But Also Marked Differences In Life Conditions

Ulrich Schneekloth and Monika Pupeter

In their everyday lives, their own family is a kind of "safe haven" for children. Normally, it meets their everyday needs while providing quality relationships, emotional security, and privacy (Schneewind 2008). The family is characterized by its specific social capital: the strong ties forged by the close and emotionally based relationships between its members (Coleman 1988). Accordingly, the family is where children and adults interact with a strong emotional commitment. However, as the two earlier Child Studies have shown, the forms the family takes can vary greatly. First, it can contain either just one or several children. Second, parents can be married to each other or live together in a domestic partnership; they can be separated but both rearing their children together or be single parents; and, finally, they can be biological parents, adoptive parents, or a combination of the two.

In this chapter, we wish to describe the familial and social background to the children's lives. Because we have already reported on this in detail in the two earlier Child Studies, this study will focus more on the relevant trends that have become recognizable since the first Child Study in 2007. Alongside the family situation, we shall consider a possible migration background (in the parents) as well as the children's social origins. Of course, one important aspect here is whether there is also a potential risk of poverty. In this new Child Study, we have broadened the indicators used to describe experiences of poverty from the children's perspective. The new findings this has generated will also be reported in this chapter. It will close by reporting on how the children themselves rate their family care situation.

U. Schneekloth (✉) • M. Pupeter
Kantar Public, München, Germany
e-mail: ulrich.schneekloth@kantarpublic.com; monika.pupeter@kantarpublic.com

S. Andresen et al. (eds.), *Well-being, Poverty and Justice from a Child's Perspective*, Children's Well-Being: Indicators and Research 17,
DOI 10.1007/978-3-319-57574-2_3

3.1 Shaped by Diversity: Today's Families Can Vary Greatly

As reported in the previous Child Studies, there have been marked changes to the characteristic form of family life over the last decades. The typical family in post-war Germany from the 1950s onward was the nuclear family composed of father, mother, and (at that time still) two children all living together in one household until the children reached adulthood. The division of labor was organized generally with the man as the sole wage earner who ensured the family livelihood and the woman as responsible for the domestic tasks of looking after the home and children-at least as long as the children were still small or attending school.

3.1.1 Faces of Families Today

It is not just recently that this ideal of the "conventional nuclear family" has lost its decisive role as a lifestyle model. This change can already be seen in the forms of family in which today's 6- to 11-year-old children are growing up.

We classified the different types of family according to the following features:

- "Marital status" of the parents
- "Completeness" in the sense of a one- or two-parent family with either biological or adoptive parents
- "Size," that is, the number of children living in the household as well as the number of generations

What has not changed at all is that children (between the ages of 6 and 11 years) still live predominately in nuclear families (Fig. 3.1).[1] Three-generation families, that is, children, parents, and grandparents all living together under one roof, are a very rare exception (they make up less than 1%). In contrast, family structures have become more differentiated: Only 39% of children in this age range live in a "two-child family" together with a sibling, and only a further 20% in a family with two or more siblings. A total of 14% of 6- to 11-year-olds are growing up as an only child. What has remained stable at approximately 17% over the last 6 years since our first Child Study is the proportion of children growing up with a single parent.[2] Findings are similar for nonmarried life partnerships and also for adoptive families (married, but at least one nonbiological parent) in which 5% and 4% of the children respectively are growing up.

---

[1] In this context, the nuclear family means the "two-generation family" living together in one household with (biological) parents. Children living in residential homes are generally not considered here, because they still make up less than 0.5% of children in this age range despite a slight absolute increase over the last few years.

[2] Here, we are referring to the results of the parent survey in which we gathered some important sociodemographic background information on the children's family situation.

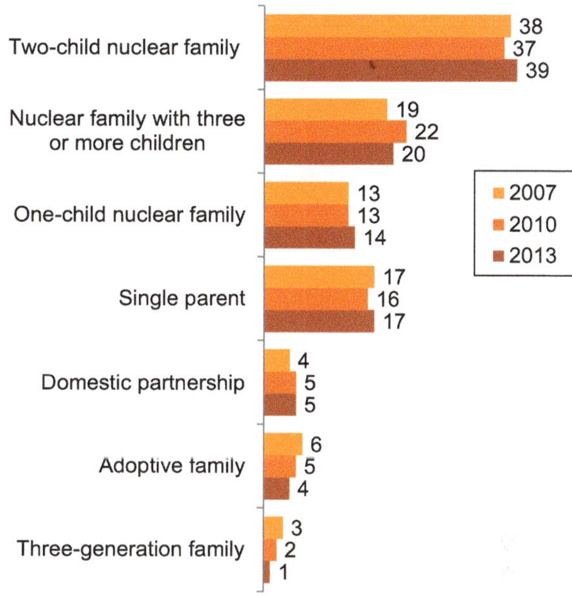

Fig. 3.1 In which families do children grow up **Children in Germany aged 6–11 years (2007: 8–11 years) (%)**

Table 3.1 Siblings in the household
Children in Germany aged 6–11 years (2007: 8–11 years) (%)

Columns in %	2007	2010	2013
Siblings in household			
No siblings	24	25	27
One sibling	50	48	49
Two siblings	18	21	17
Three and more siblings	8	6	7

If we just look at the number of siblings, regardless of which type of family they belong to, we can see a trend toward a slow but continuous growth in the proportion of children growing up in households without siblings over the last 6 years (Table 3.1).[3] We had already observed this trend in the last Child Study. Against this background, we also see no reason to change our conclusion that the proportion of children growing up without their own siblings will probably increase even further in the future. Because a major proportion of children will accordingly experience neither older nor younger siblings in their own family, experiences with "peers" will need to be organized in other ways. In early childhood, this can be provided either informally through self-organized nursery groups but also, of course, through institutional care services such as day nurseries or preschools.

[3] Here, we are referring specifically to those siblings (of all age groups) who are living in the same household. However, also including those siblings who have left the parental home and are (already) living in their own households does not alter the trend reported here.

Taken together, 73% of children are growing up in a "normal family" with their married biological parents. A further 21% are living in a recombined family either with a single parent or also with one adoptive parent. Finally, 5% are growing up with unmarried (biological or also nonbiological) parents. Even though these proportions have remained relatively stable over the last 6 years, as pointed out in the last Child Study, this makes absolutely no difference to the need to respond to the challenge to deliver child-friendly social policies that will also ensure material security and equal opportunities for children growing up in patchwork families or with unmarried parents.

3.2 Labor Participation of Parents: A Distribution of Roles and No Longer "Just the Father's Business"

In the last Child Study, we already pointed to the trend toward a changing distribution of roles within families. Being gainfully employed and thus securing the family's subsistence is no longer primarily the concern of fathers. In the current Child Study, we also surveyed the parents alongside their children, and these findings confirm the further decline in the traditional "one-male-breadwinner" family (Fig. 3.2).

Only 32% of children are still growing up in nuclear families (in this case, families with two parents without taking marriage status into account) in which only one parent—usually the father—is gainfully employed. In our last Child Study in 2010, this group still contained 40% of children, and in our first Child Study of 2007, it

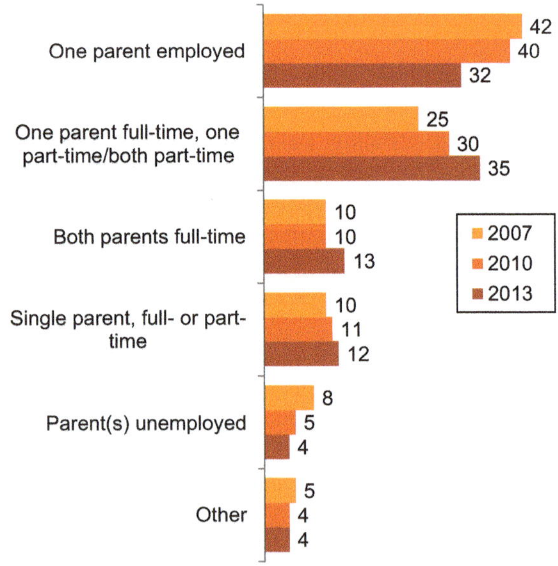

Fig. 3.2 Labor participation of Parents **Children in Germany aged 6–11 years (2007: 8–11 years) (%)**

was even 42%. These children are joined once again by 12% who are growing up with a single parent who is simultaneously gainfully employed. The most frequent constellation that is now found in 35% of 6- to 11-year-olds is two gainfully employed parents—mostly the father working full-time and the mother either part-time or at least marginally. "Both parents working full-time" now applies to 13% of the children in our age group, thereby showing a slight increase. Only 4% of children are growing up in families with one (or at least one) unemployed parent, and a further 4% in other constellations (parents or single parent in training or studying, parents or single parent not gainfully employed for other reasons).

There is a tendency for somewhat older children to have two gainfully employed parents. However, the real relationship is to the number of children in the household: the more children in the household, the greater the probability that only one parent—generally the father—will pursue gainful employment. When there is only one child (in the household), this applies to 17%; for children with one sibling in the household, to 31%; and for children with two or more siblings, to 56%. Vice versa, 19% of single children have two full-time employed parents, 12%, of those with one sibling, and no more than 8% of those with two or more siblings.

The increase in the gainful employment of both parents is due decisively to the strong recovery of the labor market in Germany over the last 6 years—and above all since the last Child Study in 2010. This allows more people in general to find gainful employment. The significance of the tendency to engage in gainful employment and, in this case, the accompanying difference in the distribution of roles within the family becomes even more visible when we also take into account where the children live—in this case, differentiated according to the old and new German states (West vs. East). Typical for the former Western states (including Berlin) is now two gainfully employed parents for 47% of the children, although generally with the father in full-time and the mother in part-time or marginal employment (36%). Only 11% of the children live in families in which both parents are employed full-time. In the Western states, 34% of children are growing up in families with one gainfully employed parent. In former East Germany (excluding Berlin), in contrast, at 30%, a large proportion of the children in this age range are growing up in families in which both parents are gainfully employed. For 25%, it is generally the father who is full-time and the mother who has part-time or marginal employment. Only 19% of the children in the East are growing up in nuclear families with only one gainfully employed parent (Table 3.2).

Table 3.2 Labor participation of parents by child's age and region
Children in Germany aged 6–11 years

Columns in %	All children	6–7 years	8–9 years	10–11 years	West[a]	East[b]
Type of labor participation						
One parent employed	32	33	34	29	34	19
One parent full-time, one part-time/ both part-time	35	33	35	36	36	25
Both parents full-time	13	13	12	14	11	30
Single parent, full- or part-time	12	13	11	13	12	14
Parents/Parent unemployed	4	5	4	3	3	7
Other	4	3	4	5	4	5

[a]West (including Berlin)
[b]East (not including Berlin)

Table 3.3 Number of hours employed mothers would like to work
Mothers of children aged 6–11 years[a]

Columns in %	All mothers	Full-time	Part-time	Marginal employment
Employment preferences				
Work more hours	18	6	18	35
Work fewer hours	14	35	8	2
Things are fine the way they are	68	59	74	63

[a]Only for children whose mothers completed the questionnaire

3.2.1 Mothers More Frequently Want Their Own (Part-Time) Gainful Employment

In the present Child Study, we ask the mothers providing information on their children to appraise their own employment situation.[4] Results are very clear: Whereas mothers who are already employed are generally satisfied with this, the majority of not employed mothers would like to have their own (part-time) gainful employment.

Among the employed mothers of children in our age range, it is those who work part-time who are most satisfied with their working hours (Table 3.3): 74% report that "things are fine the way they are." Findings are similar for marginally employed mothers with 63% reporting that they are satisfied. Nonetheless, 35% of this group

[4] Strictly speaking, the children's mothers in our survey are not a representative random selection. We recruited a representative sample of children and then gathered some background information from one of the parents. In 83% of cases, this was the mother; in the remaining 17%, in contrast, our information came from the father. In these latter cases, we have no self-reports on personal preferences from the mothers. There are many signs that the father more frequently gave information when the mother had no time because, for example, she was gainfully employed. However, because we analyzed the desired working hours separately for employed and nonemployed mothers, potential distortions should tend to be negligible.

Table 3.4 Type of employment nonemployed mothers would like
Mothers of children aged 6–11 years[a]

Columns in %	All mothers	On parental leave	Unemployed	Housewife/ Other
Desired employment				
Yes, full-time	8	2	31	3
Yes, part-time	45	43	55	43
Things are fine the way they are	47	54	14	54
No reply	0	1	0	0

[a]Only for children whose mothers completed the questionnaire

would like to work more. Among mothers with full-time employment, the majority at 59% are also satisfied with their working hours. However, 35% would prefer to work fewer hours.[5]

The situation of mothers who are not gainfully employed is completely the opposite (Table 3.4). Of those who describe themselves as unemployed, 31% would like to work full-time and 55% part-time. From the otherwise not gainfully employed mothers, that is, those who are studying, in training, or who describe themselves as housewives, 42% say that they would like to work part-time. However, 54% say that "things are fine the way they are." Finally, interesting reports come from the group of mothers who are currently on parental leave (generally because of a younger sibling living in the household). Of the mothers on parental leave, 43% would like to work part-time, whereas 54% report that things are fine the way they are. In this exceptionally small group in numerical terms, we are unable to distinguish between mothers who are purely on parental leave and those in marginal or part-time employment. Nonetheless, their reports are interesting and underline the mothers' desire to have their own jobs and generally to work part-time.

To enable a comparison, here are the findings on the actual labor market participation of the mothers providing the information: in full-time employment: 20% (West: 17%, East: 40%), part-time: 43% (West: 44%, East: 35%), marginal: 11% (West: 12%, East: 6%), unemployed: 4% (West: 3%, East: 9%), and not working for other reasons: 22% (West: 23%, East: 10%).

Combining the findings on desired and actual participation in employment, mothers from the old German states (including Berlin) most frequently prefer a part-time job. A total of 43% reported that they would prefer to work part-time or that they are satisfied with their own part-time employment; or if they work full-time, that they would prefer to work fewer hours. Only 19% prefer to work full-time, whereas 24% of this subgroup prefer marginal employment. Among mothers from the new German states, 39% prefer part-time employment, whereas 45% desire

[5]A recent study based on the German Socio-Economic Panel (SOEP) reveals that women working full-time more frequently desire fewer working hours per week, whereas women working part-time desire more working hours (Holst and Seifert 2012). However, these results are drawn on the population of all women in gainful employment and not just those with children (aged 6–11 years).

Table 3.5 Biography: Earlier attendance of a day care and a kindergarten
Children in Germany aged 6–11 years

Yes, child used to attend a day care or Kindergarten Columns in %	All children	West[a]	East[b]
Childcare			
Day care (children under the age of 3)	26	20	67
Kindergarten (children over the age of 3)	93	93	97

[a]West (including Berlin)
[b]East (excluding Berlin)

full-time employment and 10% would most prefer marginal employment.[6] Both the desire for a gainful employment in principle and the desire for full-time employment are markedly stronger in Eastern compared to Western Germany.

3.2.2 *Early Childhood Care Helps to Ensure Parental Labor Market Participation*

These different traditions in labor market participation and hence in the distribution of family roles have quite material backgrounds. When we asked parents whether their children had at some stage in the past attended a childcare institution, we found marked East–West differences—particularly for children under the age of 3 years. In former West Germany, 19% of parents report that the child we are surveying had attended a day care. In former East Germany, this is 61%. In contrast, more than 90% of parents in both East and West report that their child had attended a Kindergarten (Table 3.5).[7]

The different traditions in familial gainful employment in former East and West Germany were—and continue to be—accompanied by a different density of services in childcare institutions. This applies particularly to the care services for

[6]Because of the differences in the questions given to employed and not employed persons, preferences do not discriminate completely between the two groups. For example, as soon as a mother reported that she worked part-time but would prefer to work less, we assumed that she wished to be marginally employed. The same applied in the other direction for full-time employed and also for marginally employed persons.

[7]These retrospective reports cannot be compared directly with official statistics. We asked whether the children had at any time attended a day nursery or a Kindergarten. If, instead, as in the official statistics, we had asked how many children per age cohort were attending a Kindergarten at that particular point in time, we would have gained lower proportions—above all in the West. Part of the detailed differences between East and West are due to terminological variations as well as to the different forms of care. For the sake of simplicity, we limited our retrospective survey to institutional forms of care (day nursery, Kindergarten, daycare center) without explicitly mentioning family day carers or other forms of privately organized care. The available official data on institutional childcare nonetheless confirm the main trend and in particular the East–West differences in the daycare of children under the age of 3 years (Bertelsmann Ländermonitor Frühkindliche Bildungssysteme, Kinderbetreuung).

children under the age of 3 years. This is why it was and continues to be usual for women in Eastern Germany to take up employment comparatively soon after the birth of a child as well as more frequently in general. There were and continue to be better framing conditions for this in the form of a greater number of childcare places.

Retrospective findings underline that women whose children had already attended childcare services under the age of 3 years far more frequently take up gainful employment again than women who looked after their under-3-year-old children at home. In Western Germany, 25% of the mothers of children who had attended a day nursery according to parent reports are in full-time employment today compared to 15% of those whose children had not attended a day nursery, whereas 44% of both groups work part-time. In Eastern Germany, the figures are even 45% with day nursery compared to 29% without day nursery who currently work full-time and 36% with day nursery compared to 33% without day nursery who work part-time. Accordingly, it seems as if women who use childcare services when their children are under the age of 3 years will more probably go to work (again) as their children grow older.

In 2008, Germany passed a law in the support and care of children under the age of 3 years at day facilities and in day care (KiFöG) that set an August 1, 2013, deadline. Since then, parents have the legal right to a childcare place for their child once she or he attains the age of 12 months. This has created framing conditions designed to level out regional disparities in the provision of daycare for children. However, its practical implementation continues to be plagued by numerous difficulties, particularly regarding the expansion of care provisions this requires. Currently, it does not look as if the legal right to a daycare place for children under the age of 3 can actually be implemented throughout Germany in the foreseeable future.[8]

3.3 Personal Cultural Backgrounds: "German" Children, Migrant Parents, and Religious Traditions

A total of 34%, that is, every third child in our 2013 World Vision Child Study, has a migration background. Most of them are born in Germany with German nationality and have parents who migrated to the country. In formal legal terms, according to parent reports, 94% of children are German according to German citizenship laws, 89% have German citizenship alone, and slightly more than 5% have dual nationality—generally German citizenship along with the nationality of a non-German parent.[9] Accordingly, the children's migration background refers predomi-

[8] On the current state of implementation, see the most recent interim report on the evaluation of the Childcare Funding Act (Kinderförderungsgesetz - Kifög) for 2012 (BMFSFJ, 2013a)

[9] In general, these are children born in Germany of non-German parents who are obliged by German law (29 StAG) to declare which nationality they have decided to take before the end of their 23rd year of life.

nantly to their background of origin, or more precisely the origin of their parents. Therefore, in the following, we talk about native German children (66%) as well as children with a migration background (34%) or, sometimes, German children with a migration background (28%) and non-German children who possess exclusively non-German citizenship (6%).[10]

For 21% of the children with a migration background, either one or both parents have, according to their own reports, emigrated from Turkey. Roughly a further 7% have an Arabic background, and almost 4% come from Africa. Approximately 16% come from the former Soviet Union and 16% from other East European countries (Ukraine, Poland, and Rumania), frequently as ethnic German immigrants who have German citizenship. A further 8% come from the countries making up the former Yugoslavia. Almost 15% of the parents of children with a migration background come from Western Europe, whereas the remaining 14% are distributed across other countries.[11]

It is conspicuous that children in Germany today have a whole range of different backgrounds. Every third child in this age range has an international and therefore also a multicultural background. A very large majority of children are not migrants but were born in Germany. As a result, the trend toward a growing proportion of the population with a migration background will increase further regardless of whether more or less people migrate directly to Germany. At the current point in time, the proportion of migrants in different regions of Germany continues to vary greatly. In our Child Study, 38% of children in the old federal states (including Berlin) have a migration background compared to only 9% in the new federal states. Findings are similar for the urban–rural distribution. In urban central areas and conurbations, almost one-half of the children have a migration background compared to no more than 25% in the peripheries or rural areas.

3.3.1 *Different Religious Cultures*

The migration background to be found in one-third of all children in Germany is also accompanied by a wide range of denominations and religions. A majority of slightly more than two out of three children in our age range come from parental

[10] One methodological comment at this point: Only 2.4% of the children in our actual sample were not German citizens and, taken together, 25.4% had a migration background. Hence, in this regard, the current sample is "better" than that in previous years. However, according to the official microcensus, 32.7% of children had a migration background of whom 5.5% were foreigners without German citizenship in the reference year 2011. Because of the significance that is now assigned to a migration background, we decided to adjust our sample here by weighting it to make it more representative. We took exactly the same approach as in the past two Child Studies and adjusted the proportion of non-German children; however, we did not explicitly adjust the proportion of children with a migration background.

[11] These findings also match the nationalities of origin reported in the microcensus. However, because of the low case numbers, we cannot differentiate further here.

Table 3.6 Parents' religion
Children in Germany aged 6–11 years[a]

Columns in %	Mother	Father
Religion		
Catholic	32	30
Protestant	32	29
Other Christian	4	3
Muslim	10	13
Other non-Christian religion	2	2
No religion	20	23

[a]Reported only when either father or mother was present

Table 3.7 Religious practice in family home
Children in Germany aged 6–11 years

Columns in %	All children	West[a]	East[b]	Native German	Migration background
Do you regularly attend religious services at a church or mosque (or other place of worship)?					
Yes, every week	10	10	7	8	13
Yes, once or twice a month	18	20	4	17	20
Less often	28	31	12	28	27
Never	44	39	77	47	40
Do you pray at home?					
Very often	13	14	4	10	18
Sometimes	20	22	9	17	26
Hardly ever	11	12	3	11	11
No	56	52	82	62	45
No reply	–	–	2	0	–

[a]West (including Berlin)
[b]East (not including Berlin)

homes with a Christian faith (mostly either Catholic or Protestant depending on the region). For at least 10% of the children, the mother is Muslim; for 13%, the father.[12] A total of 20% of the mothers and 23% of the fathers have no formal religious belief; other religions are almost completely nonsignificant (Table 3.6).

In our last Child Study, we talked about the "three religious cultures": the nonreligious East, the more plural West, and from a further perspective, the more strongly religious migrants. This description of conditions remains unchanged. A total of 33% of the families of the children we surveyed "sometimes" or "very often" say prayers (36% from the old and 13% from the new federal states). A total of 44% of children with a migration background report that prayers are said at home (Table 3.7).

[12]In this case, we always consider only the children with parents providing information on their partner. These reports are missing for single parents. Because the proportion of single parents in Germany is much lower among migrants from Muslim cultures (less than 10%), slightly more fathers than mothers are reported as being Muslim.

In our last Child Study in 2010, 39% of the children reported that prayers are said at home: 43% from the old federal states, 15% from the new federal states, and 51% of children with a migration background.

In terms of religious affiliations, 37% of the children from a Christian parental home report that they pray at home (23% "sometimes" and 14% "very often"). As to be expected, only 9% of children from a parental home with no religious affiliation (both parents with no religious affiliation) report saying prayers at home. In contrast, 64% of children with either one or two Muslim parents pray at home (37% "sometimes" and 27% "very often").

3.3.2 The Majority of Native German Children Do Not Attend Church Services on a Regular Basis

In all, 28% of the children attend a church, a mosque, or other place of worship "every week" or "once or twice a month." Of these, 30% come from the old federal states, 11% come from the new federal states, and 33% have a migration background (Table 3.7). In our 2010 Child Study, the total was 27%, with 30% coming from the old federal states, 10% coming from the new federal states, and 28% with a migration background. Looking at the religious affiliations in the parental home here as well, 34% of the children from a Christian parental home attend church services (22% "once or twice a month" and 12% "every week"). A total of 10% of children whose parents have no religious affiliation report attending church services, whereas 42% of children with a Muslim parent report attending services in a mosque (25% "once or twice a month" and 17% "every week").

Results show some slight fluctuation over time. Praying seems to be slightly in decline (from 39% to 33%), whereas attending religious services continues to be the usual practice for 28% of children. All in all, religion continues to have an influence on everyday life for only a smaller proportion of the children, and this depends on whether they are growing up in the old or the new federal states. Children with a migration background have a stronger religious involvement. This would seem to be due particularly to the fact that by upholding religious traditions, parents can also uphold and communicate the cultural values of their country of origin. For migrants, particularly those with roots in a Muslim culture, religiosity contributes to their sense of identity and is accordingly more important in everyday life than is generally the case for native German families.

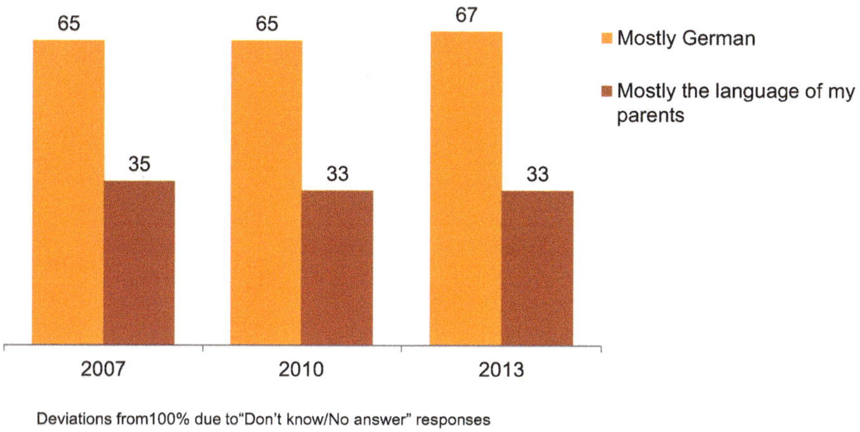

Fig. 3.3 Migration background: Which language is spoken at home
Children with a migration background in Germany aged 6–11 years (2007: 8–11 years) (%)

3.3.3 Tradition and Native Language

We also asked the children with a migration background which language they generally speak at home in their family. Looking at the trend, 67% of the children with a migration background, and thus slightly fewer than in our two prior Child Studies, report generally speaking German at home. Approximately one-third speak the native language of their parents at home (Fig. 3.3).

The question on the language that is spoken at home should not be used as a direct indicator for the frequently criticized lack of German language competence. Multilingualism is not a deficit. It is far more the case that children have very robust language acquisition abilities and can easily learn more than one language. Nonetheless, the precondition for this is the presence of both languages in everyday life and also, when needed, their focused promotion (see Jampert et al. 2009; Tracy 2007, on growing up multilingually). On the one hand, language transports and conveys culture and tradition: the stronger the cultural ties of the family with the country of origin, the more important it is for parents to speak their native language at home and, in particular, with their own children. On the other hand, it is often completely practical considerations or habit that leads parents to speak their native language at home.

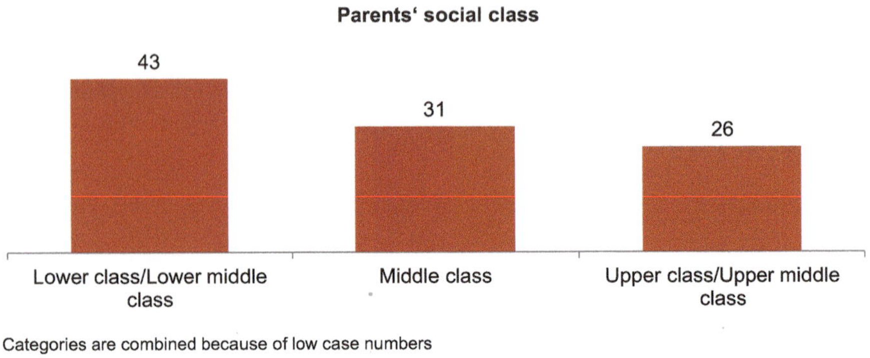

Fig. 3.4 Migration background: Language spoken at home by social class
"At home we mostly speak the language of my parents"
Children in Germany aged 6–11 years (2007: 8–11 years) (%)

3.3.4 The Less Well-Educated the Class of Origin, the More Frequently German Is Not Spoken at Home

Everyday language can also be a risk factor for children with a migration background. Language acquisition and language competence are general intervention topics for children from less well-educated parental homes. This is just as much the case for children whose parents were born and grew up in Germany as it is for those whose parents migrated and speak another native language. A migration background and the use of the native language in the family can given a corresponding context, naturally also represent a hindrance in acquiring German.

The five-level class index used to differentiate the social backgrounds of children in the World Vision Child Study also delivers important findings here. Its construction is based decisively on the parents' educational background (see also Sect. 3.5 and Appendix 2, for the following).

It is conspicuous to see that, at 43%, children in the two lower social classes far more frequently speak their parent's native language at home. For middle-class children, the proportion is 31%, and in the two upper classes, it is 26% (Fig. 3.4). Disproportionally frequently, the parents' native language tends to be used in the homes of children with a Turkish (56%) and Arabic background (45%), but also in the homes of children whose parents come from Russia and the former Soviet Union (40%). Results are similar for children from Muslim parental homes at 52%. Here, results correlate with class membership. Children with the corresponding migration backgrounds belong markedly more frequently to the poorly educated lower classes than is the case for children with parents who have migrated from other European countries or from overseas (so-called OECD migrants).

However, another finding gives cause for concern: Looking at the children with a migration background who speak more German at home, we find that parents report that 28% of them used to attend a day nursery and 93% a Kindergarten. For children with a migration background who speak the native language of their parents more at home, in contrast, only 15% used to attend a day nursery and 77% a Kindergarten. At 23%, the proportion of children who had not attended a preschool care institution is by far the largest here (children with a migration background in total: 23% attending a day nursery and 88% attending a Kindergarten). For native German children, in contrast, parents report that 27% had attended a day nursery and 96% had at some time attended a Kindergarten.

The results underline the significance of focused language interventions for certain groups of children with a migration background. Institutional care provisions could play an important role in this. Particularly in the last 10 years and in the context of what has been called a sustainable family policy, the function of the classic daycare facilities in Germany has changed from what was primarily a care service designed to reduce the strain on the family to an agency of early childhood education. In this context, the comprehensive care of preschool-age children is conceived as an active education process that offers additional opportunities for interventions. As reported in the Twelfth Report on Children and Youth to the German federal government (BMFSFJ 2005):

> The family can pass on to and initiate in the child only that which is available to it within the framework of its social and cultural resources. The educational background of the parents, the real life situation, and the concrete living conditions have a strongly modifying influence on which opportunities for development and education are available to children in their family environment. (p. 33, translated)

Therefore, the report justly points out that a major task for society is to deliver quality interventions within preschool childcare that are appropriate to a child's state of development.

The results of our Child Study also show that early childhood language interventions will succeed only if they are applied in a "culture-sensitive" manner and link up with the traditions and values of the family of origin.

3.4 Experiencing Poverty: A Harsh Reality for Some Children

In Germany, the poverty risk for children (under 18 years) currently varies depending on the source of the data between about 16% and 19% (EU-SILK 2010: 17.5%, 2011: 15.7%; Mikrozensus 2011: 18.9%; SOEP 2010: 16.5%). This places it 3–4 percentage points above the rate for the general population (BMAS 2013, p 110). Measurements of poverty are based on the relative risk of poverty rate, that is, the proportion of children and youths living in households with less than 60% of the average net income of all households in Germany at their disposal.[13] The measure

[13] This was weighted according to need under the assumption that the economy of size in larger households decreases the need per household member. According to the new OECD scale, the main bread earner in a household is weighted with the factor 1.0. All other household members

for computing "income poverty" is relative and determined through comparisons with the available annual income in all private households: In this case, as pointed out above, it is set at 60% of median available net income.

Although the trend varies somewhat depending on the data source, all available data indicate a relatively continuous increase in child poverty from 2005 to 2010 followed by what currently seems to be a slight decline. Nonetheless, it has to be borne in mind that decline in this context means mostly that the proportion of families with "alleviated poverty" has increased. Poverty is taken to be alleviated when eligible income has been raised successfully above the subsistence level that qualifies people for the unemployment supplements known as ALG II in Germany. In recent years, it has been possible to achieve this with, for example, supplementary child benefits directed particularly toward families whose income is slightly below the unemployment supplements threshold. These families and their children thereby avoid the frequently stigmatizing dependence on welfare payments (Hartz IV). However, their social position is only secure when they are able to generate the income this requires "through their own effort" and thereby, in the long term, through their own participation in the labor market.

In the Child Study, we ask the children about their own experiences of poverty. In this case, the poverty concept is oriented toward the concept of material deprivation. We assess whether children report that certain typical goods are not available to the household because of its financial situation. These are the goods that define a minimum standard of living with their lack being described as "material deprivation." We thoroughly revised and extended the deprivation indicators for the latest 2013 Child Study. Once again, it is important for us to assess the children's world of experience and their own needs. We orient ourselves toward the typical minimum need indicators that should be available for all children without linking this to any claim to reflect a "basket of goods that ensures a complete fulfilment of needs."

To introduce the topic and thereby to identify the group who should be asked to assess the deprivation indicators,[14] we have followed the same approach as in the 2010 Child Study and once again asked all children to reply to the same two items:

- We have enough money for everything we need
- We are often short of money in our family

Only children who answered "no" to Statement 1 or "yes" to Statement 2 were asked to answer the following items on the experience of poverty that we have formulated as poverty indicators:

- Because there is not enough money in my family, I can hardly ever go to the movies or to the swimming pool (*more like things are* or *less like things are*?)

over the age of 14 are weighed at 0.4 and children under 14 at 0.3. Hence, in a four-person household with two adult parents and two children under the age of 14, the net income of the household is divided by the need factor 2.0 (1.0 + 0.4 + 0.3 + 0.3) and allocated to the individuals.

[14] In both the Second Child Study and the pretest for 2013, it proved inexpedient to present our poverty indicators to all children. The two introductory questions served to screen for the group of children who have probably experienced deprivation in their everyday lives.

- Sometimes we cannot afford to buy things for school such as exercise books or pens
- I can't join a club or learn to play a musical instrument because my family cannot afford to pay for it
- We hardly ever have children's birthday parties because they cost too much
- From time to time, we get food for free, for example, from the "*Tafel*" (an organization that collects surplus food from supermarkets to distribute to the poor)
- Sometimes I am cold in winter because I do not have any warm clothes
- Within the last year, my parents have had to borrow money from my own savings
- Every year we take at least a one-week vacation away from home
- In our home, we normally eat breakfast at home before I go to school
- I generally have at least one hot meal a day[15]

In this context, we no longer define poverty exclusively in relative terms by comparing it to the average income in society, but in material terms based on the restrictions to access and participation that children experience in their everyday lives (labeled "experienced poverty" in the following).

A total of 77% of the children give positive answers to the statement "We have enough money for everything we need," whereas 13% give negative answers and 10% do not reply (compared to 70% "yes," 16% "no," and 14% "no answer" in 2010).

In contrast, as in 2010, 21% of the children in the present Child Study report that "We are often short of money in our family," whereas 60% reject this statement and 19% give no answer (compared to 21% "yes," 61% "no," and 18% "no answer" in 2010).

We then went on to ask whether the children eat breakfast before they go to school or whether they generally eat a hot meal every day. A total of 88% say they eat breakfast; 12% said they do not. In contrast, 98% of the children say that they generally eat a hot meal every day compared to 2% who say they do not.

By combining the two introductory statements on the financial situation ("We have enough money for everything we need": yes; and "We are often short of money in our family": no) as shown in Fig. 3.5, we find that, as in 2010, roughly one-quarter of the children indicate experiencing financial constraints in their everyday lives (2013: 24%, 2010: 25%).[16]

If we also include the single "poverty indicators" used to determine the population living in poverty and look at the percentages for all children (and not just those experiencing financial constraints who were given the questions), we can see that 11% of children report that they generally do not go on vacation for financial reasons; 8% that they hardly ever go to the movies or the open-air swimming pool for

[15] This statement was presented to all children. However, in this context, we include only the answers from those for whom the introductory questions had indicated financial constraints.

[16] Currently, in 2013, 69% report no financial constraints compared to 65% in 2010. Currently, 7% give no reply to both statements compared to 9% in 2010.

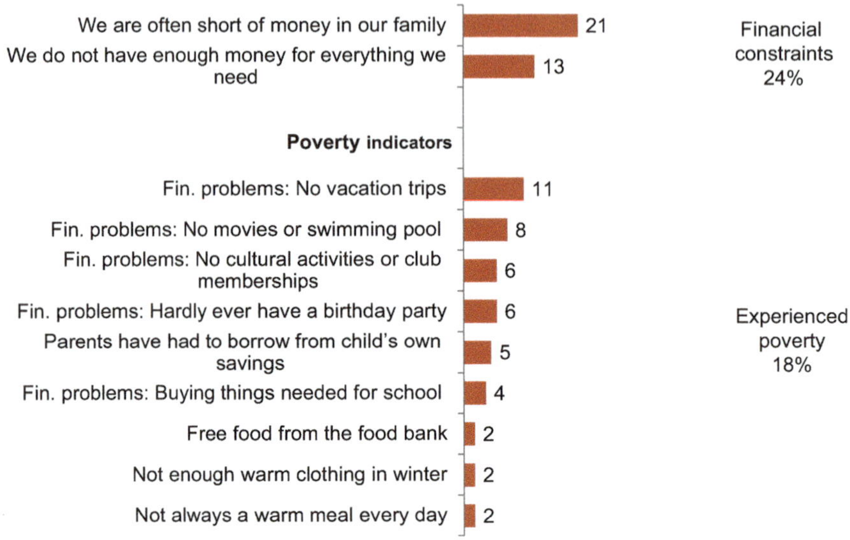

Fig. 3.5 Material deprivation and experienced poverty from the children's perspective
Children in Germany aged 6–11 years (%)

financial reasons; and 6% that their families cannot afford to pay for their membership of a club or for them to engage in other activities such as learning to play a musical instrument. Likewise, 6% report that they can hardly ever have a birthday party, 5% that their parents have had to borrow from the child's own savings during the past year, and 4% that they sometimes cannot immediately afford the things they need for school (exercise books, pens, etc.), 2% that they need to get free food from the "*Tafel*," 2% that they sometimes lack warm clothing in winter, and 2% that they do not get a warm meal every day.

As mentioned above, we revised the poverty indicators for 2013. Among those indicators that can still be compared, proportions even seem to have increased slightly since 2010. However, statistically speaking and when taking the numbers of cases into account, the deviations are mostly not significant.[17]

[17] This is subject to further methodological limitations such as the larger proportions of children who gave no answer to the introductory questions in 2010. Therefore, we did not compare the results on the single poverty indicators that had already been assessed in the last Child Study.

3.4.1 Avoiding Poverty Means Strengthening Parents' Participation on the Labor Market

Taking all poverty indicators together, 18% of all children report experiencing at least one of the indicators we surveyed when assessing experienced poverty in the family; 12% report two or more indicators; and 8% report three or more experiences of poverty.[18]

A central safeguard against poverty is for the parents to be regularly employed. Differentiated according to participation in the labor market, children with two parents holding down regular jobs have the lowest rates of experienced poverty. When both parents are employed full-time, only 12% of the children report experiencing poverty, and when one parent is employed full-time and the other part-time or even both are employed part-time, then the proportion of experienced poverty even goes down to 9%. The latter indicates that models in which both parents may be employed part-time are evidently to be found more often in families earning a higher income. The rate is markedly higher at 18% in families in which only one parent is employed. A completely different dimension of exposure to poverty is found, in contrast, among 30% of single parents even when they have a job. However, if none of the parents living in the household work, the rate of poverty reported by the children even reaches 55% (Fig. 3.6).

Findings are quite clear here as well. The way to avoid poverty is to strengthen the parents' participation on the labor market. Under the given conditions in society, a partnership model with a joint gainful employment of both parents also seems to be most appropriate here in order to secure the material framing conditions that will ensure that children are not excluded from major fields of social life for financial reasons. As pointed out in Sect. 3.2, this also corresponds to the parents' wishes. In cases in which this cannot be achieved, appropriate social provisions should ensure that children exposed to poverty receive corresponding assistance without any great access barriers, in other words, in easy ways. The results on experienced poverty as the children see it nonetheless show the importance of guaranteeing the possibility to go on day excursions; to be given midday meals in Kindergarten, daycare center, and school; and to participate in music, sport, and recreation in associations and groups.

---

[18] In the latest reports on the social situation in Europe, material deprivation (MD) is measured through indicators based on data from the EU Statistics on Income and Living Conditions (EU-SILC). According to the EU concept of MD, a person is considered materially deprived if three of the nine following items are missing from the household for financial reasons: (a) coping with unexpected expenses; (b) one week annual holiday away from home; (c) avoiding arrears (in mortgage or rent, utility bills- or hire purchase instalments); (d) a meal with meat, chicken, fish, or vegetarian equivalent every second day; (e) keeping the home adequately warm; (f) a washing machine; (g) a color television; (h) a telephone; and (i) a personal car. The more items are missing in a person's life, the more the person is considered materially deprived. According to the EU concept of MD, we speak of serious MD if four out of the nine items are missing (Sikorski and Kuchla 2011, p. 485). Current results of EU-SILC data analyses (2011) show that 5.9% of 6- to 11-year-old children in Germany experience serious MD.

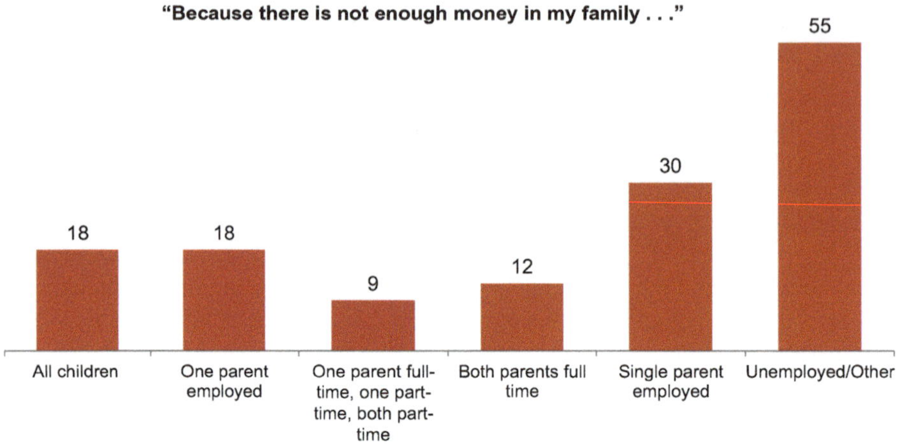

Fig. 3.6 Material deprivation: Experienced poverty by parents' employment
Children in Germany aged 6–11 years (%)

3.5 Social Background: Social Origins Continue to Determine the Difference

In the present Child Study, we once again use the 5-point class index to analyze social origins that we already introduced for the first World Vision Child Study in 2007. We assign children to a social class of origin on two dimensions: first, the parents' educational background (education dimension); and, second, the material state of the household (material participation dimension). This taps the children's central home-related and material starting and framing conditions. It focuses on the family's level of education within the context of a sufficient availability of the necessary financial resources.

Empirically, we draw on parental reports on their school-leaving qualifications supplemented by a rating of the number of books in the household gathered during the child survey, the parental evaluation of their financial situation, and the residential status (rented accommodation or home ownership). This information is comparatively easy to ask for and can, therefore, be gathered almost completely within a child study without any exceptional effort (on the formation of the index, see Appendix 2).

Lower class and lower middle-class children accordingly come from less well-educated parental homes that also tend to have low incomes, whereas children from the upper middle class and the upper class have more highly educated family backgrounds and can also draw on a higher income (Schneekloth and Pupeter 2010a, pp. 75–79).

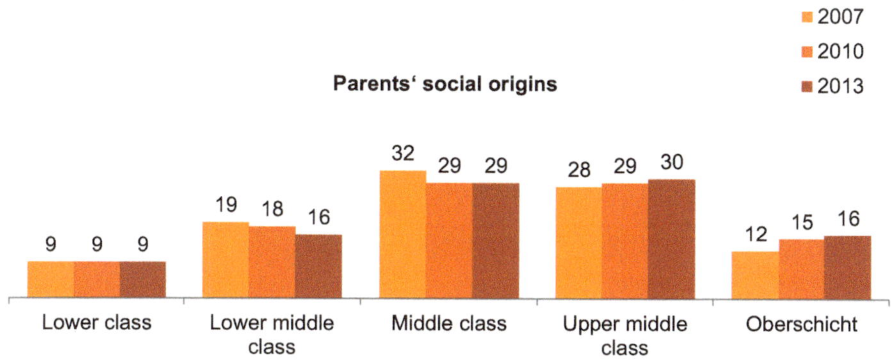

Fig. 3.7 Social Origins: Educational background and family's financial resources
Children in Germany aged 6–11 years (2007: 8–11 years) (%)

Over the course of time, our index shows a slight trend toward upward social mobility since our first Child Study in 2007 (Fig. 3.7). One particularly conspicuous feature is the higher education that the current parent cohorts were able to obtain during their school education phase. In 2007, a *Hauptschulabschluss* [basic secondary school] was the highest general school qualification for 27% of mothers and 31% of fathers; *mittlere Reife* [intermediate], the highest for 45% of mothers and 34% of fathers; *Abitur* [general university entrance] or *Fachabitur* [specific university entrance] for 26% of mothers and 32% of fathers. In the current 2013 Child Study, the proportion of *Hauptschule* graduates is 22% among mothers and 24% among fathers; the proportion with *mittlere Reife* is 40% among mothers and 34% among fathers; and the proportion with *Abitur* or *Fachabitur* is 35% among mothers and 39% among fathers.[19]

As a result, the proportion of children from the lower middle class has dropped from 19% in 2007 to 16% in 2013 and the proportion of children from the middle class from 32% to 29%. In contrast, the proportion of the upper middle class has risen from 28% to 30% and that of the upper class from 12% to 16%. Because we calculated the class index itself in the same way for each survey, the social change that has occurred is clear to see. Hence, there has been a slight increase in the "educational capital" of the families. Nonetheless, the complexity of both working and everyday life has also increased in our society. This makes it all the more worrying when we see that the proportion of children from the lowest social class has remained constant at 9%. In this the most poorly educated and also the most socially deprived class, the "educational losers" continue to accumulate—those who have not managed to move upward and have remained excluded. At this point, our class index

[19] These reports also refer to parents rearing 6- to 11-year-old children (in 2007: 8- to 11-year-olds). For single parents, in contrast, we have no information on the other parent. This means that our reports on fathers are also incomplete here and refer only to fathers and stepfathers living in the same household.

Table 3.8 Social risk states and social origin
Children in Germany aged 6–11 years

Affirmed, columns in %	All children	Lower class	Lower middle class	Middle class	Upper middle class	Upper class
Social risk state						
Experienced deprivation/ Experienced poverty	18	57	32	16	10	4
Father or mother unemployed (during the previous 3 months)	17	43	29	16	11	4
Fear of aggressive youth or adults in residential area	18	37	23	17	15	10

Table 3.9 Further social variables and social origin
Children in Germany aged 6–11 years

Affirmed, columns in %	All children	Lower class	Lower middle class	Middle class	Upper middle class	Upper class
Social variables						
Migration background	35	59	41	34	36	16
Child attended Kindergarten	93	78	92	96	95	97
Child attended day care	26	15	22	25	31	28

also measures a "negative educational homogeneity": Whereas some families also manage to move up because one parent, for example, the mother, brings a better education with her, members of the lowest class remain "among themselves" (at times also as single parents with insufficient education), and their family situation grants them almost no chances of upward mobility.

This is a good point at which to summarize those indicators that provide information on potential risks (Tables 3.8 and 3.9). As to be expected, children from the two lower classes are disproportionately frequently exposed to poverty. A total of 57% of lower class and 32% of lower middle-class children experience poverty in their daily lives and report at least one of the experiences of poverty we surveyed. The proportions of children from the higher classes are significantly lower (middle-class children: 16%, upper middle-class: 10%, upper class: 4%). Generally, these are specific subgroups such as families with a high educational background who are currently unemployed or passing through special status passages in the life course such as students with children, more highly educated single parents, or other special constellations in families with more highly educated parents. The findings emphasize once again that our class index does not primarily assess the current income situation in a household, but starts with the educational background and educational milieu of the parents and links this to the evaluation of the personal financial situation.

However, the general risk of unemployment is markedly higher in both of the lower social classes. For 43% of lower class and 29% of lower middle-class children, at least one parent has been unemployed during the previous 3 months (middle-class children: 16%; upper middle-class: 11%; upper class: 4%).

A further interesting finding here is that children from the lower social classes markedly more frequently perceive their residential environment to be threatening and report being afraid of aggressive gangs of youths or of adults. This is the case for 37% of lower class children and also 23% of lower middle-class children. This compares with 17% for middle-class children, 15% for upper middle-class children, and 10% for upper class children.

What is less surprising is that 59% of lower class children and also 41% of lower middle-class children more frequently have a migration background (middle class: 34%, upper middle class 36%, upper class: 16%). Some migrants are highly qualified people who frequently come from Western OECD countries. However, the majority of migrants such as those from Turkey or the Muslim world, from the former Yugoslavia or Eastern Europe, and also those of German descent from the former Soviet Union, frequently have a lower level of education so that their children born in Germany accordingly more frequently have lower and less well-educated social origins.

What is also notable here is the aforementioned finding that it is particularly lower class children who have less frequently attended institutional childcare facilities. No more than 16% of the lower class children ever attended a day nursery according to their parents' reports, and only 78% attended a Kindergarten. For all other social classes, the proportion that attended a Kindergarten is over 90%. Attending a day nursery, in contrast, is reported for 22% of lower middle-class children, 25% of middle-class children, 31% of upper middle-class children, and 28% of upper class children. This shows that attending a Kindergarten has now become standard. However, this is not yet the case for lower class children. Attending a day nursery is more frequent for children from the higher social classes; here as well, lower class children are in the minority. As mentioned above, this distribution can be traced back particularly to the fact that children with a migration background markedly less frequently attend institutional childcare facilities. If early childhood education is viewed as a provision that is particularly for children from less well-educated social classes, one cannot avoid seeing that there continues to be a marked gap between ambition and reality.

Social risks, as the findings from our latest 20,913 Child Study show once more, are distributed unequally and clearly to the disadvantage of children from the lowest social class. At this point, our class index points to the close relation between educational background and the children's chances of social participation. As the following chapters will show, this applies not only to parental participation on the labor market and use of institutional childcare but also to many other areas of the children's lives. Children from the lower class are the most socially deprived class (a total of 9% of all children) and continue to be excluded. However, children from the lower middle class (a total of 16% of all children) also reveal markedly less

Table 3.10 Whether my parents give me enough of their time: Trends from the children's perspective
Children in Germany aged 6–11 years (2007: 8–11 years)

Columns in %	2007	2010	2013
My mother gives me enough of her time			
Yes	67	64	64
Sometimes yes, sometimes no	27	29	29
No	5	6	6
Mother not present	1	1	1
My father gives me enough of his time			
Yes	34	32	34
Sometimes yes, sometimes no	43	44	42
No	16	16	16
Father not present	7	8	8

favorable starting conditions and therefore a clear need for social and societal support.

3.6 Care and Attention: Reconciling Family and Working Life

How do the children in our survey rate the care they receive at home? In the last Child Study, we already showed that children are generally highly satisfied with their parental care, that is, how their parents look after them. This has not changed. No more than 11% give a negative to neutral (2010 Child Study: 18%); 34%, a positive; and 54%, even a very positive rating (2010: 38% positive and 44% very positive). We asked the children the following question: "Generally speaking, how happy are you about the way your parents look after you?" Once again, the children could reply to this with our 5-point smiley scale.

We gain a more differentiated picture as soon as we pose more specific questions and ask the children whether they think that their parents give them enough of their time (Table 3.10). We have been posing this question ever since the first Child Study in 2007. Two out of three children (64%) consider that their mothers give them enough of their time; 29% reply "sometimes yes, sometimes no"; and 6% say their mothers do not give them enough of their time. The general trend in the findings is very consistent. The slight deviation in 2007 is due to the fact that we surveyed only 8- to 11-year-old children at that time. The older the children, the greater the proportion who are satisfied with the time their mothers devote to them (6- to 7-year-olds: 61%, 8- to 9-year-olds: 63%, 10- to 11-year-olds: 70%). At 63%, 6- to 7-year-old boys are more satisfied than girls at 57%. The same applies for 8- to 9-year-olds: 64% of boys compared to 61% of girls. Among 10- to 11-year-olds, this inverts slightly with 67% of boys being satisfied with the time their mother spends with

Table 3.11 Whether my parents give me enough of their time by age and gender
Children in Germany aged 6–11 years

Columns in %	All children	Girls	Boys	6–7 years	8–9 years	10–11 years
My mother gives me enough of her time						
Yes	64	64	65	61	63	70
Sometimes	29	29	28	29	31	25
No	6	7	6	9	5	4
Mother not present	1	0	1	1	1	1
My father gives me enough of his time						
Yes	34	34	34	35	33	35
Sometimes	42	43	40	37	45	41
No	16	14	18	20	15	14
Father not present	8	9	8	8	7	10

them compared to 73% of girls. However, the general trend is for the ratings of boys and girls to remain on a comparable level (Table 3.11).

Results are similar for rating time with fathers. Here, however, only one in three children (34%) consider that their father gives them enough of their time, 42% reply "sometimes yes, sometimes no," and 16% say their fathers do not give them enough of their time. No clear trend can be ascertained here, because although children's reports very slightly from study to study, statistical differences are only slight. Differentiating according to age also reveals a similar picture: In each age group, approximately one-third of the children are satisfied with the time their father spends with them. However, 20% of the younger children aged 6–7 years answer "no" when asked whether their father gives them enough of their time. Differentiating according to gender also reveals slight differences with boys somewhat more frequently saying "no" than girls.

3.6.1 Fourteen Percent of Children Complain About Explicit Parental Care Deficits

Summarizing the children's ratings on whether their parents give them enough of their time reveals the following picture (Fig. 3.8): At 33% (2010: 31%), one-third of children report that all parents give them enough of their time. In this case, "all" means "all parents who live with them." For single parents, this is only one parent; for patchwork families, this may also be more than two parents.

The majority of children reveal a typical constellation: one parent either sufficient time or sometimes yes, sometimes no. This is reported by 44% of the children (2010: 47%). In contrast, one single parent not sufficient time (answer "no," but excluding single parents) is named continuously by 9% of children.

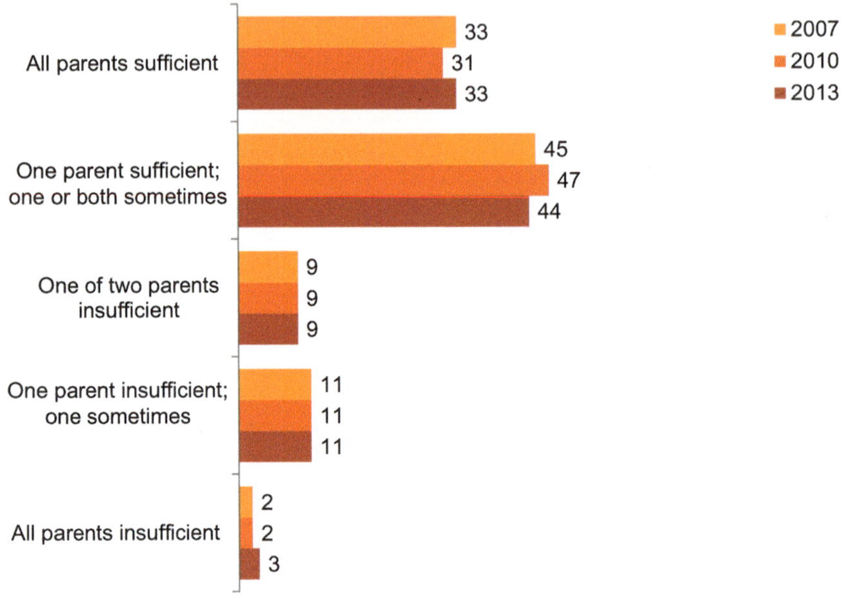

Fig. 3.8 Deficits in parental care: Children's reports on time parents spend with them
Children in Germany aged 6–11 years (2007: 8–11 years) (%)

Insufficient care is reported by 11% of children with "one parent insufficient; the other sometimes yes, sometimes no" (2010: 1%) and 3% (2010: 2%) with "all parents insufficient" (here including single parents). We classify both these constellations as a care deficit. Hence, according to their own reports, this holds for 14% of children.

3.6.2 Gainful Employment of Parents Does Not Have to Be Accompanied by Care Deficits

Our latest Child Study also confirms the finding that increased gainful employment of parents and sufficient time for children do not have to contradict each other (Fig. 3.9). The least care deficits are named by children whose parents have jobs. If only one parent is gainfully employed, then 9% of children report a care deficit. If both parents are gainfully employed (either one full-time or both part-time), it is also no more than 8% who report a care deficit. If both parents are gainfully employed full-time, this proportion rises to 16%.

However, the situation is markedly different for children of gainfully employed single parents. Here, 32% complain about a care deficit. However, at 29%, a similar

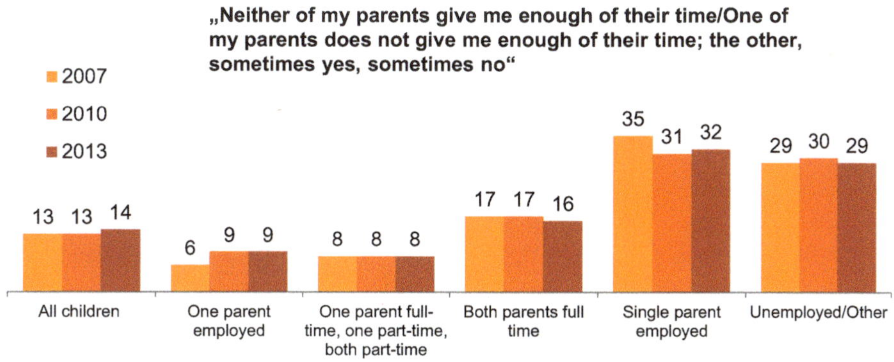

Fig. 3.9 Deficits in parental care and parents' labor market participation from the children's perspective
Children in Germany aged 6–11 years (2007: 8–11 years) (%)

level is reported by children whose parents are unemployed or do not pursue gainful employment for other reasons.[20]

3.6.3 Reconciling Family and Working Life: How the Parents See It

In the latest Child Study, we ask not only the children but also parents about reconciling family and working life.[21] A total of 14% of parents say reconcilability works "very well" and a further 52% that it works "well." This compares with 26% for "just about okay," 5% for "less well," and 1% "not well at all" (2% gave no reply; see Fig. 3.10).

The child's age and gender make no difference here. As to be expected, the economic situation of the family plays a strong role in rating reconcilability. In every second family in which one of the children surveyed reports (at least) one of the poverty indicators we surveyed (see Sect. 3.4), the reconcilability of family and working life is reported to work only "just about okay" (33%) or "(less well) not well at all" (17%).

Differentiating the answers of the parents providing the information according to type of family, we find that every second single parents reports that reconcilability works either "just about okay" (38%) or "(less well) not well at all" (13%). For families with three or more children, 23% report that it works "just about okay" and

[20] Adding the children who report a lack of time with one parent to the children with a care deficit results in a comparable trend.

[21] Questions on the family and on the parental background were reported by one information source on behalf of the other—83% by the mother and 17% by the father.

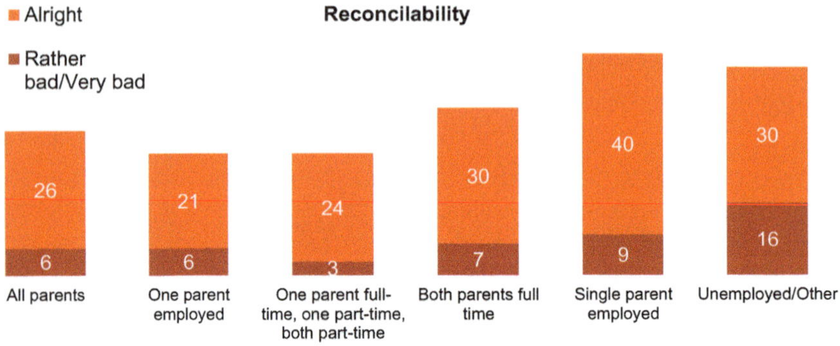

Fig. 3.10 Labor market participation and reconciling family and working life — the parents' perspective
Children in Germany aged 6–11 years (%)

9% "(less well) not well at all." Among two-child families, 23% report that reconcilability works "just about okay" and 4% "(less well) not well at all"; and in one-child families, 27% "just about okay" and 2% "(less well) not well at all."

Finally, differentiating according to participation on the labor market, we find the following picture: The most frequent complaints come from 49% of single parents who are gainfully employed: 40% report that reconcilability works "just about okay" and 9% that it works "not well at all." This is followed by 46% of those families in which both parents are unemployed or do not work for other reasons. Here, 30% report that reconcilability of family and working life works "just about okay" and even 16% that it works "(less well) not well at all."

When both parents are gainfully employed full-time, 37% complain about reconcilability: In this case, 30% report that reconcilability works is "just about okay" and 7% "(less well) not well at all." As before, these percentages are lower than those in the other groups. When one parent works full-time and the other part-time, or both part-time, then it is only 27% who complain with 24% "just about okay" and 3% "(less well) not well at all." Results are similar for the constellation "one parent gainfully employed" at 27% with 21% "just about okay" and 6% "(less well) not well at all."

In summary, a constellation of several factors—low level of education, unemployment, and risk of poverty, and/or type of family (single-parent)—lead more frequently to a moderate to poor reconcilability between family and working life. In a constellation of two full-time gainfully employed parents, there are also more frequent reports on problems with reconciling family and working life, but they are less frequent than among parents in precarious employment situations. In contrast, families that have organized their division of labor with a combination of full- and part-time gainful employment do not report problems in reconciling family and working life more frequently than families in which only one parent goes to work.

From both the children's and the parents' perspective, both caring for and having time for children seem to work best when the family situation is stable and predictable. It is highly evident that this is best resolved when parents have succeeded in ensuring a viable participation on the labor market. In contrast, the family care situation is markedly problematic and deficient when conditions are unstable—be this because a single parent does not have enough time through own gainful employment or because both parents are unable to achieve a sufficient intensity of care because of unemployment or other precarious situations. Hence, time is an important precondition for a good and reliable care of children. However, here as well, a potential "more" does not always mean a "better." Alongside time, it is, above all, the quality of the relationship that is important—hence, taken together, the "quality time." According to both the children and their parents, this can work better in a stable family constellation based on shared and well-coordinated gainful employment of both parents than in an economically and/or emotionally insecure situation that both children and parents perceive to be unsatisfactory or stressful.

For single parents, there is no alternative here to having appropriate institutional childcare facilities at their disposal. Otherwise they can hardly avoid being dependent on transfer payments to counter poverty (e.g., Hartz IV or social welfare benefits). However, it is also notable that families with more than two children also more frequently complain about problems in reconciling family and working life. This is certainly due to the lack of family friendliness in German society. This is perceived by both the children (see Sect. 2.7) and their parents. Here as well, meeting the demand for more time, money, and infrastructure—the most important strategies for delivering a sustained family policy according to the 7th Family Report to the German government (BMFSFJ 2006)—would also make an important contribution to ensuring the well-being of both children and their parents.

References

BMAS (Bundesministerium für Arbeit und Soziales). (2013). *Lebenslagen in Deutschland.* Der vierte Armuts- und Reichtumsbericht der Bundesregierung. (Endfassung: 06.03.2013). Verfügbar unter. http://www.bmas.de/.

BMFSFJ. (2005). 12. Kinder- und Jugendbericht. Berlin: BT. Drs. 15/6014.

BMFSFJ. (2006). *Familie zwischen Flexibilität und Verlässlichkeit. Perspektiven für eine lebenslaufbezogene Familienpolitik.* 7. Familienbericht. Berlin: BT. Drs. 16/1360.

Coleman, J. (1988). Social capital and the creating of human capital. *American Journal of Sociology, 94*, 95–120.

Holst, E., & Seifert, H. (2012). Arbeitszeitpolitische Kontroversen im Spiegel der Arbeitszeitwünsche. *WSI-Mitteilungen*, 2/2012, S. 141–149.

Jampert, K., Zehnbauer, A., Sens, A., Leuckefeld, K., & Laier, M. (Hrsg.). (2009). *Kinder-Sprache stärken. Aufwachsen mit mehreren Sprachen. Praxismaterial.* Weimar/Berlin: Das Netz.

Schneekloth, U., & Pupeter, M. (2010a). Familie als Zentrum: Bunt und vielfältig, aber nicht für alle Kinder gleich verlässlich. In World Vision Deutschland. (Hrsg.), Kinder in Deutschland 2010a. 2. World Vision Kinderstudie (S. 61 – 94). Frankfurt a. M.: Fischer.

Schneewind, K. A. (2008). Sozialisation in der Familie. In Hurrelmann, K., Grundmann, M., & Walper, S. (Hrsg.), *Handbuch Sozialisationsforschung* (7. vollst. überarbeitete Auflage, S. 256–273). Weinheim: Beltz.

Sikorski, U., & Kuchler, B. (2011). Wer muss worauf verzichten? Einschätzungen zur Wohn- und Lebenssituation der privaten Haushalte. *Wirtschaft und Statistik, 5*/2011, S. 484–492.

Tracy, R. (2007). *Wie Kinder Sprachen lernen. Und wie wir sie dabei unterstützen können.* Tübingen: Francke.

Chapter 4
School: An Increasingly Important Field of Experience

Monika Pupeter and Klaus Hurrelmann

School plays a major role in the daily lives of 6- to 11-year-olds—and not just in terms of the time spent there and the structuring of the day through school attendance. It also imposes completely new social and intellectual demands on children, because they now have a range of different things to learn, and they need to acquire not only knowledge but also basic competencies such as reading, writing, and arithmetic. School admission also marks the beginning of a new phase of life in a new community in which children first have to find and claim their place. This is because school is a social location in which children can meet their friends and forge new friendships. Hence, alongside confronting them with the actual contents of learning, it also places greater demands on children's abilities to socialize and adapt to their surroundings while simultaneously coming to terms with new spatial conditions. Put briefly, school has many facets for children, and for each individual child, school admission is accompanied not only by opportunities, scopes for making new discoveries, and new chances but also by constraints, disappointments, and trials to be mastered. School becomes an increasingly important life space for childhood experience.

In most German federal states, elementary school lasts only 4 years. As a result, one of the most pressing questions regarding the further academic career already emerges in the third year of school: Which transition option will become available at the end of elementary school? Will the parents' wishes be fulfilled enabling the child to transfer to a *Gymnasium* or another school offering a university entrance track? This parental wish has become even stronger in recent years, particularly

M. Pupeter (✉)
Kantar Public, München, Germany
e-mail: monika.pupeter@kantarpublic.com

K. Hurrelmann
Hertie School of Governance, Berlin, Germany
e-mail: hurrelmann@hertie-school.org

S. Andresen et al. (eds.), *Well-being, Poverty and Justice from a Child's Perspective*, Children's Well-Being: Indicators and Research 17,
DOI 10.1007/978-3-319-57574-2_4

because of the long-lasting labor market problems and the financial crisis. It is particularly apparent in the transition rates to Gymnasium and other schools offering a university entrance track that are now far above 50% throughout Germany (Autorengruppe Bildungsberichterstattung 2012, p. 253). This places children under a great pressure to maintain their position and perform well right from the start of elementary school.

This summarizes the reasons why the topic of "school" plays such a major role in the World Vision Child Studies. As the latest study shows once again, the children themselves also have a lot to say about the topic. They are very aware of the importance of this life domain, and when it comes to questions about school, they express clear opinions and attitudes. These are what we shall be addressing in the present chapter: We shall start by reporting on the children's perspectives and aspirations for their further school careers and how these differ in line with their social origins—that is, the status of the parental home. Then we shall address what children expect from an all-day school and how they would like it to be. This is followed by an overview of children's appraisals regarding how far and in which domains they can codetermine daily life at school and in school lessons as well as the design of their school. Finally, at the end of the chapter, we shall ask how fair children perceive their school to be and how satisfied they are with their daily schooling.

4.1 Social Origins Shape Educational Expectations

The results of international comparative studies (above all, IGLU, PISA, and TIMSS) have shown that social origins shape a child's school achievement more strongly in Germany than in most other countries (Baumert et al. 2006; Bos et al. 2010). When the parents are well off economically, possess a high social status, and are themselves well-educated, then this transfers to the expectations and mostly also to the actual school achievements of their children. When the parents have either low or no school-leaving qualifications, and/or are in an economically weak position, then their children mostly do comparatively less well at school (Hadjar and Becker 2006; Quenzel and Hurrelmann 2010).

The reason for this close relationship is that parents in Germany are traditionally granted particularly strong freedoms in shaping and influencing how their children are reared and educated. Compared to other countries, day nursery and preschool provisions and all-day schools expanded much more slowly after World War 2. It was only new legislation to promote child development in the late 1990s (the *Kinderförderungsgesetz*) that finally resulted in parents having a legal right to early childhood care in a daycare center for children over the age of 12 months from August 1, 2013, onward. Even before it came into force, this law triggered an impressive increase in the proportion of under-3-year-old children attending preschool. All-day schools have been promoted since the German government introduced a program to invest in future education and care (the *Investitionsprogramm Zukunft Bildung und Betreuung*) in 2003. Nonetheless, even today, it is still

Table 4.1 Children by school grade and social origin
Children in Germany aged 6–11 years

Columns in %	All children	Lower class	Lower middle class	Middle class	Upper middle class	Upper class
1st grade	19	26	19	19	19	17
2nd grade	18	15	18	20	19	15
3rd grade	19	19	18	18	19	20
4th grade	17	19	21	19	15	15
5th grade	19	17	18	18	19	21
6th grade[a]	8	4	6	6	9	12

[a]Including 7th grade (proportion under 1%)

questionable whether the reforms introduced so far have been sufficient to overcome the high level of unequal starting conditions in families.

4.1.1 The Children's Educational Paths

The World Vision Child Study can be used to analyze the relation between children's social origins and the educational track they are pursuing in 2013. We shall first look at which grade the 6- to 11-year-old children are attending at the beginning of 2013, the time point of the survey (Table 4.1). The total column shows that the children are distributed relatively equally across Grades 1– 5 (from 17% to 19% per grade). Roughly 8% of the children are already attending 6th grade. However, major differences emerge when we take social origins into account: Whereas more than one-quarter of the lower class children (26%) are attending 1st grade, this is the case for only 17% of the upper class. In the 5th and 6th grades, the numbers reverse with 21% of the 6- to 11-year-olds coming from the lower class and 33% from the upper class.

This unequal distribution of the children across school grades is due to children from higher social classes already having better starting positions right at the beginning of schooling. Because their parents have prepared them better for school admission, these children are less frequently told to wait one further year before starting school, and a larger proportion can take advantage of the "can rule" permitting early school enrolment under favorable circumstances. Together with the focused support that these children receive from their parents at home, this enables them to adapt more quickly to the rhythm of work and the social rules of school life than children from lower social classes. Hence, they start off with a temporal advantage that they can build on increasingly over the course of elementary school. Eventually, this leads to greater achievement and far better chances of transferring to the academic track of the *Gymnasium* (Hadjar and Becker 2006; Maaz et al. 2010; Stubbe 2009).

Table 4.2 shows how elementary school careers influence transitions to the different types of secondary school. The majority of the 6- to 11-year-olds surveyed

Table 4.2 Type of schools children attended (Parents' reports) of different social origins
Children in Germany aged 6–11 years

Columns in %	All children	Lower class	Lower middle class	Middle class	Upper middle class	Upper class
Elementary school	68	68	67	70	70	64
Hauptschule	5	12	10	6	1	1
Realschule	8	4	9	8	7	7
Gymnasium	11	1	4	7	15	21
School with several tracks	4	2	3	5	5	6
Special needs school	4	13	7	4	2	1

are still attending elementary school, but the one-third who have already left are distributed very unequally across the different types of secondary school. Whereas the majority from the lower class are attending *Hauptschule* (12%), the majority from the upper class are attending *Gymnasium* (21%) or schools offering a range of tracks (6%; composed of comprehensive schools, integrated secondary schools, city district schools, etc.) providing direct access to the academic university entrance track.

When we compare these findings with those from 2007 and 2010, we can see hardly any changes. In the two prior World Vision Child Studies as well, the proportion of lower class children attending a Gymnasium was, according to parent reports, about 1% compared to about 20% of upper class children. The comparison across time also reveals hardly any changes in the attendance of other types of school.

How can we interpret these findings? Our impression is that the relation between social origins and school careers has consolidated over the 6-year period covered by our studies. It is evident that the aforementioned education policy reforms (expansion of preschool and all-day provisions) and the intensive public discussion on the topic of unequal educational opportunities have had no measurable impact. The social inequalities that children bring with them from their parental homes continue to be neither balanced out nor overcome by the educational effects of school despite the policy reforms introduced for this purpose (Hurrelmann et al. 2011).

4.1.2 The Children's Educational Aspirations

As in the two previous World Vision Child Studies, we also asked the 6- to 11-year-olds in the current study what sort of school-leaving qualification they would like to attain. The question given to elementary school children was: "What type of school do you want to go to later when you leave elementary school: *Hauptschule* (*Hauptschulabschluss*), *Realschule* (*Realschulabschluss*), *Gymnasium* (*Abitur*), or Don't know/Don't care?" We asked children who were already attending a

Table 4.3 Desired school-leaving qualification by child's age
Children in Germany aged 6–11 years

Columns in %	All children	Girls	Boys	6–7 years	8–9 years	10–11 years
Basic secondary school leaving certificate (*Hauptschulabschluss*)	5	4	6	5	4	5
Intermediate secondary school leaving certificate (*Realschulabschluss*)	27	25	28	13	31	33
University entrance qualification (*Abitur*)	45	49	42	37	44	52
Don't know	23	22	24	45	21	10

secondary school: "What kind of school-leaving qualification would you like to attain: *Hauptschulabschluss*, *Realschulabschluss*, *Abitur*, or Don't know/Don't care."

Table 4.3 reports the children's answers. Not surprisingly, the proportion who have not reached any decision is relatively high among the younger children with 45% of the 6- to 7-year-olds who do not yet know or care about which type of secondary school they will eventually attend. Among the 10- to 11-year-olds, this proportion has already dropped to 10%. There is a clear trend in educational aspirations: Whereas 37% of the younger children are also striving for an *Abitur*, this proportion rises to 52% among the older children. The preference for a *Realschulabschluss* also increases as children grow older. Only the *Hauptschulabschluss* remains unattractive, ranking at only about 5% among both younger and older children.

As these data show, children are already aware of the value of different school-leaving qualifications at an early age: One-third aspire to an intermediate qualification; more than one-half, to an *Abitur*. Hence, in summary, an impressive majority of 85% of the 10- and 11-year-olds set themselves demanding goals for their school careers. There can be no doubt that this reflects both the wishes and the admonitions of their parents who point out that a successful career is hard to achieve without a high-quality school-leaving qualification. It is interesting to see how more ambitious the educational aspirations of girls are compared to boys. This replicates the strong growth in the motivation for education among girls found in other studies. It continues to grow in secondary school and is now leading to an ever larger relative disadvantaging of boys (Hurrelmann and Schultz 2012). Differences between Eastern and Western German, in contrast, are minimal.

Figure 4.1 presents the relation between social origin and the aspirations for school-leaving qualifications.[1] This reveals major inequalities in the distributions:

[1] We used an in-depth multivariate analysis to test all factors influencing whether 6- to 11-year-old children consider that they will complete secondary schooling with an *Abitur* (university entrance qualification). The children's social origins proved to have the greatest explanatory power. The influence of the child's age also persisted in the analysis. A further factor was the children's leisure-time behavior. Looking at the leisure types, compared to the "all-rounders" at 58%, the "media consumers" had a much lower interest in attaining the *Abitur* at 29%. Residential structure, which essentially reflects the structure of school provisions, contributes a further explanatory

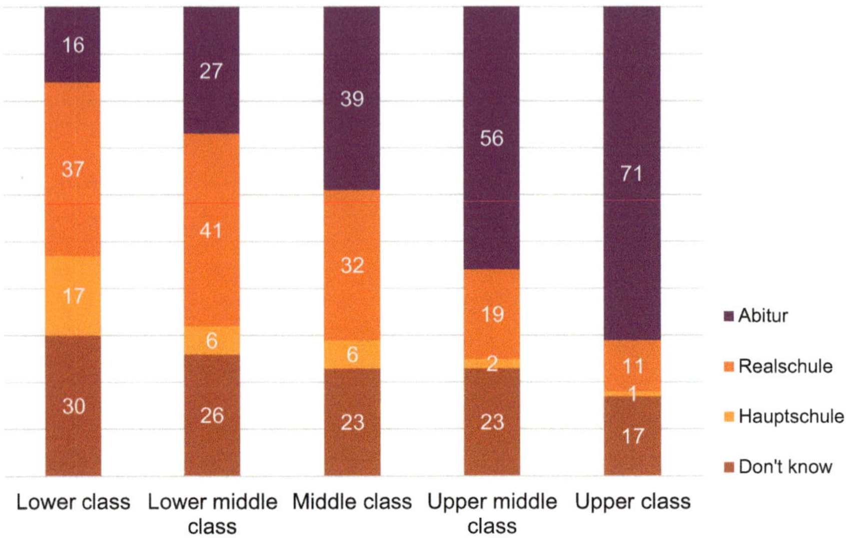

Fig. 4.1 Aspirations for school-leaving qualification by social origins
Children in Germany aged 6–11 years (%)

Among the upper class children, 71% wish to attend the *Gymnasium* after leaving elementary school; 11%, the *Realschule*; and only 1%, the *Hauptschule*. In contrast, only 16% of lower class children aspire to the *Abitur*; 37% want a *Realschulabschluss*; and 17%, a *Hauptschulabschluss*. Hence, more than four times as many children from the upper class than the lower class aspire to the most desirable highest school-leaving qualification, the *Abitur*. Whereas 17% of the upper class children are uncertain about which school-leaving qualification they aspire to, this proportion is almost twice as high among lower class children at 30%. The children from the middle of these three social classes give reports that lie between these two extremes.

These findings can be interpreted as indicating that even early in life, children in Germany sense the effects of their social origins on their later educational careers. They are at least intuitively aware of the social status of their parental home, how this influences their current achievement position, and which perspectives and developmental chances it provides. Apparently, their family, school, neighborhood, and environment gives them so many hints and signals regarding their achievement and developmental potential that they are able to derive an appraisal of their own chances in further education. As they grow older, this appraisal becomes increasingly

effect. Rural areas have fewer schools leading to higher school-leaving certificates. Children in rural areas who wish to attend a Gymnasium generally have to accept longer routes to school. This aspect also plays a major role in considerations on which qualification to strive toward. Big cities, in contrast, offer several different types of school to choose from that are also in easy travelling distance. This is also reflected in the anticipation of being able to achieve the *Abitur* (49% vs. 39%).

Table 4.4 Desire to attain university entrance qualification (*Abitur*) across time
Children in Germany aged 6–11 years (%)

Columns in %	All children	Lower class	Lower middle class	Middle class	Upper middle class	Upper class
6- to 11-year-olds						
2010	50	19	30	45	64	76
2013	45	16	27	39	56	70
8- to 11-year-olds						
2007	49	21	32	36	68	82
2010	53	16	28	50	70	82
2013	48	19	27	42	61	73

more precise: "Don't knows" become less frequent, and the differences in future perspectives become larger and larger.

Scientific studies have shown how important educational aspirations are for the motivation and learning style of students. In the majority of cases, those who set themselves high goals also cultivate the necessary energy and persistence to attain them (Hopf 2010). This is why the school-leaving qualification aspirations gathered here are such strong predictors of the educational goals that children actually attain.

The trends to be seen in these relations have changed hardly at all compared to the 2007 and 2010 World Vision Child Studies. We evaluate this as indicating two trends: First, as pointed out above, despite all the debates on reform, there has been no actual improvement in educational chances in relation to social origins. Second, despite all the problems that educational policy is facing in relation to this great inequality, we can at least conclude that the pressure on children to attain the high-ranking *Abitur* school-leaving qualification has not increased any further since 2007.

4.1.3 Educational Aspirations Across Time

A closer look at the data across the years on the aspirations for an *Abitur* school-leaving qualification confirms this second conclusion. As Table 4.4 shows, the children's desire to attain the *Abitur* has not increased over the course of our studies; indeed, it has slightly weakened. Because the 2007 survey did not yet include 6- to 7-year-olds, the upper part of the table reports only findings for 2010 and 2013. However, the trend is clear: In all social classes, a lower percentage is striving toward the *Abitur* in 2013 compared to 2010. Findings are not so clear in the lower part of the table that compares the results on 8- to 11-year-old children across all three World Vision Child Studies. Despite strong variations in the percentages, one can predominantly see a decline in the aspiration toward the *Abitur* school-leaving qualification. Moreover, ideas on which secondary school and which school-leaving qualification can be attained seem to have become less clear over time, as indicated by the increase in the proportion of "don't know/don't care" answers (not reported in the table).

If such a trend persists in the next World Vision Child Study, it could be evaluated as a sign of uncertainty regarding whether one can or should strive toward which particular school-leaving qualification at elementary school age. Because the children's reports also reflect their parents' perspectives, the findings may also point to a shifting trend and be one first sign of an easing of the prestige- and status-dominated decisions on the future career paths of children. Many parents are uncomfortable with the pressure of having to get their children to grasp the significance of the "elementary school *Abitur*" and already take this seriously in their third year of schooling. As a result, they prefer schools offering a range of educational pathways that also include the *Abitur* but make it possible to postpone this decision until a later time when already attending secondary school.

4.2 Children Expect a Great Deal from All-Day School

The gradual introduction of all-day schools in Germany, since 2003 has been a reaction to the social fact that both parents increasingly go out to work. However, it simultaneously follows the goal of balancing out the aforementioned differences in educational opportunities and enabling children from poorly educated parental homes to receive additional support. School courses in the afternoon supplemented by sports, musical and cultural "leisure-time" activities should particularly support children with a low education background and offer them developmental opportunities going beyond the traditional framework of the half-day school with its emphasis on teaching and imparting knowledge (Bremm 2013; Fischer et al. 2011).

4.2.1 More All-Day Schools

According to the official definition given by the Standing Conference of the Ministers of Education and Cultural Affairs of the Länder (KMK), a school can be viewed as an all-day school when children spend 7 h a day there on at least 3 days in the week. All-day provisions at schools with an "open" concept allow children and their families to decide for themselves whether they wish to take advantage of the school's afternoon care provisions. In this open form, the teaching and leisure-time units in the afternoon are purely optional and do not have to be attended by all the children in a class. The KMK talks about "partially compulsory" or "completely compulsory" all-day schools when the children are obliged to attend at least some of the afternoon provisions in some areas for certain periods of time (KMK Sekretariat 2012). According to official reports, more than one-half of all schools now meet this comprehensive definition of an all-day school. The leaders in this field are comprehensive schools, special education schools, and *Hauptschule*. In

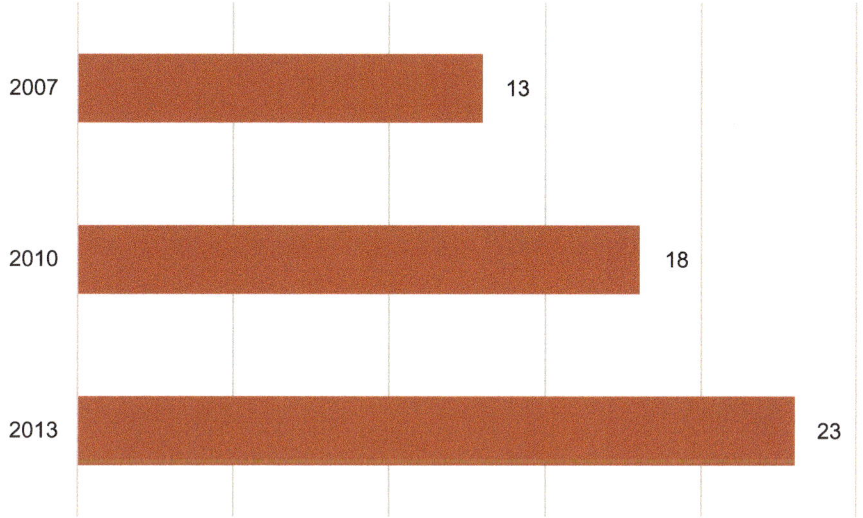

Fig. 4.2 Trends in the proportion of children attending all-day schools
Children in Germany aged 8–11 years (%)

2010, a total of 44% of elementary schools were classified as all-day schools, although only about 6% as compulsory and the remaining 38% as voluntary (Autorengruppe Bildungsberichterstattung 2012, p. 78).

Information from children can be used to track the actual development of all-day schooling in recent years. The children themselves can provide more succinct and authentic reports than the official statistics on how many of them actually take advantage of the all-day provisions of their school regardless of whether this is either compulsory or voluntary. Their reports give a clear picture and show a marked increase in the number of children attending all-day provisions since 2007. Indeed, it has almost doubled: In 2007, only 13% of the 8- to 11-year-olds reported attending an all-day school; 6 years later, this is already 23% (Fig. 4.2).

When also including the 6- to 7-year-old children in the 2013 study, the proportion attending all-day schools totals 24%. According to the latest survey findings, more than one 1st-grade child in four (26%) remains at school in the afternoon. These figures indicate that the use of all-day provisions is on the increase. According to the children's own reports, the proportion of children attending all-day schools is 20% for elementary school, 27% for *Hauptschule*, 19% for *Realschule*, 60% for special education schools, and 55% for comprehensive schools (no table).

Our study confirms the KMK's statistics showing that the various German federal states and regions vary greatly in how far they have introduced all-day schooling. Children and their parents can consider attending an all-day school only if it is available in the region where they live. According to the children's reports, this is far more frequently the case in Eastern Germany at 39% than Western Germany at 21%. In addition, the proportion of all-day students in big cities (30%) and

Table 4.5 Type of schools attended by region and settlement structure
Children in Germany aged 6–11 years.

Columns in %	All children	West	East	Big city	Big city suburbs	Conurbations	Rural areas
Half-day school	76	79	61	70	81	77	81
All-day school	24	21	39	30	19	23	19

conurbations (23%) is higher than in other regions (Table 4.5). The difference between the old and new German states is particularly large in elementary schools: It is particularly high in the East at 41% compared to 16% in the West (no table).

An analysis of the statistical relations after holding the regional supply factors (old/new German states and settlement structure) constant reveals no further significant explanations of all-day school attendance based on personal and social variables (no table). Individual characteristics such as age and gender seem to play only a secondary role. A migration background in the children's families also reveals no particular effect. The main explanatory power for attending an all-day school lies in the supply structure. Accordingly, the decisive aspect is where a family lives and whether they have a realistic opportunity to choose freely in favor of an all-day place for their children.

4.2.2 Social Origins of Children Attending All-Day Schools

As pointed out above, the expansion of all-day schools called for by policymakers also has to be seen as a response to the unsatisfactory performance of children from the lower social classes in international comparisons. Broadening and deepening the learning opportunities in all-day schools should supplement the familial support for children's educational careers and improve their relatively less favorable educational opportunities.

What do the results of the current Child Study tell us about this? In 2013, roughly every third child from the lower class reported attending an all-day school; for upper class children, this was only every fifth, and for middle-class children, slightly more than every fifth (Fig. 4.3). At first glance, this outcome would seem to basically support the political intentions behind setting up this new type of school: Lower class children coming from particularly poorly educated parental homes personally report an above-average use of all-day school provisions.

When we compare these findings with those from the 2007 and 2010 World Vision Child Studies, we can see interesting trends. In 2007, the differences in the attendance of all-day schools between children from the lower class and other classes were much less marked than in 2013 (Fig. 4.4). Since 2007, children from all classes, and particularly those from the upper class as well, have increased their

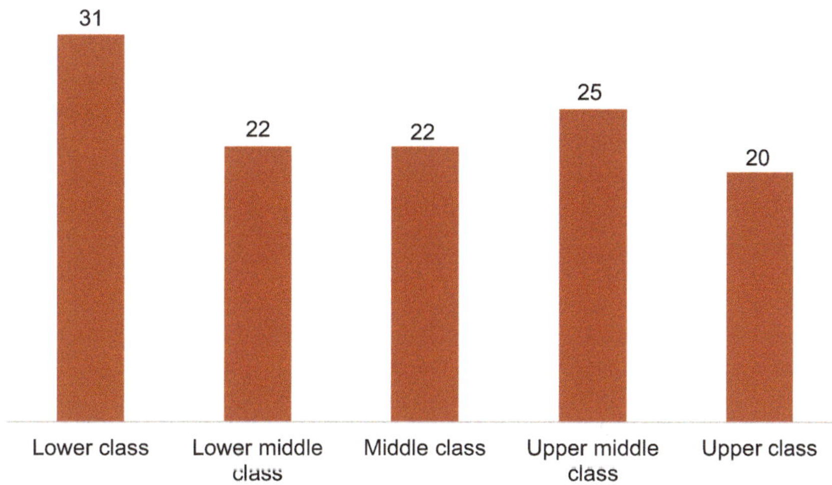

Fig. 4.3 Social origins of children attending all-day schools in 2013
Children in Germany aged 6–11 years (%)

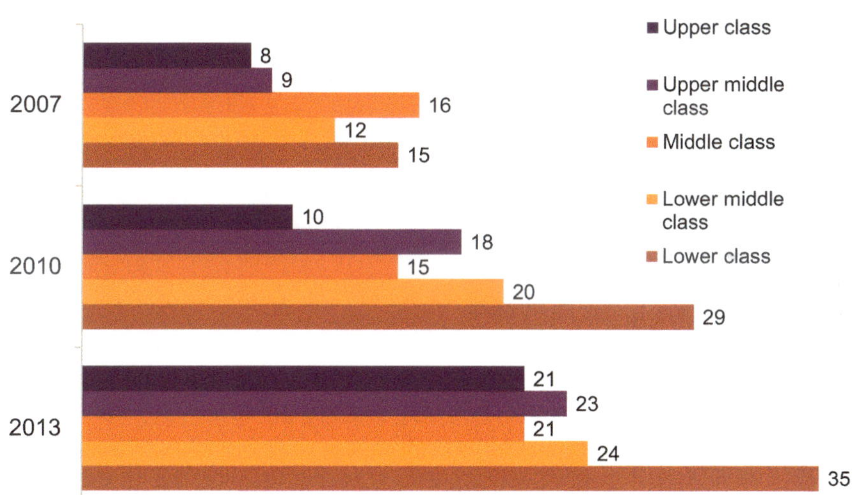

Fig. 4.4 Trends in social origins of children attending all-day schools
Children in Germany aged 8–11 years (%)

participation in this type of school. At the same time, there has been a renewed increase in the proportion of lower class children, and in 2013, a good 10% more of them attend than all other social classes.

Our study is unable to say whether more frequently attending all-day schools has also resulted in better school performance among lower class children. The KMK statistics can be interpreted as indicating that the high attendance rates for all-day schools are due particularly to the use of the partially compulsory and completely compulsory forms of provisions. However, these provisions are found to be particularly frequent in the types of school attended by an above-average proportion of lower class children; that is, comprehensive schools, special education schools, and *Hauptschule* (Autorengruppe Bildungsberichterstattung 2012, p. 81). By applying (mostly compulsory) all-day provisions, these schools should achieve particularly intensive and sustained learning effects and compensate the influence of the parental homes. However, there are various reasons for attending these types of school, and attendance is not always voluntary. Future studies will reveal whether this educational policy is really a success under these circumstances and whether it can compensate the disadvantages in the educational careers of those from poorly educated parental homes. Our results, however, cast some doubt on this.

4.2.3 How Well Do Children Accept All-Day Schools?

Support for our doubts comes from the children's reports on their acceptance of all-day schools. We first asked children whether they would prefer to attend a school in which teaching ends at midday. This is rejected by 61% of the children attending all-day schools; 30% would prefer a morning-only school, and 10% are undecided. Hence, although the acceptance of this type of school is good among the students attending it, it is not exactly overwhelmingly high.

Differentiating the answers to this question according to the children's social origins shows that only 41% of lower class children accept this type of school. This is well below the average of 61%. In contrast, three-quarters of the upper class children find all-day school good. Hence, the group of children in which a particularly large proportion attends this type of school is simultaneously the group that is least satisfied with all-day schooling. Our study cannot explain why this is so. Perhaps it relates to the aforementioned fact that attending an all-day school is not always voluntary for lower class children and that a difficult student clientele accumulates at these schools. The more than averagely high acceptance of all-day schools among upper class children could correspondingly be traced back to the particularly high proportion of students that the KMK reports as voluntarily attending all-day schools (Autorengruppe Bildungsberichterstattung, 2012, p. 80).

4.2.4 What Children Expect from an All-Day School

The very differentiated answers that we find throughout the World Vision Child Study when asking children to describe their own life situation leave us in no doubt about their ability to appraise their situation at school both appropriately and accurately. As a result, we consider the relatively high level of dissatisfaction and the worryingly large lack of appreciation of all-day schooling among lower class children to be based on sound and well-justified reasons. The most recent German LBS-Kinderbarometer study confirms this. A questionnaire survey of 4th- to 7th-grade students revealed that the less happy children feel at school, the more frequently they reject afternoon school provisions (LBS-Kinderbarometer 2011, p. 153).

This has important implications for the discussion on extending all-day schooling. The children's statements show not only how inadequate it is to simply increase the quantity of places in all-day schools without ensuring an appropriate quality and sufficient resources but also the problems that arise when all-day school attendance is not voluntary. As our study shows, such a strategy does result in more lower class children attending this type of school. However, given their internal self-distancing from these schools, it is questionable whether they profit from this. The future concern is not just a quantitative expansion of all-day provisions. It will be far more necessary to pay greater attention to the quality of the care and services provided and to ensure that the children themselves appreciate them. At the end of the day, children who spend almost the entire day attending such a school will benefit from it only if they feel happy there and are able to experience the services provided as beneficial to their development (see the research findings reported in Stecher et al. 2011).

As documented in the last two World Vision Child Studies, children have very precise ideas about what a "good" all-day school should be like. Studies on urban facilities for children including playgrounds show repeatedly that these are accepted most readily and best fulfil their goals when their future users are actively involved in their planning and design (Stange et al. 2009). Such findings should be transferred to the school environment and particularly to that of the all-day school. The need is to develop a program for afternoon schooling that the children accept because they have helped design it.

Our surveys show that children attending half-day schools can also imagine taking part in school activities in the afternoon. In 2010, the majority of half-day students (76%) expressed an interest in afternoon sports (Leven and Schneekloth 2010, p. 171). The children were also interested in art and theater groups (65%), projects (56%), and homework supervision (38%). In contrast, only 17% of half-day students were in favor of normal teaching lessons in the afternoon, and only 8% were not interested in any of the proposed afternoon activities. These findings are also confirmed by the latest LBS-Kinderbarometer survey reporting that children are less interested in using the afternoon to revise the morning's lessons in more depth or to receive extra tuition. What they are interested in is new and exciting subjects and lessons, topic-related projects, sport and leisure-time provisions, and also quite simply phases of creative relaxation (LBS-Kinderbarometer 2011, p. 154).

In summary, the majority of children are in favor of all-day schools, but they have very precise expectations regarding what this new type of school in Germany should be like. They are only unreservedly in favor of all-day school when this brings subject-related and social benefits. The value of drawing on the children's subjective well-being as an indicator for the quality of their socioecological habitat becomes clear. If the all-day school delivers additional incentives and services, the children welcome it. If it represents only a lengthening of the traditional half-day school, then acceptance is only moderate.

4.3 Still Much to Be Desired Regarding Codetermination

The type and extent of child codetermination of lessons and school life varies greatly from school to school. The only standardized child participation in school is that regulated by laws and directives: the right to elect a class speaker. Just about anything going beyond this established participation structure is at the discretion of the teaching staff: the integration of students in determining the rules in the class, in shaping the daily life at school ranging from how the classroom is decorated to joint decisions on school trips and projects, and the organization of events or activities involving more than one class. Whether or not they are involved in such tasks and procedures makes a great deal of difference for children. Numerous studies confirm a close relation between greater possibilities of codetermination in a school and both the children's subjective well-being and their trust in their teachers (Bacher et al. 2007).

4.3.1 Possible Fields of Codetermination in School

In the 2013 World Vision Child Study, we wanted to ascertain how children appraise the possibilities of codetermination in their schools. We presented items referring to seven domains in which the students and their teachers can negotiate the rules and conditions of daily school life. We asked the children:

In your school, are you allowed to help decide:

- How your classroom is decorated?
- Whom are you allowed to sit next to?
- How the desks, chairs, and tables are arranged in your classroom?
- On working out the rules in your class; in other words, how everybody treats each other in the class?

For children attending 2nd grade and above, we added two more questions:

- Where you will all go on school outings?
- On suggesting possible topics for future class projects?
- On organizing school events?.[2]

[2] The response categories available to the children were "often," "sometimes," and "hardly ever." A greater number of younger children gave no answer, which was reflected in a slightly higher number of "no reply" and "don't know" responses—particularly for the questions given to children only from Grade 2 onward.

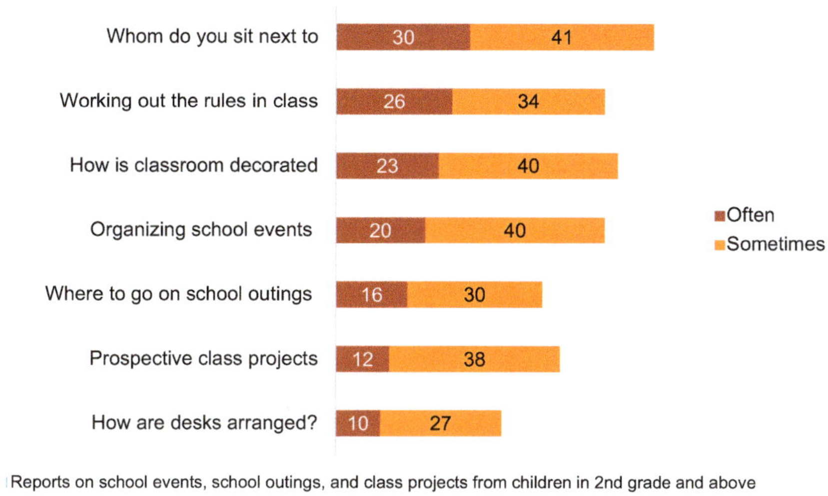

Fig. 4.5 Domains of codetermination at school
Children in Germany aged 6–11 years (%)

The results are presented in Fig. 4.5. The most frequent domain of codetermination is reported to be "whom you are allowed to sit next to." A total of 30% of children report that they can decide this "often"; 41%, "sometimes"; and 28%, "hardly ever." When it comes to "working out the rules in your class," 26% report that they can codetermine this "often"; 34%, "sometimes"; and 37%, "hardly ever." When "deciding how your classroom is decorated," 23% said they can codetermine this "often"; 40%, "sometimes"; and 34%, "hardly ever."

From 2nd grade onward, we asked the children about codetermining school events, where to go on outings, and topics for their projects. This produced the following results: For helping to decide "on organizing school events," 20% say they can do this "often"; 40%, "sometimes"; and 35%, "hardly ever." For "where you will all go on school outing," 16% say they can do this "often" and a further 30%, "sometimes," whereas one-half (50%) can do this "hardly ever." When "suggesting possible topics for future class projects," 12% report that they can codetermine this "often"; and a further 38%, "sometimes." In contrast, 45% say they can do this "hardly ever." From all seven of the domains surveyed, the children can least frequently codetermine "how the desks, chairs, and tables are arranged in your classroom." Only 10% of the children say they can do this "often"; a further 27%, "sometimes;" but 61%, "hardly ever."

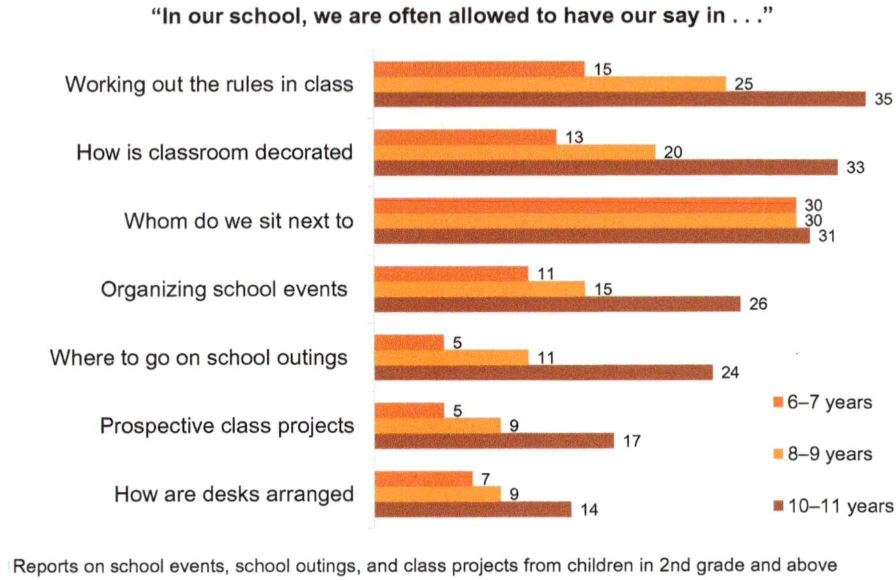

Fig. 4.6 Codetermination at school by age
Children in Germany aged 6–11 years (%)

4.3.2 Codetermination in Relation to Age, Frequency, and Gender

There are major differences between age groups with a tendency for older students to have more codetermination than younger ones. At 30%, just about every third 10- to 11-year-old reports "often" participating in decisions on at least three of the domains surveyed. Nonetheless, 26% of children in this age group report never being integrated into school life in this way. Among the 6- to 7-year-olds, only 5%; and among the 8- to 9-year-olds, 17% report that they "often" codetermine at least three domains, but 57% of the 6- to 7-year-olds and 40% of the- to 9-year-olds say that this is "hardly ever" the case. An inspection of the individual domains also reveals that older children more frequently report "often" on all domains except for "whom you are allowed to sit next to." This is about equal in all three age groups at circa 30% (Fig. 4.6).

The distribution of school codetermination according to age also reflects the type of school the children attend. Children in secondary schools report far more frequent codetermination than those attending elementary schools. Age effects can also be seen within elementary schools. Children in higher grades more frequently report that they are "often" involved in codetermination than those in lower grades (no table).

Child codetermination in school varies in terms of its extent and frequency. We find that 40% of all children aged 6–11 years do not feel well-integrated in the seven

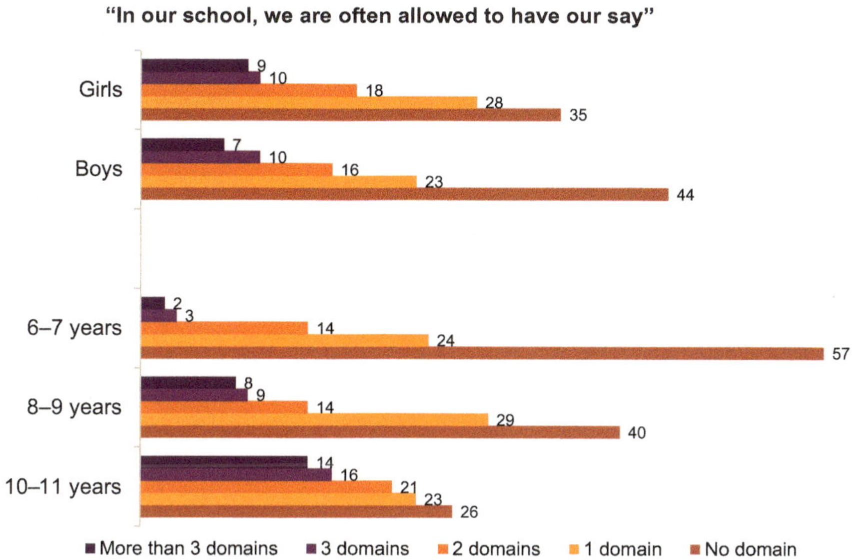

Fig. 4.7 Frequency of codetermination at school by gender and age
Children in Germany aged 6–11 years (%)

domains surveyed and feel unable to codetermine any of the domains "often. "Boys gain this impression far more frequently than girls (44% vs. 35%), and 6- to 7-year olds at 57% far more strongly than 10- to 11-year-olds at 26% (Fig. 4.7).

These reports show the broad possibilities for further extending the degree of participation in life at school. This is particularly the case for the youngest children, who are basically 1st- and 2nd-grade elementary school students and, above all, it is the case for school beginners. Here, the teaching staff should focus on thinking about new and stronger forms of participation that will let the children know right at the beginning of their school careers that their wishes and opinions are being valued and taken seriously. Up to now, many schools do not seem to have taken full advantage of these opportunities. This is poor educational policy, because impressions gained right at the beginning of schooling are very decisive. When children become aware right from the start of their school careers that they are able to participate in organizational and negotiation processes, their commitment to achievement also increases (Olk and Roth 2007). The first years at school are particularly decisive and set the pattern in every way. This is why they also form the foundation for all later experiences in life at school.

In this respect, there is a great need to improve things for boys. As pointed out above, their educational aspirations are lower than those of girls (Table 4.3). This relates to their notably lower frequency of codetermination in school. In all seven domains, girls perceive stronger codetermination at school than boys. Girls have a clear advantage in all activities relating to the communicative situation in the class-

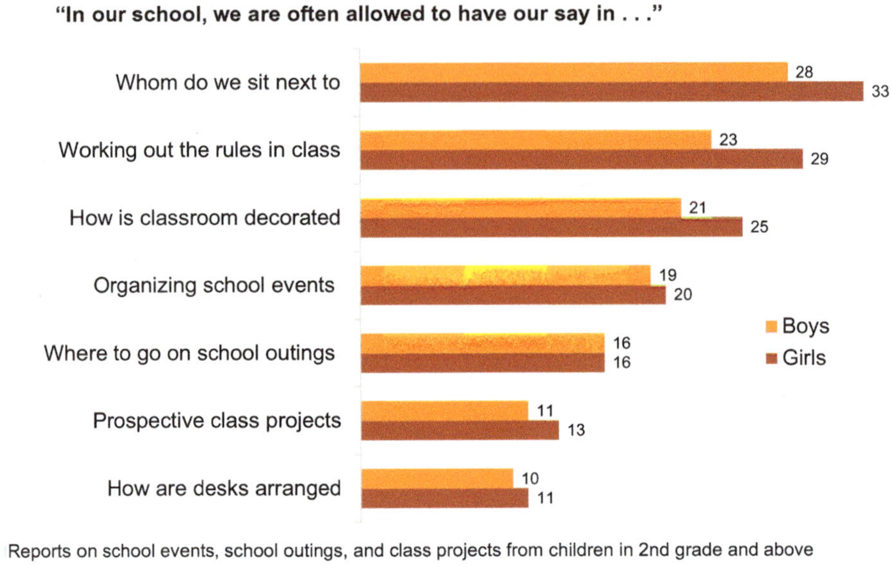

Fig. 4.8 Codetermination at school by gender
Children in Germany aged 6–11 years (%)

room and during lessons. Girls more "often" report codetermination in "working out the rules in your class" (29% vs. 23% in boys), "whom you are allowed to sit next to" (33% vs. 28%), and deciding "how your classroom is decorated" (25% vs. 21%; see Fig. 4.8).

A look at the close relations between codetermination, commitment, and performance shows that these findings deliver important indications regarding the urgently needed efforts to improve the performance of boys. One strategy to encourage more intensive integration of boys in lessons and school life could be to use increased commitment to social rules and regulations to achieve greater commitment to performance. Previous research on these topics has shown how important it is to build up the same trust in and willingness to get involved in social activities at school in boys as in girls. This is necessary to counteract their current reluctance to comply with the social demands of the school that is often due to the performance-deriding influences of the male peer group. Codetermination could be one way to encourage their interest in learning and achieving (Hurrelmann and Schultz 2012).

4.4 Most Consider Life at School to Be Fair

Chapter 2 has already pointed out how believing that they have their say in major decisions in their life world is fundamentally important for children's sense of justice or fairness. The more they see themselves as being integrated into the process

Table 4.6 Relation between perceived justice at school and frequency of codetermination
Children in Germany aged 6–11 years

	Number of domains that are "often" codetermined				
Columns in %	Total	None	One	2–3	4 or more
Very fair	22	20	23	22	31
Quite fair	56	51	56	62	58
Rather unfair	16	20	16	13	8
Very unfair	3	4	2	2	2
Don't know, no reply	3	5	3	1	1

of formulating and further developing rules, the greater their subjective sense of experiencing fairness.

In the next section, we want to transfer this finding to a life space that has become so important for children today: the school. We particularly want to look at how the codetermination children are able to perceive relates to their sense of justice in their school. Then we shall also turn to the question of how satisfied children are with their school.

4.4.1 Relation Between the Sense of Justice and Codetermination

The 2013 questionnaire asks "And how fair do you think things are in general?" It poses this question in relation to the family, to the circle of friends, and to school. In relation to school, the question is "And in your school? Are things there very fair, quite fair, rather unfair, or very unfair?"

The majority of children surveyed judge their school to be "very fair" or "quite fair." As Table 4.6 shows, 22% find their school "very fair" and 56% "quite fair." Negative reports are very weak at 16% "rather unfair" and 3% "very unfair." Hence, at 78%, the majority of children give their school quite good grades in the domain of balancing interests and distributing opportunities. Although, as reported in Chap. 2, the family and circle of friends are evaluated even more positively, this high fairness rating is quite remarkable considering that it is being given to an institution that makes decisive decisions on awarding those certificates that determine future educational careers, and, in turn, the opportunities for social development. Hence, the majority of children consider that the school operates and makes its judgments according to comprehensible criteria. This positive appraisal by children can be interpreted as indicating that they hold their teachers in high esteem.

Table 4.6 also shows how strongly the sense of justice relates to the level of potential codetermination in the school: the greater the number of domains in which they can participate and the greater the variety of design options, the higher their judgments on fairness. Children who report that they are often able to codetermine in four or more domains significantly more frequently consider that their school is "very fair." Children who rate justice negatively (taken together, only just 10%) are infrequent in this group. However, in the group of children with no possibilities of codetermination, 24% find school either "rather unfair" or "very unfair."

How far children consider their teacher to take their opinion seriously (assessed in Chap. 7) also relates to their sense of justice (no table). On average, almost one-third of the children say that they feel respected by their teacher. The proportion of children who see their school as being "very fair" is markedly higher here at 43%. Children who see their school as unfair, in contrast, are well below the average here. A further finding is also interesting in this context: Children who rate school life as "rather unfair" or "very unfair" classify themselves as performing less well than the average student.

These findings show how closely the children's sense of justice relates not only to the degree of inclusion in school affairs but also to the recognition they receive from their teachers both personally and in terms of assessing their performance. The children's replies suggest that inclusion in school activities and their teachers' respect for their opinions and achievements can positively promote their sense of justice. Children who feel involved in the daily issues at school and taken into account when decisions are made evidently have a better understanding of how schools are run and how they reach their decisions, have a more empathic understanding of how things are interrelated, and therefore perceive the school as being more fair than those who feel excluded and remain passive. This can be seen clearly in the three domains of codetermination that are most important for the children (Fig. 4.9).

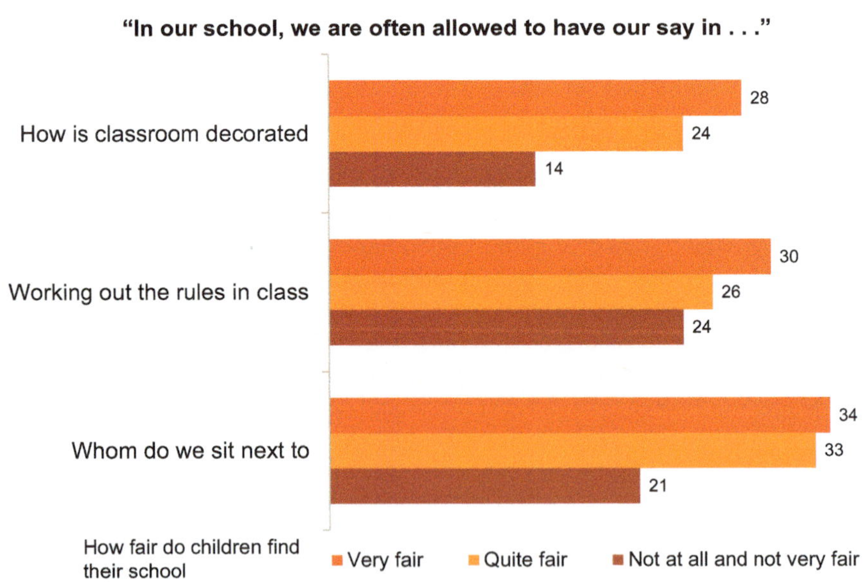

Fig. 4.9 Sense of justice in school by selected domains of codetermination
Children in Germany aged 6–11 years (%)

Table 4.7 Satisfaction with school by gender and age
Children in Germany aged 6–11 years

Columns in %	All children	Girs	Boys	6–7 years	8–9 years	10–11 years
Very positive	42	46	38	59	40	32
Positive	37	36	37	26	40	42
Neutral	16	14	19	11	15	22
Negative	3	2	4	2	3	3
Very negative	2	2	2	2	2	1

As the figure shows, children who rate their school as being "very fair" report being able to codetermine how the classroom is decorated almost twice as frequently (at 28%) as children who do not consider their school to be fair (14%). This difference can also be seen in choosing whom they sit next to and codetermining the rules in the class. The more strongly children are involved in shaping important procedures and the more they can also exert an influence on their social surroundings, the most positively they rate their school on the fairness scale. This clearly indicates starting points for reform. Not only satisfaction but also the sense of justice relate (at least indirectly) to the children's achievement at school. Any plan to strengthen achievement cannot just be attained through a greater encouragement of learning in the teaching of individual subjects, but also through including children in the sociospatial design of the workplace known as school.

4.4.2 Relation Between the Sense of Justice and Satisfaction

When asked how much they like school, the children's answers on a 5-point smiley scale are generally positive. A total of 42% give very positive answers and 37% positive ones (Table 4.7). Only 16% give a neutral rating; 3%, a negative one; and 2%, a very negative one. This means that 79% of the children associate school with positive feelings. Compared to 2010, this rating has gone up 9% (pointing to positive developments in the elementary school domain).

Girls in general are far more satisfied with school than boys with 82% giving "very positive" and "positive" reports compared to 75% among boys. This confirms the trends we have already reported for the domain of educational aspirations and particularly for which school leaving qualification children aspire to (Table 4.3). The distribution of ratings on satisfaction with school also varies according to age. Younger children have a far more positive perception of school with 59% of 6- to 7-year-olds finding it "very positive" and a further 26% finding it "positive." Among older age groups, the "very positives" decline. Whereas 40% of the 8- to 9- year-olds consider school to be "very positive" and a further 40% to be "positive," among the 10- to 11- year-olds, this drops to 32% "very positive" and 40% "positive."

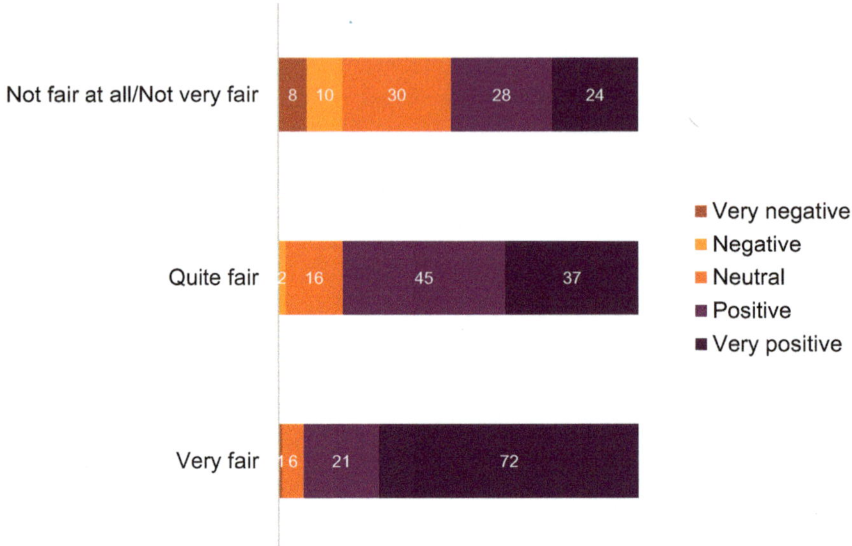

Fig. 4.10 Relation between satisfaction with school and sense of justice
Children in Germany aged 6–11 years (%)

The children's sense of justice also shows a close relation to general satisfaction with school. Students who consider school to be "rather unfair" or "very unfair" are also less satisfied with school in general and vice versa (Fig. 4.10). More than two-thirds of the students who view school as "very fair" are also very satisfied with their school (72%). This indicates once again how strongly the children sense whether they are treated fairly or not and whether they are included in important decision making in daily school life. Positive experiences in these domains increase satisfaction with the school.

References

Autorengruppe Bildungsberichterstattung. (2012). *Bildung in Deutschland 2012*. Ein indikatorengestützter Bericht mit einer Analyse zu Perspektiven des Bildungswesens im demografischen Wandel. Bielefeld: W. Bertelsmann Verlag.

Bacher, J., Winkelhofer, U., & Teubner, M. (2007). Partizipation von Kindern in der Grundschule. In Alt, C. (Hrsg.), *Kinderleben – Start in die Grundschule* (Band 3: Ergebnisse aus der zweiten Welle, S. 137–163). Wiesbaden: Verlag für Sozialwissenschaften.

Baumert, J., Stanat, P., & Watermann, R. (Hrsg.). (2006). *Herkunftsbedingte Disparitäten im Bildungswesen*. Wiesbaden: Verlag für Sozialwissenschaften.

Bos, W., Klieme, E., & Köller, O. (Hrsg.). (2010). *Schulische Lerngelegenheiten und Kompetenzentwicklung*. Münster: Waxmann.

Bremm, N. (2013). Schulen mit ganztägigem Angebot. Vorbereitung einer Typologie. *Diskurs Kindheits- und Jugendforschung* 12, S. 23–38.

Fischer, N., Holtappels, H. G., Rauschenbach, T., Stecher, L., & Zürchner, I. (Hrsg.). (2011). *Ganztagsschule; Entwicklung, Qualität, Wirkungen*. Weinheim: Beltz Juventa.
Hadjar, A., & Becker, R. (Hrsg.). (2006). *Die Bildungsexpansion*. Wiesbaden: Verlag für Sozialwissenschaften.
Hopf, W. (2010). *Freiheit-Leistung-Ungleichheit. Bildung und soziale Herkunft in Deutschland*. Weinheim: Beltz.
Hurrelmann, K., & Schultz, T., (Hrsg.). (2012). *Jungen als Bildungsverlierer*. Weinheim: Beltz Juventa.
Hurrelmann, K., Quenzel, G., & Rathmann, K. (2011). Bildungspolitik als Bestandteil moderner Wohlfahrtspolitik. *Zeitschrift für Soziologie der Erziehung und Sozialisation, 31*, S. 313–328.
KMK Sekretariat. (2012). *Allgemein bildende Schulen in Ganztagsform in Ländern der Bundesrepublik Deutschland*. Bonn und Berlin: KMK.
LBS-Kinderbarometer. (2011). *Stimmungen, Trends und Meinungen von Kindern aus Deutschland*. Recklinghausen: RDN Verlag.
Leven, I., & Schneekloth, U. (2010). Die Schule: Frühe Vergabe von Lebenschancen. In World Vision Deutschland. (Hrsg.), *Kinder in Deutschland 2010* (S. 161–185). Frankfurt a. M.: Fischer.
Maaz, K., Baumert, J., Gresch, C., & McElvany, N. (Hrsg.). (2010) *Der Übergang von der Grundschule in die weiterführenden Schulen*. Berlin und Bonn: BMBF.
Olk, T., & Roth, R. (2007). *Mehr Partizipation wagen*. Gütersloh: Bertelsmann Stiftung.
Quenzel, G., & Hurrelmann, K. (Hrsg.). (2010). *Bildungsverlierer*. Wiesbaden: Verlag für Sozialwissenschaften.
Stange, W., Meinhold-Henschel, S., & Schack, S. (2009). Mitwirkung (er)leben. *Handbuch zur Durchführung von Beteiligungsprojekten mit Kindern und Jugendlichen*. Gütersloh: Bertelsmann Stiftung.
Stecher, L., Krüger, H. H., & Rauschenbach, T. (Hrsg.). (2011). *Ganztagsschule – neue Schule?* Wiesbaden: Verlag für Sozialwissenschaften.
Stubbe, T. (2009). *Bildungsentscheidungen und sekundäre Herkunftseffekte*. Münster: Waxmann.

Chapter 5
Leisure Time: Varied and Colorful, but Not For All Children

Agnes Jänsch and Ulrich Schneekloth

Together with attending school, spending leisure time both together with and apart from the family is a major life domain for 6- to 11-year old children. It offers opportunities to gain important experiences and acquire knowledge beyond that at school. The 2007 and 2010 Child Studies have already shown how strongly leisure time differs according to not only age group and social class but also personal dispositions. To make the different patterns of leisure activities easier to grasp, we developed a leisure typology (Leven and Schneekloth 2007) that permits a more detailed analysis of the specific preferences of media consumers, normal leisure users, and all-rounders.

After giving a general report on the current leisure-time activities of 6- to 11-year-old children while paying particular attention to age effects, gender effects, and the use of electronic media, we shall take a closer look at the three leisure types and how they use their leisure time. We are particularly interested in how family support structures differ in the three groups and how their leisure behavior has changed since 2007. A further important aspect is institutional leisure activities. How are children integrated into clubs or other service structures in the musical and cultural domain, and have children from financially and socially disadvantaged families managed to gain more access? Then we shall take a look at one specific aspect of leisure activities: the use of the Internet and mobile phones as components of contemporary communication that are becoming increasingly just as important for children as they are for adults.

These different aspects of our analysis finally lead us to ask how far children themselves are satisfied with their leisure time and which factors they consider to be decisive for their level of satisfaction.

A. Jänsch (✉) • U. Schneekloth
Kantar Public, München, Germany
e-mail: info.de@kantarpublic.com; ulrich.schneekloth@kantarpublic.com

S. Andresen et al. (eds.), *Well-being, Poverty and Justice from a Child's Perspective*, Children's Well-Being: Indicators and Research 17,
DOI 10.1007/978-3-319-57574-2_5

5.1 Children's Leisure Activities

5.1.1 Wide Range of Popular Activities from Making Things to Television and Sports

As in the previous Child Studies, we also asked the children how frequently they engage in different activities in their leisure time in 2013. They could use one of three response categories: "hardly ever," "sometimes," and "very often." Since the first Child Study, our intention has been to develop a list that will cover the entire spectrum of childhood leisure activities. Therefore, we have updated and extended our list repeatedly. Compared to the first two Child Studies, we have modified our list of possible leisure activities in line with two goals: (1) to make our survey more gender-neutral by avoiding a one-sided bias in favor of typical activities for girls; and (2) to adequately reflect the entire breadth of childhood leisure activities by broadening single items or summarizing related activities. For example, "riding my bike" has been extended to include "inline skating or "skateboarding." "Making things" first introduced in 2010 has been modified to "making things with tools" and "building things with Lego©" has been supplemented by "or playing with Playmobil©." We have changed "doing things with animals," to "engaging with nature or animals" as a relevant leisure-time category, and we introduced "playing outside on the street" as being a typical childhood leisure activity. Finally, we added "listening to audio plays or stories" to our list.

According to their own reports, the children in our survey most frequently play at home with their toys (54% "very often"). They also engage particularly frequently in sports (53%), listen to music (52%), watch television (50%), or meet their friends (51%).

Alongside these possible leisure activities, a relatively large proportion of children (30% and more) report engaging in the following activities "very often": "riding a bike, inline skating, or skateboarding" (38%), "reading (looking at) books or magazines" (31 %), "handicrafts, painting, or drawing" (35%), "engaging with nature or animals" (32%), and "playing outside on the street" (30%).

For a slightly smaller proportion of children, "playing a musical instrument, making music" (20%), "PlayStation, Nintendo, Wii, computer games" (23%), "building things with Lego or playing with Playmobil©" (28%), "doing things together with my family" (27%), and "listening to audio plays or stories" (24%) are a very frequent part of their daily lives.

In contrast, only 14% of the children report "theater group, dance, or ballet" as an activity they engage in "very often"; and, at 8%, "making things with tools" is one of the less popular leisure activities. Both options are relatively gender-typical activities, although we shifted "theater" to the front of the first item in order to make it more accessible to boys. A separate analysis reveals that 26% of the girls report belonging to a theater, dance, or ballet group "very often" compared to only 3% of boys. Parent reports on club memberships reveal that ballet and dance are clearly more popular than theater among girls. Boys, in contrast, are clearly in the majority

Table 5.1 What do children do most often in their lesiure time
Children in Germany aged 6–11 years

Columns in %	All children	Girls	Boys	6–7 years	8–9 years	10–11 years
Playing with my toys at home	54	52	56	72	59	37
Sports	53	45	61	45	56	57
Listening to music	52	58	47	44	52	59
Meeting friends	51	52	50	45	51	55
Watching television	50	45	54	50	50	49
Bike, inline skates, or skateboard	38	35	41	33	40	40
Handicrafts, painting, or drawing	35	46	25	45	41	23
Nature or animals	32	37	28	29	34	34
Reading/Looking at books or magazines	31	36	27	31	32	31
Playing outside on the street	30	26	34	27	32	30
Playing with Lego™/Playmobil™	28	15	40	38	31	17
Excursions with family	27	28	26	28	29	25
Listening to audio plays/stories	24	27	21	31	26	17
Playstation, Nintendo, Wii, computer games	23	17	29	16	26	26
Playing an instrument, making music	20	26	15	16	22	22
Theater/Dance/Ballet	14	26	3	13	17	12
Making things with tools	8	3	13	8	10	7

when it comes to making things with tools; 13% report that they engage in this activity "very often" in their leisure time compared to only 3% of girls.

Table 5.1 presents an overview on the frequencies of the various leisure activities itemized according to gender and age group. To make the table easier to follow, activities are ranked according to how frequently they are named by all children and not according to the sequence in which they were presented in the questionnaire (see the appendix for the questionnaire).

5.1.2 Age-Specific Structure of Leisure Activities: Range of Activities Increases and Children Have a Wider Range of Different Media Devices

Whereas some leisure activities such as looking at books or magazines and playing on the street are engaged in equally frequently by children of all age groups, others reveal an age-specific course. Younger children far more frequently report playing at home "very often" than older children. A total of 72% of 6- to 7-year-olds frequently play with their toys at home, compared to only 37% of 10- to 11-year-olds. The activities "making things, painting, or drawing," "building things with Lego or playing with Playmobil©," and "listening to audio plays or stories" also reveal a similar age trend. Although this may be due to different leisure preferences, it may also be due to external factors: Whereas younger children generally receive far more care and supervision from their parents and thereby have closer ties to their home environments, older children are already granted more autonomy and freedom, and they can take advantage of this to engage in other leisure pursuits that are more frequently outside the parental home. The increased naming of activities such as "sports," "meeting friends," and "riding a bike, inline skating, or skateboarding" support this hypothesis because these all tend to take place outside the home. Nonetheless, 10- to 11-year-olds also engage in activities predominantly at home such as "listening to music," "PlayStation, Nintendo, Wii, computer games," or "playing a musical instrument, making music." However, all these pursuits require children to have certain equipment at their disposal – be this a hi-fi system, a PlayStation, or a musical instrument – and this is far less frequently the case for younger children. Sixty-five percent of 6- to 7-year-olds report having their own radio compared to 75% of 10- to 11-year-olds. Whereas 12% of the youngest children have their own laptop or computer, among the older children, this is 45%. Eighteen percent of the 6- to 7-year-olds have their own games console (42% their own Gameboy) compared to 41% of 10- to 11-year-olds (68% their own Gameboy). Their own CD or MP3 player is found in 64% versus 82% of children's rooms and a DVD or Blu-Ray player in 13% versus 29%. This age-related increase in media equipment is also reflected in the use of the available equipment, and thereby contributes to different leisure activities in different age groups. What is conspicuous here is that this does not apply to the frequency of watching television. Whereas 20% of the youngest age group and 43% of the 10- to 11-year-olds report having their own television, the extent of television consumption remains surprisingly constant across age groups. Approximately one-half of each age group reports watching television "very often." Evidently, even when younger children do not have a television in their own room, the one in the parental household is relatively freely accessible to them.

5.1.3 Gender-Specific Differences in Leisure Activities: Sport and Media for Boys; Music and Creative Activities for Girls

Leisure preferences do not just differ according to age but also according to gender. Boys name movement-related activities more frequently: that is, they engage more often in sports (61% vs. 45%); ride bikes, inline skates, or skateboards more (41% vs. 35%); and play on the street more (34% vs. 26%). However, they also engage more in passive leisure options such as watching television (54% vs. 45%) and playing with PlayStation or computers (29% vs. 17%). Although girls engage less frequently in sports such as swimming or soccer, they are more active, as mentioned above, in the field of "theater group, dance, or ballet" (26% vs. 3%). Hence, they combine sports with music and creative activities in their leisure time. They tend to be more creative in general, as shown by the frequency reports for "handicrafts, painting, or drawing" (46% vs. 25%), "reading (or looking at) books or magazines" (36% vs. 27%), and "playing a musical instrument, making music" (26% vs. 15%). In addition, girls listen to music more frequently than boys (58% vs. 47%) and spend more time "engaging with nature or animals" (37% vs. 28%).

As already reported in the 2010 Child Study under the heading *Der kulturell-musische Freizeitbereich – Jungen verlieren hier den Anschluss* [Boys are losing touch with the cultural and musical domain], boys in general far less frequently belong to cultural and musical clubs and groups than girls. According to parent reports, 47% of all girls have at least one club membership in this domain compared to only 19% of boys. At 27% in girls and 16% in boys, the most popular cultural and musical leisure activity is membership of a music group or music school. Girls also very frequently belong to a ballet group or dance club (25%), whereas this is very much the exception among boys at only 2%. Painting and theater groups are among the least frequently attended organized leisure activities in both genders with only 3% of girls and 1% of boys belonging to a painting group. Whereas 4% of girls participate in a theater or movie group, boys are almost completely absent here. In particular, multiple memberships are something for girls – 11% of them belong to more than one organized group in the cultural and musical domain compared to only 1% of boys.

5.1.4 Computer Games: An Everyday Pastime for Many Children

The most recent study on children's use of the media, computers, and the Internet in Germany, the KIM study (Medienpädagogischer Forschungsverbunds Südwest 2013) confirms that adults often disapprove of "the use of digital games – on computers, game consoles, or the Internet. Nonetheless, for one-quarter of all children (particularly boys), playing such games is one of their favorite leisure activities and is – similar to television and radio – something they take for granted in daily media life" (p. 46, translated).

As Table 5.1 shows, for 23% of the 6- to 11-year-olds in the current Child Study, computer games and game consoles are not just part of daily life but are even played "very often." Since 2007, the proportion of 8- to 11-year-olds[1] who report playing with a computer or game console "very often" has declined slightly from 29% to 26%. However, since 2010 when the breadth of use was assessed in more detail ("What about computer games, Gameboy, PlayStation, and the like? How often do you play with them?"), it has proved to be relatively constant. Among 6- to

[1] The group of 6- to 7-year-olds was not included in these analyses, because it was not surveyed in 2007, making a direct comparison across all children impossible.

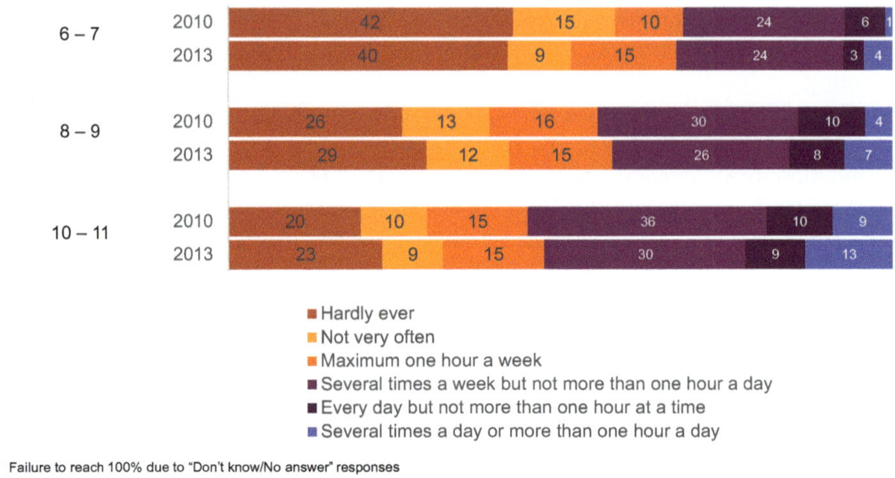

Fig. 5.1 Frequency of playing computer games by age groups over time
Children in Germany aged 6–11 years (%)

11-year-olds,[2] 14% in 2010 and 15% in 2013 play computer games "at the most, one hour a week"; 31% in 2010 and 27% in 2013, "several times a week for up to one hour a day"; 9% in 2010 and 7% in 2013, "every day, but up to one hour a day"; and 5% in 2010 and 8% in 2013, "several times a day for more than one hour a day." In contrast, roughly 30% of children at each assessment "hardly ever" spend their leisure time playing with computers and game consoles.

Figure 5.1 presents the frequencies of computer game use in different age groups. It reveals a clear increase with age: Whereas 40% of 6- and 7-year-olds hardly ever play with a computer or game console, this drops to 29% in the intermediate age group, and to 23% in the 10- to 11-year-olds.

A comparison between those girls and boys who "very often" or "sometimes" spend their time playing computer games reveals a gender effect: When girls are asked to give more detailed reports on the extent of their use of computers or game consoles, 24% say that they hardly ever or only sometimes play with computers. Only 13% of boys report such a low usage. Twenty-three percent of girls spend a maximum of one hour a week on computer games compared to 18% of boys. In contrast, 65% of boys report using computers several times a week or even every day, whereas, at 50%, notably fewer girls report such intensive use (Fig. 5.2).

Both the findings on the increasing frequency of playing computer games as children grow older and the gender differences found here are in line with the results of the German KIM study on children and the media. This confirmed a greater affin-

[2] This question has been posed only since the 2010 Child Study that also surveyed 6- to 7-year-old children. This permits a comparison of trends across age groups.

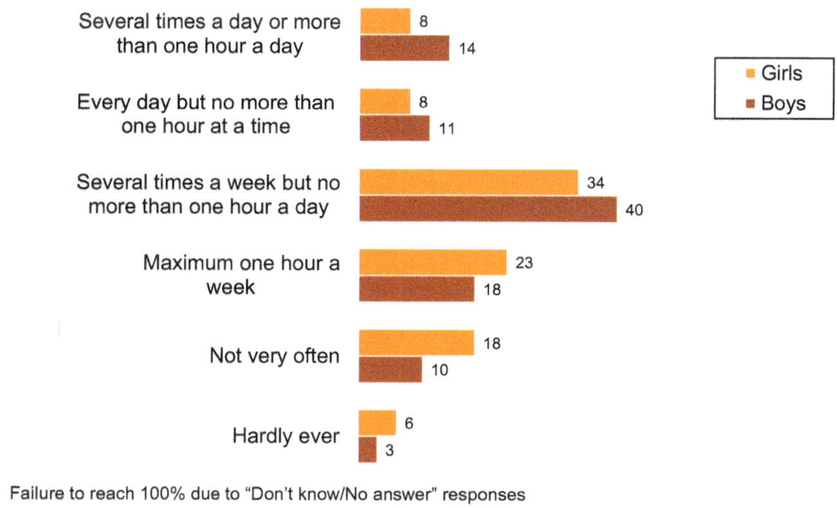

Fig. 5.2 Frequency of playing computer games by gender
Children in Germany aged 6–11 years who previously reported playing computer/Playstation "very often" or "sometimes" (%)

ity to digital games among boys and a decline in the number of nonplayers with increasing age (Medienpädagogischer Forschungsverbunds Südwest 2013).

5.2 A Typology of Leisure Time: Groups Differ in Reading and Media Consumption

The typology of leisure time developed for the World Vision Child Study is based on the list of leisure activities reported in Table 5.1. A factor analysis of the frequency reports revealed four different domains of leisure activities. These could be labeled Culture, Sport/Exercise, Media, and Play (at home). These factors then formed the starting point for a cluster analysis that resulted in a typology containing three groups of children: "media consumers," "normal leisure users," and "all-rounders."

According to the present data for 2013, approximately one-quarter of the children can be assigned to media consumers (26%) and one-quarter to the all-rounders (25%). The remaining one-half (49%) are normal leisure users. This corresponds roughly with the distribution across the different groups found in both the First and Second World Vision Child Studies.

Figure 5.3 shows that whereas some leisure activities are engaged in equally frequently by children in all three groups, others are particularly characteristic of one of the two extreme groups: media consumers or all-rounders. Hence, these activities can be used to differentiate between the two. For example, media consum-

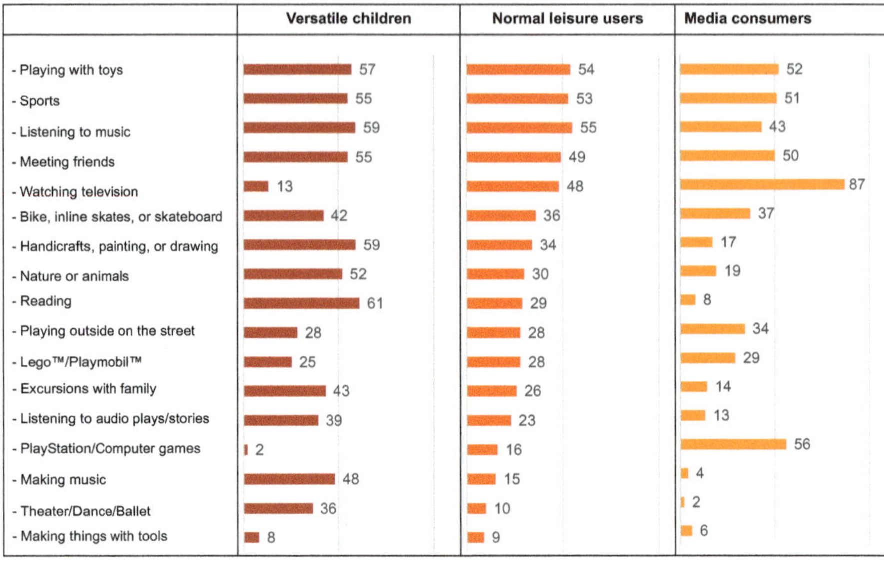

Fig. 5.3 Typical activities from different leisure types in 2013
Children in Germany aged 6–11 years (%)

ers are characterized by a particularly frequent use of electronic media such as television, computers, and game consoles. They very infrequently engage in creative and cultural activities such as reading, making things, and painting or making music. Normal leisure users can be found in all activities; however, there are no domains in which they stand out through extreme engagement or a complete lack of interest. Finally, as already reported in the previous Child Studies, all-rounders engage particularly frequently in musical and cultural activities in which media consumers show hardly any interest. The former read, make things and paint a lot, make music, play theater, or they take ballet lessons. They are also characterized by a particularly low television consumption and extremely infrequent use of computer games.

As already seen in 2010, all-rounders engage in significantly more different leisure activities in 2013 as well. However, as well as differing in the number of leisure activities, the leisure types also differ in their content. Around one-third of all-rounders say that they very often take part in a theater group, dance, or ballet, whereas less than 10% of the normal leisure users and media consumers engage in such activities very often. Results are similar for playing a musical instrument: Almost one-half of the all-rounders do this frequently, but normal leisure users and media consumers do so markedly less often. All-rounders also predominantly view handicrafts, painting, and drawing as an integral part of their leisure time. More than one-half of them report engaging in such activities very often compared to only roughly one-third of normal leisure users and one-fifth of media consumers.

This difference between all-rounders and media consumers is particularly drastic when it comes to reading – a leisure activity that is a particularly important basic cultural technique in the musical and cultural domain. More than 60% of all-rounders report that reading is one of the activities they engage in very often compared to less than 10% of media consumers. Evidently, in many cases, media consumers drop reading as a source of information and inspiration with all its creative potential in favor of the markedly more passive medium of television. A total of 87% of the children in this group report watching television very often compared to only 13% of all-rounders. A clear difference can even be found when looking at those children in both groups who report watching television very often: Media consumers most frequently report watching television for 1–2 hours per day; all-rounders, for 0.5–1 hour per day. This also shows how the children's evaluation standards differ: Whereas all-rounders already consider 30–60 min a day of television as very often, this category stands for several hours a day in media-oriented children. A correlation analysis reveals a significant negative relation between the amount of television watching and the frequency of reading:[3] Children who watch a lot of television have less to do with books and vice versa.

Media consumers are also characterized quite clearly by a more frequent use of further electronic media such as PlayStation, Nintendo, Wii, and other computer games. In contrast, all-rounders hardly use these, with only 2% reporting that they play with them often. More detailed questions on the extent of use reveal that 14% of all-rounders play computer games several times a week or even daily compared to 71% of media consumers. Hence, all-rounders and media consumers differ not only in their self-reports on how far computer games belong to their preferred leisure activities but also in the number of hours they report playing them. Here as well, a rank correlation reveals a significant negative relation between the extent of media use and the frequency of reading.

5.2.1 Different Family Incentive Structures: Broad Range of Media Equipment Versus Books and Doing Things Together

It is not just the reported leisure activities in the musical and creative domain and media use that differentiate clearly between the various leisure groups. They also show fundamental differences in what is available to them within their family framework.

Whereas 44% of media consumers report having their own television in their room, this is the case for only 18% of all-rounders. Approximately one-third of media consumers have their own DVD or Blu-ray player compared to only about 10% of all-rounders. Likewise, an own computer (32%), a game console (51%), and a Gameboy (72%) are to be found far more frequently in the media consumers' rooms than in those of the all-rounders (computer: 24%, game console: 14%,

[3] Nonparametric test: Spearman's correlation coefficient significant on the 5% level.

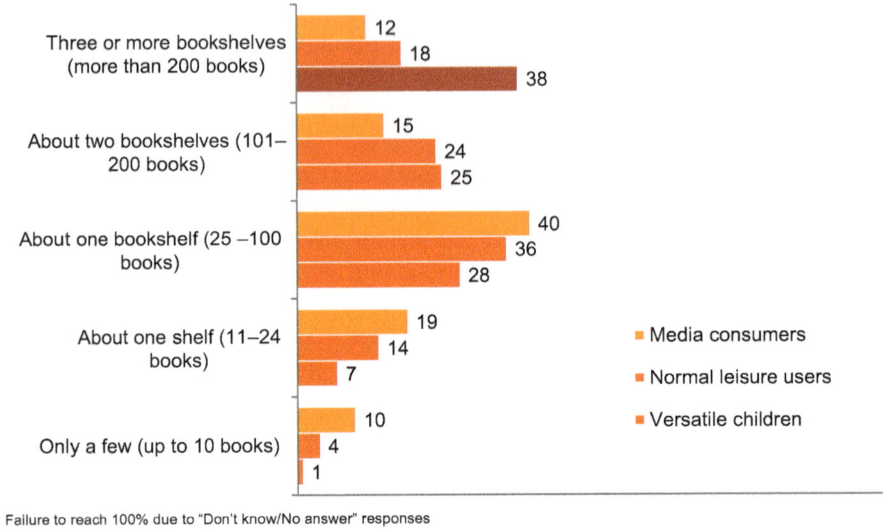

Fig. 5.4 Number of books in the family home by different leisure types
Children in Germany aged 6–11 years (%)

Gameboy: 44%). However, the two groups hardly differ when it comes to having their own mobile phone: 42% of media consumers and 38% of all-rounders. However, at 48%, media consumers more frequently have their own Internet access than all-rounders (42%).

The comparatively greater range of electronic media in the children's rooms contrasts with the presence of books in the home (Fig. 5.4). When we ask both media consumers and normal leisure users how many books there are in their homes, their most frequent answer is "about one shelf (25–100 books)." All-rounders, in contrast, most frequently answer "three or more shelves (more than 200 books)." Even when this is not explicitly literature for children, that is, books with which the respondent's themselves can spend their leisure time, answers do indicate the status of reading in that household. Whereas all-rounders evidently grow up particularly frequently in families in which books are considered to be important and are correspondingly granted a great deal of space within the family home, media consumers and normal leisure-time users live in less book-friendly environments.

Spending leisure time actively together is also particularly characteristic of families with all-rounders. We find that 43% of these children report very frequently going on excursions together with their families. This contrasts with only 26% of normal leisure users and 14% of media consumers. In addition, parents of all-rounders grant their children more codetermination about potential leisure activities. Whereas 68% of media consumers say that they can "sometimes" codetermine what the family does together during leisure time, this compares with 75% of normal leisure users and even 83% of all-rounders. Interestingly, all-rounders have more codetermination over what they do in general. A total of 90% are allowed to codetermine what they do in their leisure time compared to 84% of normal leisure users and 83% of media consumers (see also Chap. 7 on codetermination).

Hence, all-rounders receive more family support and encouragement in general, and this expresses itself not only in an emphasis on musical and creative activities but also in a broader family leisure program. Their particularly caring parents do not prescribe the planning activities together with the family or leisure time in general. In contrast, they coordinate them more closely with their children than parents of the other two leisure types.

5.2.2 *Social and Material Constraints as Risk Factors for Excessive Media Consumption*

We computed a nominal regression to take a closer look at which factors in the family influence the membership of one of the three leisure groups (Table 5.2).[4] Results show that girls belong more frequently to the all-rounders and less frequently to the media consumers than boys. This is not surprising because there is a relatively strong agreement between the leisure pursuits that girls report engaging in particularly often and those preferred by all-rounders. Already in 2010, we found that three times as many girls as boys were all-rounders. This is also confirmed in the present study, along with the finding that this relation inverts for media consumers. The age groups differ insofar as children in the youngest age group belong significantly less often to the media consumers than members of the other two age groups. Computations also show that children from the lower social classes are less likely to belong to the all-rounder group than those from the more educated classes, and there is a very strong probability of finding them among the media consumers. A care deficit from one or both parents is also a risk factor for children who spend their leisure time as media consumers. In addition, children who report having experienced poverty significantly less frequently belong to the group of all-rounders compared to their more affluent peers.

Hence, both material and social deficits within the family continue to impose decisive constraints on the versatility of children's leisure time. On the one hand, the parents' lack of financial resources makes it harder for them to offer their children a comparable range of opportunities as in more affluent families. On the other hand, deficits in social care from either one or both parents can lead a child to turn to the media as an alternative source of stimulation. In contrast, no fundamental cultural differences can be ascertained. A possible migration background does not, in itself, have any effect in either one or the other direction. What is decisive here is how class membership moderates the relation. Whereas 20% of native German children belong to the lower class or the lower middle class, this applies to 34% of children

[4] Relations reported here are statistically significant on the 5% level.

Table 5.2 Significant relations between leisure types and personal and social variables[a]
Children in Germany aged 6–11 years

% (per line)	Versatile children	Normal leisure users	Media consumers
Total	25	49	26
Gender			
Girls	**38**[b]	49	13
Boys	12	49	**39**[b]
Social origin			
Lower class	**7**[b]	47	**46**[b]
Lower middle class	**13**[b]	53	34
Middle class	20	50	30
Upper middle class	**31**[b]	48	**21**[b]
Upper class	**45**[b]	44	**11**[b]
Experienced poverty			
No experience of poverty	27	48	25
Constraints	22	51	27
Specific experience of poverty	**14**[b]	52	34
Age			
6–7 years	26	51	**23**[b]
8–9 years	26	47	27
10–11 years	23	48	29
Parental care and attention			
No deficit	26	50	24
Deficit in one parent	20	45	**35**[b]
Care deficit	20	44	**36**[b]

[a]The relationship was tested with a multivariate nominal regression on the variable "leisure" Variables included: age, gender, social origin, experience of poverty, care deficit, and migration background

[b]For ease of presentation, bivariate values are presented as percentages in the table. Notable deviations for variables that were also significant within the multivariate statistical analysis are printed in bold ($p < .05$)

with a migration background, and this leads to a basically greater probability of spending leisure time as a media consumer.

5.2.3 *Leisure-Time Types and Their Activities Across Time: Increasingly Less Time for Reading*

As pointed out above, "reading," "watching television," and "PlayStation/computer games" are types of leisure activity that distinguish particularly clearly between the two extreme groups in our leisure typology: media consumers and all-rounders. Hence, it is particularly worth taking a look at the trends in these three leisure activities. When tracked across time in all three leisure groups, we can see a slight decline in television consumption. Whereas in 2007, 56% of children reported watching television very often, this dropped to 48% in 2010 before rising again slightly to 49% in 2013.[5] In all three survey years, frequent computer use varies between 25% and 30%, and about one-third of all children read very often.

However, the two extreme groups reveal a somewhat different trend: Whereas television viewing remains on a constantly high level of approximately 80% to 90% in media consumers, it is declining among all-rounders. Whereas in 2007, 24% of the latter still reported watching television very frequently; in 2013, it is only 12%. It is not only the proportion of all-rounders who watch a lot of television that is in decline, but also the amount of time they spend watching each day. Of the 8- to 11-year-old all-rounders who reported watching television very often in 2007, 23% watched for 2–3 hours per day. In 2013, this has dropped to only 14%. Among media consumers, in contrast, we observe an opposite trend. Whereas in 2007, approximately 30% watched television for 2–3 hours or more a day, in 2013, approximately 40% of those who say they watch television very often do so for 2–3 hours or more.

All-rounders also reveal a decline in playing computer games. Whereas approximately 60% of 8- to 11-year-old media consumers report playing on computers or game consoles very often in all three surveys, the proportion of all-rounders here has dropped from 10% to 2%. Moreover, when asked in more detail, the proportion of all-rounders who report spending time on computer games several times a week or even daily has dropped from 18% in 2010 to the aforementioned 14% in 2013. For the media-oriented children, in contrast, the proportion reporting several times a week or daily continues to be 71%.

Regarding reading, we can initially determine no clear trend. About 10% of media consumers report reading "very often" in all three surveys. In 2007, 63% of the all-rounders reported very often spending their leisure time reading; in 2010, this even rose to 76%, and in 2013, this returned to almost the same frequency as in 2007 at 62%. Hence, the subjectively perceived frequency of spending time with books seems to remain more or less constant or is subject to fluctuations that fail to form any clear trend. However, when questioned more closely as to how often they read or look at books in their homes, we can see that the frequency of spending time with books is declining. Among media consumers, it was 9% in 2007, 5% in 2010, and now 6% in 2013 who spend time with books every day. Among all-rounders, this was 42% in 2007, 39% in 2010, and is now only 28% in 2013. It is precisely in this group in which frequent reading is a fundamental part of leisure that we can see a particularly significant decline in its actual frequency.

[5] To ensure comparability, only the trend calculations were included for 8- to 11-year-olds covering the years 2007, 2010, and 2013.

5.3 Institutional Leisure Activities: A Possible Compensatory Source of Stimulation When the Family Is Unable to Provide It?

As pointed out above, family factors exert a major influence on how children shape their leisure. Whereas those from more affluent social classes more frequently belong to the all-rounder group and spend their leisure in a variety of ways with a focus on musical and creative activities, children from the lower social classes tend toward a more one-sided media-oriented use of leisure. Government interventions such as special social transfers to children (for extra tuition or school materials) should help to ensure that children from lower social classes can also take advantage of social, cultural, and educational facilities. Funds are made available for these children to, for example, join a sports club or attend a music school. On the one hand, this can offer them experiences that their own families are unable to provide because of limited income, and, on the other hand, it could compensate for any potential care deficits. In view of the finding that 10% of children from the lower class report a lack of attention from one parent and even 28% a lack of attention from both, it is precisely the second aspect that would seem to indicate the most important task for extrafamilial and leisure services.

Germany has a wide range of institutional leisure and cultural provisions. These are traditionally organized in the form of clubs and associations – particularly when it comes to sports. There are also church-run provisions as well as what are frequently private and commercial services provided by music, dance, and ballet schools. In the Child Study, we asked parents to tell us whether their child is a member of such a club, association or other kind of organized group.

With a few individual exceptions, trends reveal a slight decline in memberships of clubs and groups or the use of other such provisions since the last Child Study. Between 2007 and 2010 in contrast, we found a slight increase.[6] Among 8- to 11-year-olds, who have been surveyed since the first Child Study, 74% belonged to at least one club in 2007 and 80% in 2010, whereas in 2013, 78% of parents report that their child is organized in at least one regular group or association. As before, it is membership of sports clubs that is strongest among the 8- to 11-year-olds. At 57%, more than one child in two is active here. This is followed by musical and cultural provisions (music groups/music schools: 21%, dance club/ballet: 13%). Activities in church-run groups are reported for 7% of children. Further memberships and use of provisions are listed in Table 5.3.

[6] We have surveyed 6- to 7-year-olds only since 2010. However, the increase in memberships identified here could be ascertained independent of age.

Table 5.3 Membership in clubs and organized groups or use of other such provisions
Children in Germany aged 6–11 years (2007: 8–11 years)

Positive answers per cell in %	2007	2010	2013
Clubs, groups, or use of other provisions (multiple responses)			
Sports club	58	62	57
Music group/music school	21	23	21
Dance club/Ballet	10	10	13
Painting/drawing group	2	2	2
Theater or movie group	3	3	2
Church group	11	10	7
Girl guides/boy scouts	2	2	2
Nature or animal protection society	1	1	1
Organized group in a child or youth club	4	3	2
Traditional costumes and folklore clubs	1	1	1
Other	7	7	5
None of the above	27	22	25

5.3.1 Declining Club Memberships in the Lower Classes

Table 5.4 reports the proportions of children who are members of clubs, belong to organized groups, or use other musical and cultural provisions across time broken down according to social origins. Trends show a conspicuous decline particularly among 6- to 7-year-olds. This applies above all to children from the lower classes.

There are also fluctuations among the 8- to 9-year-olds and the 10- to 11-year-olds, although these do not relate to social class so clearly. Looking just at the lower class, the proportion of 8- to 9-year-olds belonging to clubs or groups in our first Child Study in 2007 was 35%. This rose to 49% in 2010, and has now dropped back to 37%. Among the 10- to 11-year-olds, memberships in the lowest social class have fluctuated from 58% over 47% to a current 53%. Among the 6- to 7-year-olds who have been included since our second Child Study, the rate is currently 18% compared to 30% in 2010.

5.3.2 Social Class and Not Type of School Determines Club Membership

When interpreting these findings, it is worth considering the influence of the type of school children are attending. Those attending an all-day school have less free time at their disposal for clubs and groups. Moreover, the all-day school provisions ranging from sports to music and theater groups already cover several activities that are otherwise organized in clubs. As reported in Chap. 4, the proportion of all-day students rose from 13% in 2007 to 17% in 2010 and is now 24% in 2013. Moreover, lower class children attend all-day schools more frequently than those from higher

Table 5.4 Membership in a club or participation in an organized group
Children in Germany aged 6–11 years

	2007			2010			2013		
Per cell in %	6–7 years	8–9 years	10–11 years	6–7 years	8–9 years	10–11 years	6–7 years	8–9 years	10–11 years
Lower class	–	35	58	30	49	47	18	37	53
Lower middle class	–	61	64	59	69	63	54	71	65
Middle class	–	67	71	75	77	81	59	80	77
Upper middle class	–	85	87	81	90	92	82	82	86
Upper class	–	91	87	94	98	94	93	86	95

social classes (31% all-day students in the lower class vs. 20% in the upper class). Hence, the greater attendance of all-day schools already at elementary school age and particularly among children from lower social classes could correspondingly lead to a lower participation in clubs and groups.

Interestingly, however, the proportions of both all-day and half-day students who are members of a club or an established group have converged strongly in recent years. Whereas in 2007, 25% of the 8- to 11-year-old half-day students and 37% of the all-day students of the same age were not in any club or using a corresponding service, in 2010, these figures had dropped to 19% and 27% respectively. In the current survey, 25% of the parents of half-day and 27% of the parents of all-day students report that their child does not belong to a club or engage in any other provisions (Table 5.5). The only relevant difference is found in sports clubs: These are used more frequently by children in this age range attending half-day (58%) than all-day schools (52%). Hence, attending a half-day or all-day school does not seem to be decisive for membership of clubs or groups in this age range.

However, as Table 5.4 has shown already, class-related differences can be seen clearly in all three Child Studies. Across all survey times and age groups, the frequency of club memberships increases clearly in line with social status. The current data from the third Child Study indicate that it is particularly children from the lowest social class who continue to be insufficiently integrated into the great range of club provisions available in Germany – even though these are basically open to every child.

Table 5.5 Membership in a club, participation in an organized group, or use of other such provisions by type of school
Children in Germany aged 6–11 years

Positive answers, Per cell in %	Total	Half-day school	All-day school
Clubs, groups or use of other provisions (multiple responses)			
Sports club	56	58	52
Music group/Music school	21	21	22
Dance club/Ballet	13	13	13
Painting/drawing group	2	2	2
Theater or movie group	2	2	2
Church group	7	8	5
Girl guides/Boy scouts	2	2	1
Nature or animal protection society	1	1	1
Organized group in a child or youth club	2	3	2
Traditional costumes and folklore clubs	1	1	1
Other	5	5	5
None of above	25	25	27

5.3.3 Music and Sport Groups Also Fail to Reach the Lower Class

As well as asking about club memberships, the items in the parent questionnaire tap a whole series of further group activities or other provisions. In the following, we want to take a closer look at memberships of sports clubs and music groups or music schools. These are both activities that the German Federal Ministry of Labor and Social Affairs has named as being exemplary for the goals of government interventions to increase the participation of socially disadvantaged children (BMAS 2013). Due to the influence of age on the frequency of club memberships, we shall examine the different age groups separately here as well.

Across all social classes, 58% of 8- to 9-year-olds and 58% of 10- to 11-year-olds belonged to a sports club in 2007. In 2010, 58% of parents reported such a membership for their 6- to 7-year-old children; 63%, for their 8- to 9-year-olds; and 64%, for their 10- to 11-year-olds. In the current study, 52% of parents of 6- to 7-year-olds report that their child is a member of a sports club compared to 59% of the parents of 8- to 9-year-olds and 58% of the parents of 10- to 11-year-olds. Hence, there is a degree of fluctuation around 60% for the two older groups and between 50% and 60% for younger children. This does not reveal any clear trend toward more or less frequent club memberships in the sports domain.

The proportion of music group and music school memberships is also relatively stable in all age groups. In 2007, 20% of 8- to 9-year-olds and 21% of 10- to 11-year-olds belonged to a music group. In 2010, it was 20% of 6- to 7-year-olds, 26% of 8- to 9-year-olds, and 22% of 10- to 11-year-olds. In the current survey, the

Table 5.6 Membership in a sports club or music group/music school
Children in Germany aged 6–11 years

Per cell in %	2007 6–7 years	2007 8–9 years	2007 10–11 years	2010 6–7 years	2010 8–9 years	2010 10–11 years	2013 6–7 years	2013 8–9 years	2013 10–11 years
Sports club									
Lower class	–	32	49	26	35	35	11	23	35
Lower middle class	–	54	49	48	51	50	43	49	47
Middle class	–	49	56	58	61	65	44	62	62
Upper middle class	–	68	66	61	72	74	65	65	60
Upper class	–	73	71	84	81	80	73	70	73
Music group									
Lower class	–	0	8	1	9	4	0	3	7
Lower middle class	–	6	13	10	12	7	11	10	7
Middle class	–	17	17	13	18	18	12	17	16
Upper middle class	–	26	30	25	38	36	21	29	29
Upper class	–	45	36	43	44	34	47	42	43

proportion of 6- to 7-year-olds is almost unchanged at 19%, and both the 8- to 9-year-olds and the 10- to 11-year-olds are at 22%.

Table 5.6 shows the trends in memberships of sports clubs and nonschool music groups and music schools since the first Child Study in 2007. Here as well, we report the proportions of different age groups and different social classes. Yet again, we can confirm hardly any positive effect on children in the lowest social class in the responses on these two prototypical items for sports and cultural activities. Regarding membership in sports clubs, we can even see a decline in the lower class among 8- to 9-year-olds from 32% in 2007, to 35% in 2010, and 23% in 2013; and among the 10- to 11-year-olds, from 49% in 2007 to 35% in both 2010 and 2013.

In the music domain, the participation of lower class children remains comparably low at less than 10% in all age groups. Outside school, these children continue to be more or less totally excluded from musical and creative education. The general questions on leisure activities also do not produce any essentially different outcome here. Within the first Child Study, 4% of lower class children reported playing a musical instrument or making music "very often." In 2010, this rose to 5%, and in 2013, to 8%. Hence, there is a very slightly positive trend, but this is still far from catching up with the opportunities for participation available to the children of families in a better social position.

If we also look at children attending a half-day school separately here in order to rule out any confounds between attendance of an all-day school and memberships of clubs or groups, we can see, as already pointed out above, that the decline in club memberships cannot be explained exclusively through an increase in attendance of all-day schools and the accompanying availability of leisure provisions within the school. The lower class 8- to 11-year-old half-day students are slightly less frequently members of a sports club or a music group in 2013 compared to either 2007 or 2010.

5.4 How Children Use the Internet

5.4.1 Social Class Continues to Be Decisive for Access to the Internet

As reported above, although the extent to which 6- to 11-year-olds use electronic media such as television and computer games varies greatly, they are nonetheless a part of the direct life worlds of children in general. Likewise, the Internet has also become a self-evident feature of the environment for children in this age range, although they vary greatly in how far and for what purposes they use this medium.

Having one's own computer is no essential precondition for access to the Internet. A total of 46% of all surveyed children reported having access to the Internet, although only 27% possess their own PC or laptop in their own room. Hence, the children have further ways of accessing the Internet such as their parents' computer, at school, or at friends' homes. Nonetheless, children who possess their own computer have, at 67%, an above-average frequency of access to the Internet. As already shown in the 2010 Child Study, there is a clear age effect here. Only 24% of the children in the youngest age group report having access to the Internet, compared to 36% in the 8- to 9-year-olds and a clear majority of 71% in the 10- to 11-year-olds. Among those with access, 40% use it regularly each week. A clear age effect can be recognized here as well. Whereas only 17% of the 6- to 7-year-olds who have access to the Internet report using it regularly, this is already 31% in the 8- to 9-year-olds and 50% in the oldest age group.

At 42%, all-rounders have somewhat less access to the Internet than normal leisure users (46%) and media consumers (48%). Differences between the various leisure groups become more apparent when we look at the regularity of Internet use. A total of 50% of media consumers with access to the Internet use it regularly compared to only 39% of normal leisure users and 30% of all-rounders.

An inspection of the social, personal, and structural variables influencing the probability of having access to the Internet reveals a significant effect of a child's social class: Lower class and lower middle-class children less frequently have access than middle-class children, whereas members of the upper middle-class more frequently have access. Likewise, 6- to 7-year-olds less frequently have access to the Internet than 8- to 9-year-olds. In contrast, children in the oldest group in the survey more frequently have access than 8- to 9-year-olds. As in 2010, the current Child Study reveals that children with a migration background significantly more frequently have access to the Internet than native German children. In the 2010 Child Study, this finding ran counter to that of 2007, but it now seems to have become a stable trend. In contrast, gender and settlement structure have no significant influence on the probability of a child having access to the Internet. Accordingly, girls and boys have equal access, and the technical limitations that still seem to have been a problem in some rural areas a few years ago have apparently been resolved. Table 5.7 reports findings on the relations between features that have a significant influence on access to the Internet.

5.4.2 Extent of Internet Use: Use of the World Wide Web Is Equally Widespread in All Leisure Types

Children reveal just as strong a trend toward increasing use of the Internet as that found in adults. However, this applies only to older children from the age of 10 to 11 years onward. In both 2007 and 2010, 13% of 8- to 9-year-olds reported regularly spending time on the Internet. Currently, this is 11% of this age group. Among 10- to 11-year-olds, the proportion regularly using the Internet every week has risen from 29% in 2007, across 32% in 2010, to a current 36%. According to their own reports, only 4% of 6- to 7-year-olds regularly use the Internet each week. We shall have to wait and see how things develop further. However, due to the increasing availability of mobile web-enabled end devices, we can assume that regular Internet use will increase even further among children.

Children who use the Internet regularly do so mostly for up to 1 hour (26%) or up to 2 hours (23%) a week. The frequencies for the other categories ("no more than half an hour," "up to 3/4/5 hours," and "more than 5 hours" per week) are all roughly 10%. A breakdown according to age groups in Fig. 5.5 shows that the proportion of 10- to 11-year-olds who spend more than 2 hours on the Internet each week is higher than that of 8- to 9-year-olds. Whereas 8- to 9-year-olds most frequently (37%) use the Internet for up to 1 hour per week, and only 25% report using it for more than 2 hours, 44% of the older children spend more than 2 hours a week online.[7]

[7] Because of the low number of cases of regular Internet users in the group of 6- to 7-year-olds (29 cases), we report no frequencies for the youngest age group here.

Table 5.7 Significant relations between access to the internet and personal and social variables[a]
Children in Germany aged 6–11 years

% (per cell)	Yes	No
All children	46	54
Age		
6–7 years	24	**76**[b]
8–9 years	36	64
10–11 years	**71**[b]	29
Social origin		
Lower class	32	**68**[b]
Lower middle class	41	**59**[b]
Middle class	45	55
Upper middle class	**51**[b]	49
Upper class	49	51
Migration background		
Native German children	45	55
Children with a migration background	**47**[b]	53

[a]The relationship was tested with a multivariate logistic regression on the criterion variable "access to the Internet: yes or no."
Variables included: age, gender, migration background, type of settlement structure, and social origin
[b]For ease of presentation, bivariate values are presented as percentages in the table. Notable deviations for variables that were also significant within the multivariate statistical analysis are printed in bold ($p < .05$)

Looking at the different leisure types, it is interesting to see that when we ask media consumers and normal leisure users who are regularly online how often they use the Internet each week, they most frequently answer "up to 1 hour," whereas the most frequent answer among all-rounders is "up to 2 hours." We find that 36% of media consumers, 41% of normal leisure users, and 36% of all-rounders use the Internet for more than 2 hours a week. Hence, we can see no clear differences between the single leisure types regarding the extent of activities on the Internet. However, when asking 6- to 11-year-olds about their Internet use, we are naturally not just interested in how much they use it but also what they do on the Internet and how the age groups and leisure types differ here.

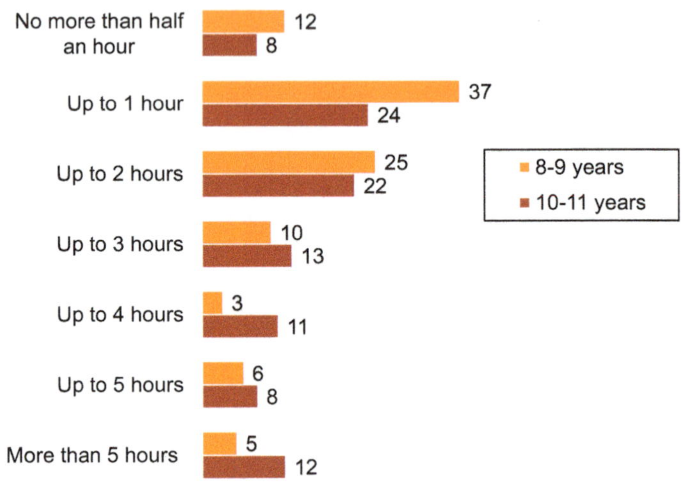

Only children who use the Internet regularly each week
Failure to reach 100% due to "Don't know/No answer" responses

Fig. 5.5 Frequency of Internet use per week by different age groups
Children in Germany aged 6–11 years who use the Internet regularly each week (%)

5.4.3 What Children Do on the Internet: Clear Differences Between Age Groups and Leisure Types

Table 5.8 presents an overview of children's activities on the Internet. It reports the frequencies of the categories receiving "very often" answers and includes only children who are regularly online.

Gender differences in Internet use are conspicuously low. The only marked exception is online games that are played by more than 40% of boys compared to only one-quarter of girls. All other functions such as downloading music and videos or making and communicating with friends over Facebook or chat lines are used almost equally frequently by both sexes.

In contrast, there are clear age differences. Whereas younger children focus more on online games and watching and downloading videos, older children reveal an increasing participation in social networks and chat lines. Although only 8% of 8- and 9-year-olds report using Facebook and the like, social networks are the most frequent activity on the Internet reported by 10- to 11-year-olds at 33%. Chat lines are also gaining in importance: Whereas these are a very frequent form of Internet use in only 15% of 8- and 9-year-olds, this rises to almost one-third in the oldest group. Older children also more frequently use e-mails as a means of communication. This is certainly not just an age-dependent change in interests, but also reflects an increase in reading and writing competence. Although social networks have very graphic displays and are based on pictures just as much as writing, basic reading and writing competencies are essential to tell things to other users and understand what

Table 5.8 What do children do on the internet
Children in Germany aged 6–11 years who use the Internet regularly[a]

Columns in %	All children	Girls	Boys	8–9 years	10–11 years	Versatile children	Normal leisure users	Media consumers
Computer games	33	24	42	44	30	17	29	46
Facebook	26	27	24	8	33	24	24	29
Specific search	25	26	23	21	27	29	28	18
Chat	25	26	24	15	29	20	24	29
Look at/ Download videos	18	20	16	24	16	13	19	19
Just surf	11	10	11	9	11	13	9	11
Send e-mails	8	8	7	2	10	14	7	6
Download music	6	4	8	3	7	1	5	10
Twitter	0	0	1	0	0	0	1	0

[a]Because of the low number of cases in each cell, separate percentages are not reported for 6- to 7-year-olds

they say in return. This is particularly true of chat lines that are frequently not characterized as being orthographically and grammatically correct, but by a high speed of information flow. An interesting fact in relation to the use of social networks is that Facebook, for example, has a minimum age of 13 years, so that the respondents in the Child Study do not yet even belong to the official circle of users. Nonetheless, children succeed in using the online service by either pretending to be older than they actually are or by gaining the help of older persons. This is in line with the findings of the latest KIM study reporting that Facebook is, at 17%, the most popular website among 6- to 13-year-olds (Medienpädagogischer Forschungsverbunds Südwest 2013). Twitter, in contrast, does not play a role in any of the age groups surveyed in the present Child Study.

Whereas there are no clear differences between the various leisure types regarding the amount of Internet use, they differ strongly in the ways they use it. Media consumers particularly frequently take part in online computer games and chat lines compared to the other two groups. They also use Facebook and other social networks slightly more frequently and download more frequently than all-rounders. Normal leisure users and all-rounders, in contrast, use the Internet particularly frequently for specific searches, and all-rounders use it particularly to send e-mails. Hence, media consumers tend to use the Internet to extend the entertainment media they already have at their disposal in order to play games online and engage in fast and uncommitted communication through chat lines. All-rounders, in contrast, use the Internet more for obtaining information and for specific and purposeful communication.

5.5 The Mobile Phone: Simply Taken for Granted by Many Children

The 2010 Child Study has already shown that the mobile phone is no longer just a part of daily life for youths; it is also increasing something that is simply taken for granted by 8- to 11-year-olds. Whereas in 2007, only 17% of 8- and 9-year-olds and 56% of 10- to 11-year-olds had a mobile phone, this already rose to 27% and 66% in 2010. Nowadays, the proportion of children in both age groups with a mobile phone is even slightly higher. In 2013, 31% of the middle group and 72% of the oldest group say they have their own mobile phone. The latest KIM study (Medienpädagogischer Forschungsverbunds Südwest 2013) also reports comparable findings on children with mobile phones. There continues to be a leap in the frequency of having one's own mobile phone between the 8- to 9-year-old and 10- to 11-year-old children. This matches the findings of the German FIM study on the family and the media that reports 10 years as the average age for children to have their own mobile phones (Medienpädagogischer Forschungsverbunds Südwest 2012). The sudden leap reflects the transition from elementary to secondary school. Whereas 59% of 10- to 11-year-olds attending an elementary school report having their own mobile phones, this rises to 78% among those attending secondary schools. The decision not to give their child a mobile phone at elementary school but to do so when changing to secondary school could relate, on the one hand, to restrictive rules at elementary school (mobile phones not being allowed); but, on the other hand, to the greater need to exchange information due to varying teaching hours at secondary schools. The youngest age group reveals a slight decline from 9% to 6%. Perhaps because mobile phones have become so much more expensive since the widespread introduction of smart phones, parents are unwilling to purchase such valuable instruments for their children.

The gender difference found in the last two Child Studies is also found in 2013. In 2007, 39% of girls and 34% of boys reported having a mobile phone. In 2010, this had risen to 50% of girls and 44% of boys among the 8- to 11-year-olds. In 2013, 56% of girls and 49% of boys in this age group report having their own mobile phone. On the one hand, this may be because parents trust their daughters to use their mobile phones more responsibly. On the other hand, it could also reflect a greater concern for girls' welfare by ensuring that they are able to contact their parents at any time.

The various leisure types reveal only slight differences in having their own mobile phone: 43% of all media consumers, 39% of normal leisure users, and 38% of all-rounders. An examination of age groups reveals that media consumers in the youngest age group tend to have their own mobile phone more often (9%) than their peers in the other leisure groups (6%). However, because the difference is only slight and the number of cases is low, this finding should be interpreted with caution.

To analyze the effect of various personal, social, and structural features on the probability of having one's own mobile phone more precisely, we computed a logistic regression (Table 5.9). This showed that children in the oldest survey group sig-

Table 5.9 Significant relations between having one's own mobile phone and personal and social variables[a] **Children in Germany aged 6–11 years**

% (per cell)	Yes	No
All children	40	60
Age		
6–7 years	6	94
8–9 years	31	69
10–11 years	**72**[b]	28
Type of family		
Single parent	**46**[b]	54
Not single parent	38	62
Type of settlement structure		
Big city	**43**[b]	57
Big city suburbs	39	61
Conurbations	33	67
Rural areas	38	62
Gender		
Girls	**42**[b]	58
Boys	37	63

[a]The relationship was tested with a multivariate logistic regression on the criterion variable "owning a mobile phone: yes or no."
Variables included: age, type of family, type of settlement structure, leisure type, gender, and social origin
[b]For ease of presentation, bivariate values are presented as percentages in the table. Notable deviations for variables that were also significant within the multivariate statistical analysis are printed in bold ($p < .05$)

nificantly more frequently have their own mobile phone than children in the younger groups. The gender effect reported above also proves to be statistically significant. Likewise, children living in urban areas more frequently have their own mobile phone than those growing up in rural areas. The finding already reported in 2010 that children growing up in single-parent households more probably have their own mobile phone than those living in other family constellations proves to be a stable trend. In 2007, 47% of 8- to 11-year-olds living with a single parent had their own mobile phone compared to 34% living in other types of family. In 2010, this rose to 52% versus 46%. And now, in 2013, 62% of the 8- to 11-year-olds living in single-parent households have their own mobile phone compared to 50% living in other types of family. Being easy to reach and able to quickly make flexible rearrangements seem to be particularly important in families with only one caregiver who needs to coordinate different obligations such as going to work, caring for children, and organizing leisure activities. In contrast, membership of a specific social class has no significant effect on the probability of having one's own mobile phone.

Hence, independent of income and education, parents equally frequently give their children a mobile phone to use. Likewise, the statistical comparison between normal leisure users and the two extreme groups of media consumers and all-rounders reveals no significant differences in having one's own mobile phone.

5.6 Satisfaction With Leisure is Also a Question of Social Class

The two previous Child Studies showed that social variables impact decisively on how satisfied children are with their leisure time. Social origins and experienced poverty determine the children's life worlds and thereby also impact directly on their subjective satisfaction with the leisure activities available to them.

Satisfaction scores are generally high. A total of 59% of all children surveyed are very satisfied with their leisure time, 33% are satisfied, and only 8% view it as being negative or neutral. In the present survey, the children are even slightly more satisfied than they were in the 2010 Child Study. Because of the very high general level of satisfaction, in the following, we shall compare only "very positive" responses with the frequency of other responses.

A comparison of the various social classes reveals that very positive ratings are significantly less frequent in lower class children compared to their middle-class peers, and that the former tend to give negative to neutral (17%) or positive (53%) ratings (Table 5.10). The drastic nature of these findings becomes apparent only when we compare them directly with the reports of the other groups in which the proportion of negative to neutral ratings lies between 6% and 11%, and positive ratings between 30% and 32%. Results are similar for experienced poverty. Children who have already experienced poverty directly in their own daily lives also tend to rate their leisure time less positively than their peers who have no prior exposure to poverty. Seventeen percent of them rate their leisure as negative to neutral and 39% as positive. Children who have already experienced constraints in their daily lives at least once due to lack of money also less frequently rate their leisure as being very positive compared to their materially more affluent peers. These reports can be compared with the ratings from children who have not experienced poverty and constraints in daily life. Only 7% view their leisure as being negative to neutral, only 31% as being positive, whereas the majority of 62% view it as being very positive.

As before, we have to assume a clear dependence of children's satisfaction on external material factors. Up to now, it has not been possible to enable lower class children to experience their leisure as positively as children from more prosperous classes do every day.

Nonetheless, there are some signs of a positive trend. Whereas in 2010, 28% of lower class children still rated their leisure as being negative to neutral, this has now dropped to 17% in 2013. These changes are not to be found in the very positive rat-

Table 5.10 Significant relations between satisfaction with leisure and personal and social variables[a]

Children in Germany aged 6–11 years

% (per cell)	Negative to neutral	Positive	Very positive
All children	8	33	59
Social origin			
Lower class	**17**[b]	**53**[b]	30
Lower middle class	11	32	57
Middle class	8	32	60
Upper middle class	6	31	63
Upper class	7	30	64
Experienced poverty			
No experience of poverty	7	31	62
Constraints	6	**45**[b]	49
Specific experience of poverty	**17**[b]	**39**[b]	44
Leisure type			
Media consumers	11	**40**[b]	49
Normal leisure users	8	34	58
Versatile children	6	**26**[b]	68

[a]The relationship was tested with a multiple analysis of variance

Variables included: age, gender, leisure type, migration background, social origin, and experienced poverty

[b]For ease of presentation, bivariate values are presented as percentages in the table. Notable deviations for variables that were also significant within the multivariate statistical analysis are printed in bold ($p < .05$)

ings, but in the positive ones. In 2010, 38% of children from the lowest social class viewed their leisure as positive; in the current Child Study, it has risen to 53%. Even when we are far from having achieved a leisure time that all children perceive as being very positive, there are at least first signs of a shift in the right direction. Nonetheless, this slightly positive trend cannot be explained through participation in groups and clubs, because, as reported in Sect. 5.3, this is declining in the lower class. It also cannot be explained by the higher proportion of all-day students in this social class. In agreement with the findings reported in Chap. 4 showing that it is particularly children from the lowest social class who are more often dissatisfied with their all-day school, there is even a decline in satisfaction with their own leisure compared to 2010 that is linked closely to the institution they are attending. Whereas in the 2010 Child Study, 43% of all-day students from the lower class still rated their leisure time very positively, this has dropped to only 29% in 2013. Here we can see a shift from very positive ratings toward the intermediate category of positive ratings. This can also be understood as indicating that the rapidly imposed expansion of all-day schools has yet to deliver qualitatively convincing results. The success of this initiative will also have to be measured in terms of how the children being cared for in these institutions appraise them. In contrast, we can see a positive trend in half-day students from the lower class. In 2010, 29% of them rated their leisure as negative to neutral and 42% as positive. In 2013, only 16% of these children still give a negative to neutral rating, and 53% of them view their leisure activities positively. The available data provide no clear explanation for this increase in satisfaction among half-day students from the lower class, because this group also reveals a decline in memberships of clubs and groups.

A comparison of the satisfaction ratings in all three leisure groups reveals that media consumers less frequently give a very positive rating than normal leisure users and significantly more frequently rate their leisure as positive. Vice versa, all-rounders more frequently rate their leisure as very positive and significantly less frequently give only a positive rating.

In contrast, we can find no statistically significant influence of age and gender or of a possible migration background on the children's ratings.

The perceived possibility of codetermination when shaping their own leisure time also proves to be an important factor for children's satisfaction. Among those whose parents let them help decide how they spend their leisure together, 60% view their leisure as "very positive" compared to only 54% among those who are given little or no codetermination. The relevance of the possibility of codetermination becomes even clearer in answers to the question: "Can you decide for yourself what you do in your free time?" Whereas 61% of the children who answered "generally yes" rated their leisure as "very positive," among those who said "generally no," only 41% gave very positive ratings. As presented in more detail in Sect. 7.1, possibilities of codetermination in daily life are an important aspect of participatory justice in children's lives. If adults integrate children into the decision-making processes that concern them and they thereby feel they are being treated fairly, then they also report greater satisfaction.

We computed a rank correlation to see whether there is a relation between satisfaction with one's own leisure time and general satisfaction with life. This shows a highly significant positive relation between the two variables. Children who report a greater satisfaction with their lives in general are also more satisfied with their leisure time.[8]

References

BMAS (Bundesministerium für Arbeit und Soziales). (2013). *Das Bildungspaket.* Das ist drin im Bildungspaket. Verfügbar unter. www.bildungspaket.bmas.de.

Leven, I., & Schneekloth, U. (2007). Die Freizeit. Anregen lassen oder fernsehen. In World Vision Deutschland. (Hrsg.), *Kinder in Deutschland 2007. 1. World Vision Kinderstudie* (S. 165–200). Frankfurt a. M.: Fischer.

Medienpädagogischer Forschungsverbund Südwest. (Hrsg.). (2012). *FIM-Studie (2011): Familie, Interaktion & Medien.* Untersuchung zur Kommunikation und Mediennutzung in Familien. Stuttgart: Medienpädagogischer Forschungsverbund Südwest: LFK.

Medienpädagogischer Forschungsverbund Südwest. (Hrsg.). (2013). KIM-Studie (2012): Kinder + Medien, Computer + Internet, Basisuntersuchung zum Medienumgang 6- bis 13-Jähriger in Deutschland. Stuttgart:Medienpädagogischer Forschungsverbund Südwest: LFK, LKM.

[8]Nonparametric test: Spearman's correlation coefficient significant on the 5% level.

Chapter 6
Friendships Among Peers

Agnes Jänsch and Monika Pupeter

Alongside children's reference persons in the family and school, it is friends who are the most important social group in their lives. Children meet their peers in the neighborhoods they live in, at school, perhaps when attending institutional daycare centers in the afternoons, and also in the clubs to which they belong. And where children interact with their peers, they can also build up friendships (Pupeter and Schneekloth 2010). In different phases of life, friendships take different forms and fulfil different developmental tasks. In early childhood, they particularly take the form of joint play, and they enable children to practice solving conflicts and controlling their emotions. In middle childhood, the focus is on being socially accepted by one's peers and avoiding rejection; and an important task during this phase is to acquire rules for expressing emotions adequately. In adolescence, friendships help young people to explore and define themselves. In this phase, they develop an understanding of the role feelings play in social relationships (Parker and Gottman 1989, as cited in Oerter and Montada 1998). Numerous studies have confirmed the importance of stable friendships for not only emotional well-being but also social competencies and problem-solving abilities in children of all ages (Salvas et al. 2011). Friends can offer emotional support when stressed, while simultaneously serving as a source of cognitive development and knowledge acquisition (Prazen et al. 2011).

In the transitional phase from infancy or preschool age to adolescence, friendships develop a new quality, because it is during this phase that children themselves begin to build up confidence and trust between equal-ranking partners and thereby also to find solutions when conflict situations arise. In the following, we want to start by taking a closer look at the extent of the circle of friends in 6- to 11-year-old children during this important phase of social development and analyzing which

A. Jänsch (✉) • M. Pupeter
Kantar Public, München, Germany
e-mail: info.de@kantarpublic.com; monika.pupeter@kantarpublic.com

S. Andresen et al. (eds.), *Well-being, Poverty and Justice from a Child's Perspective*, Children's Well-Being: Indicators and Research 17,
DOI 10.1007/978-3-319-57574-2_6

factors are relevant for the formation of peer relationships. Then, we want to ask where children meet their friends, whereby we shall also pay particular attention to the possibilities of virtual contacts. Finally, we shall turn to the topic of trust and being appreciated in friendships in order to look at how children appraise their satisfaction with this aspect of their lives.

6.1 Quantity and Quality of the Circle of Friends

6.1.1 Personal Freedoms as an Important Precondition for Friendships

To gain an idea of the size of the peer groups in which children locate themselves, we first asked them to tell us how many friends they have. At 34%, the most frequent response to this question is "10 or more." About one-quarter report 6–9; another one-quarter, 4–5 friends. This leaves 13% who count only two to three peers in their circle of friends, and 1% who report having only one friend or no friends at all. A comparison of boys and girls reveals no significant gender differences. As Fig. 6.1 shows, the namings in the different response categories are about equal in both groups.

In contrast, there is a marked increase in friendships as children grow older (Table 6.1). Whereas 17% of 6- to 7-year-olds cultivate friendships with two to three other children, only 11 to 12% of older children report having such a small circle. Only roughly one-quarter of the members of the youngest group view 10 or more children as their friends, whereas this grows to 33% in the 8- and 9-year-olds and even 44% in the 10- to 11-year-olds. This increase in the size of the circle of friends also reflects the children's growing autonomy. Forty-five percent of the 6- and 7-year-olds report "meeting friends" as a very frequent leisure-time pursuit compared to 51% of the intermediate age group and 55% of the oldest children (see Sect. 5.1). Hence, as they grow older, children acquire more opportunities to meet

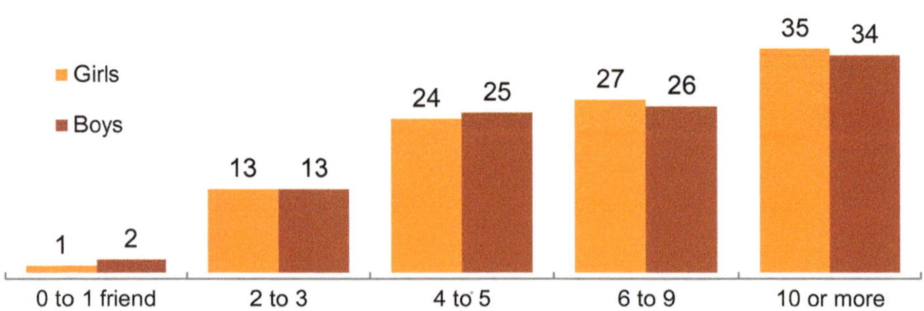

Fig. 6.1 Size of friend circles for girls and boys
Children in Germany aged 6–11 years (%)

Table 6.1 Number of friends by age and leisure type
Children in Germany aged 6–11 years

Columns in % Number of friends	6–7 years	8–9 years	10–11 years	Media consumers	Normal leisure users	Versatile children
0–1 friend	2	2	1	2	2	1
2–3	17	11	12	16	13	10
4–5	27	26	22	28	24	22
6–9	30	28	22	24	26	28
10 or more	24	33	43	30	35	39

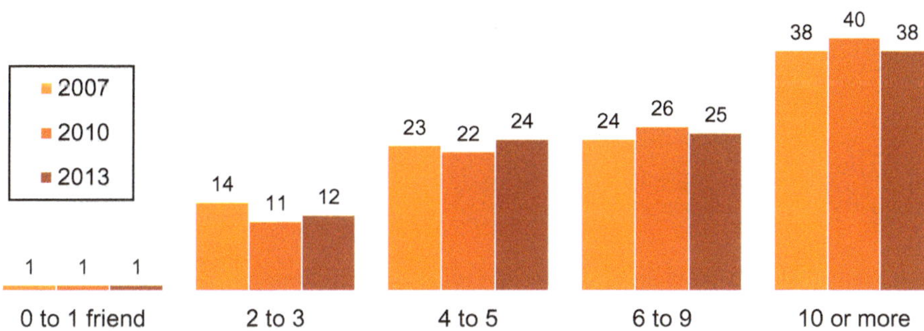

Fig. 6.2 Size of friend circles over time
Children in Germany aged 8–11 years (%)

their peers and thereby cultivate and intensify their friendships. In addition, older children report having more rights to codetermine whom they meet and how many friends they can invite back to their homes (see Sect. 7.1). Even 81% of the youngest group feel that they have the right to codetermine their choice of social contacts. By the age of 10–11 years, this proportion rises even further to 92%. Forty-six percent of 6- to 7-year-olds, 43% of 8- to 9-year-olds, and 54% of 10- to 11-year-olds can decide how many friends they can bring home with them. Whereas adults exert a stronger control over the social contacts of younger children, the greater freedom of decision making granted to older children enables them to purposefully build up, cultivate, and deepen contacts with peers toward whom they feel a special empathy. As a result, they are able to acquire an increasingly large circle of friends. As reported in Sect. 5.3, older children are also more frequently members of clubs or leisure-time groups that also offer opportunities to make further social contacts and extend their circle of acquaintances and friends.

Over time, in contrast, results are highly consistent. As Fig. 6.2 shows, approximately 40% of 8- to 11-year-olds report a large circle of friends containing 10 or more peers in all three Child Studies. Roughly one-half of children report having between 5 and 9 friends. And slightly more than 10% of respondents have only a small or no circle of friends. Without reporting on the type and quality of these

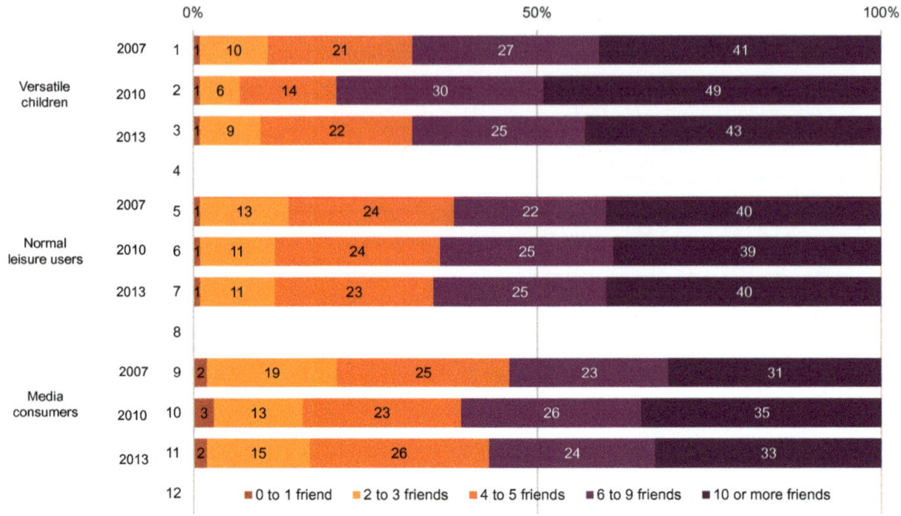

Fig. 6.3 Size of children's friend circles by leisure type
Children in Germany aged 8–11 years (%)

social contacts at this stage, we can already see that at least the size of the social networks of children surveyed in the three Child Studies has not been subject to any major change up to the present.

6.1.2 Friends Are Not Made In Front of the Computer or Television

Marked differences in the size of the circle of friends relate not only to age but also to the different leisure groups (see Sect. 5.2). Whereas media consumers more frequently report having a relatively small circle of friends, all-rounders generally have a larger circle with 16% of the former group reporting that they have two to three friends compared to only 10% of the latter. Thirty percent of media consumers report having a circle of friends containing more than 10 children compared to 39% of all-rounders. Table 6.1 presents an overview of responses broken down into age groups and leisure types.

As Fig. 6.3 shows, relations between the various leisure types are stable across time. Only about one-third of media consumers report having a circle of friends containing more than 10 children across all three surveys compared to more than 40% of all-rounders and about 40% of normal leisure users. In contrast, small circles containing three or less children are more typical for the media consumers. In all three Child Studies, 16 to 21% of this group reported only one to three friends compared to 12 to 14% of normal leisure users and 7 to 11% of all-rounders.

An inspection of the preferred leisure pursuits of the children reveals that media consumers meet up with their friends somewhat less often than all-rounders (50% vs. 55% "very often"). In addition, the leisure pursuits of media consumers far more frequently include computer games and television, as reported in Chap. 5. Fifty-six percent of them report playing computer games very often and 87% watch television very often, whereas only 2% of all-rounders play computer games very often and only 13% watch television very often. Whereas the leisure behavior of all-rounders with its stronger focus on social contacts rather than media consumption helps to build up a circle of friends, the passive activities of media consumers characterized by a lack of direct interactions are inappropriate for making new contacts and cultivating them. Nonetheless, we have to ask what is the cause and what is the effect here. It would seem just as plausible to assume that children who find it hard to make friends and do not manage to build up a stable circle of friends will tend to withdraw and spend their leisure time with activities that they can carry out alone.

6.1.3 Lower Class Children Are also Disadvantaged Among Their Peers

To analyze which social and structural factors are decisive for the size of the circle of friends in more detail, we summarized the responses into three categories and computed a logistic regression. Zero to three friends represented a small circle; four to nine, a normal or middle-sized circle; and 10 or more, a large circle of friends. Then we compared the middle group named by 40–50% of the children in each age group with the other two groups.

As Table 6.2 shows, children from the lowest social class significantly more frequently have a small or no circle of friends and less frequently a large circle of friends than middle-class children. Members of the lower middle class also tend to have a smaller circle of friends, whereas upper class children cultivate markedly more friendships. Whether the child is a native German or has a migration background proves to have no significant effect on the size of the circle of friends. However, the way that leisure time is organized plays a decisive role. Children who belong to no clubs or leisure-time groups name significantly fewer friends than children who are organized into at least one group. Regularly meeting up in clubs and leisure-time groups gives children an opportunity to build up stable contacts outside of school as well. Moreover, the shared interests in the group activities already provide a basis for possible friendships. Hence, members of the lower social classes simultaneously have a less varied leisure time and a particularly small circle of friends. Instead of being able to compensate for the constraints on leisure activities through numerous positive social contacts, these children also have to come to terms with constraints on their friendships. In contrast, however, the type of school has no influence on the size of the circle of friends. Children attending all-day schools do not have more contacts with friends through the longer daily interactions

Table 6.2 Significant relations between size of friend circles and personal and social variables[a]
Children in Germany aged 6–11 years

% (per cell)	No/Small circle of friends	Medium-sized circle of friends	Large circle of friends
All children	15	51	35
Age			
6–7 years	19	57	**24**[b]
8–9 years	15	51	34
10–11 years	12	45	**44**[b]
Social origin			
Lower class	**30**[b]	53	**17**[b]
Lower middle class	**20**[b]	51	29
Middle class	14	54	32
Upper middle class	11	51	38
Upper class	8	45	**47**[b]
Club membership			
Yes	10	51	39
No	**28**[b]	52	**20**[b]
Parental care and attention			
No deficit	13	50	37
Deficit in one parent	21	54	**25**[b]
Care deficit	19	55	**26**[b]

[a]The relationship was tested with a multivariate nominal regression on the variable "size of circle of friends

Variables included: age, social origin, club membership, migration background, type of school (half-day/all-day), and care and attention deficit

[b]For ease of presentation, bivariate values are presented as percentages in the table. Notable deviations for variables that were also significant within the multivariate statistical analysis are printed in bold ($p < .05$)

at school than children attending half-day schools who possibly spend more time alone at home. Time spent together at school or in afternoon daycare is accordingly not enough to form friendships. Hence, further bonding elements such as shared hobbies are just as relevant. For children who receive insufficient care and attention from one or both parents, friendships seem to be a particularly important social anchor and to some extent a possible way of compensating for the lack of parental attention and appreciation.[1] However, it is particularly in this group that a large circle of friends is most unusual. Children who complain about not receiving enough attention from either one or two parents significantly less frequently report having 10 friends or more than children who do not lack attention from their parents.

[1]"Having friends is more important for children whose family relationships are less satisfying, supportive, and positive than it is for children in higher-functioning families, and families contribute more heavily to children's adjustment when they do not have close friends" (Gauze et al. 1996, cited in Gifford-Smith and Brownell 2002).

Children who report meeting their friends very often during their leisure time have a larger circle of friends than children who only sometimes or hardly ever meet their peers. Whereas 41% of the former report having a large circle of friends with 10 or more peers, this is only the case for 28% (several times a week) or 19% (hardly ever) of the remaining children. We assume that a bidirectional effect is to be found here, because those who have a larger number of friends will generally also meet up with these more often in their free time, whereas, at the same time, regular contacts are necessary to maintain and strengthen social relationships.

6.1.4 Really Good Friends And How to Make Them

We took those children who reported having at least one friend when questioned about the size of their circle of friends, and we asked them how many really close friends they have in order to determine the size of the core peer group. Roughly one-quarter report having two and a further one-quarter having three really close friends, and 10–15% report having either only one or four to five very close friends. This leaves 8% who report having six to nine very close friends and 4% who have 10 or more. As to be expected, a correlation analysis[2] reveals a significantly positive relation between the size of the circle of friends in total and the number of very close friends. This correlation is slightly lower for children in the youngest group than for the 8-to 9-year-olds and the 10- to 11- year-olds. This indicates that younger children still do not have such a differentiated concept of social relations at their disposal and are less able to distinguish between friends and acquaintances.

When we ask the children whether they find it easy or difficult to make new friends, the majority (66%) report having no difficulty; 27% find it more difficult; and 7% are not certain—with the largest proportion of "uncertains" in the group of 6- to 7-year-olds (9%). This may be because social contacts are still organized and determined more strongly by their parents as pointed out at the beginning of this chapter, and they may still have little experience in making friends by themselves. On the whole, children find it increasingly easy to make friends the older they become. At 6–7 years, 63% report that they find it easy to forge new contacts; in the group of 8-to 9-year-olds, this already rises to 66%; and in the 10- to 11-year-olds, it is 69%.

Not very surprisingly, children who find it easy to forge social contacts generally also have a larger circle of friends than children who find it hard to make friends. Forty percent of those who report no difficulties have 10 or more friends, whereas only 26% of those who find it more difficult to make friends have a comparably large circle.

However, social competencies do not just influence the forging of all friendships, however superficial these may be. We can also see an effect on the number of very close ones. Whereas approximately one-half of the children who report that they

[2] Nonparametric test: Spearman's correlation coefficient significant on the 5% level.

find it more difficult to forge friendships, have one to two very close friends, only one-third of those who find it easy to make friends have so few close friends. Vice versa, only 8% of children who find it more difficult to make friends have six or more very close friends compared to 15% of those who find it easy. Nonetheless, when interpreting such findings, it has to be noted that extraverted children, who approach others more easily, may have a different understanding of what really good friends are than introverted children: The former may more quickly consider another child to be a good friend, whereas the latter may be more restrained in their appraisals.

6.2 Where Children Meet Their Friends

6.2.1 The Traditional Meeting Places: School, the Home Neighborhood, and Clubs

A further question that links up closely with how children forge their relations to peers and how they cultivate them is naturally where they meet their friends. Fig. 6.4 provides an overview of the locations involved.

The absolute frontrunner among regular opportunities for contact is the school. A total of 78% of children see their friends here just about every day and 17% at least several times a week. This holds for nearly all types of school. The proportion is only slightly lower at 69% among children attending a special needs school. Because schools for children with special needs are frequently not located where children live and they have to travel some distance, this may result in a separation between the school and the rest of daily life— including existing friendships. Students attending basic secondary school (*Hauptschule*) in contrast particularly frequently (86%) report meeting their friends every day at school. Hence, schools are not just important locations of learning and development in the sense of academic education; they make a fundamental contribution to making and keeping friends. The relevance of the school as a meeting place also continues into secondary school. This indicates that when children are confronted with new situations—following the transfer to secondary school—they react flexibly and make new friends, as is also revealed in the larger circles of friends they report.

A further important meeting place for many children is their own home and the homes of their friends. About 60% meet their friends at home either almost daily or several times a week, and an equally high proportion report being guests at friends' homes almost daily or several times a week.

Closely linked to the own home is the immediate neighborhood with its surrounding streets, parks, and playgrounds. Seventeen percent of the children meet their peer group here almost every day and a further 50% see their friends here several times a week. We can find no mentionable trends indicating a shift in meeting friends from the parental home to public spaces with increasing age. In all three

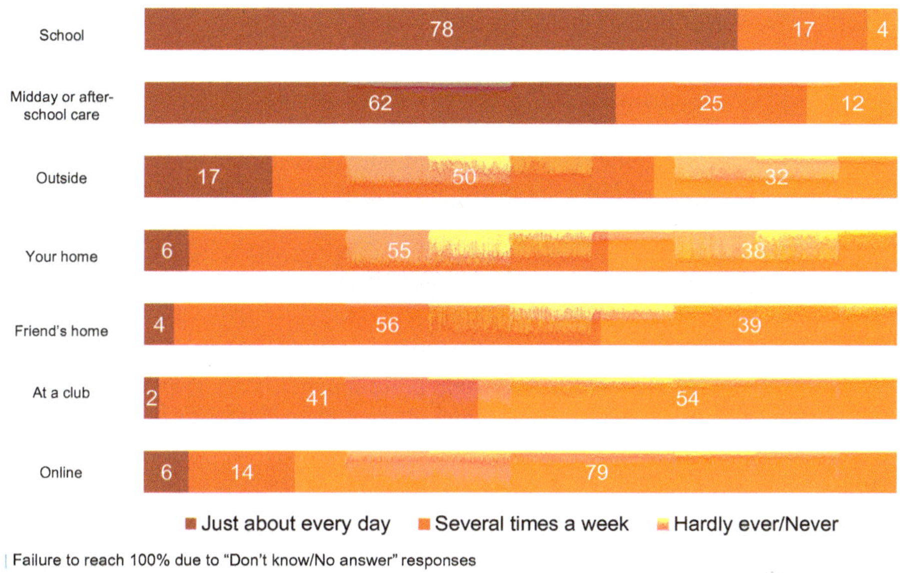

Fig. 6.4 Where do children meet their friends
Children in Germany aged 6–11 years (%)

age groups, children almost equally frequently use the own home, that of their friends, or the neighborhood streets and playgrounds for their meetings.

The neighborhood in which children live can facilitate or impede contacts with friends, and this can influence the frequency of meeting them. In 2007 and 2013, we asked the children whether there are enough friends to play with living in their neighborhood. In 2013, the neighborhood seems to be somewhat less suitable for meeting friends in leisure time than it was in the first Child Study. Whereas in the current Child Study, 63% of 8- to 11-year-olds report having enough friends to play with in their immediate neighborhood, in 2007, this was 66%. Hence, the children see less opportunity to meet other children in their neighborhood than they did 6 years ago. Nonetheless, the difference is too slight to be able to assume that it indicates any real trend.

As reported above, clubs assume an important function in the social life of 6- to 11-year-olds. This can also be seen in the meeting places they name. Forty-three percent of the children report meeting their friends in clubs just about every day or several times a week.

For children attending some kind of daycare center after school in the afternoon, these institutions offer an almost equally important opportunity to see their friends as the school itself. Nearly two-thirds of these children meet their friends just about every day here; and one-quarter, at least several times a week.

6.2.2 The Internet: New Meeting Place for Digital Natives?

Approximately one-quarter of the children with access to the Internet report being very frequent users of Facebook or other social networks (see Sect. 5.4). As shown in Fig. 6.4, every fifth child who has access to the Internet and is regularly online reports interacting with friends there just about every day or several times a week. Based on all children, the proportion who meet their friends online is 3% just about every day and 6% at least several times a week. Answers to the question where meetings with friends occur also reveal the age effect reported in Sect. 5.4 indicating that younger children hardly ever use social networks and chat lines, whereas 10- to 11-year-olds use them particularly widely. Children in the youngest group hardly ever report the Internet as a possible place to meet, 10% of 8- to 9- year-old Internet users meet their friends there, and almost 30% of 10- to 11-year-olds use this option.

It remains to be seen how the use of social networks by children in this age range develops, because this is measured for the first time in the 2013 Child Study. However, we can already see a trend toward children meeting up personally with their friends less often. Looking at the group of 8- to 11-year-olds surveyed since 2007, we can observe an almost drastic decline in the frequency of personal contacts to friends during leisure time. In both the first and second Child Studies, 68% reported meeting their friends very often. In 2013, there has been a clear drop to 53%.

This raises the question how far this trend should be viewed in relation to the Internet and the shifting of social contacts to virtual space. Are today's children already interacting with their peers in chat lines and forums rather than meeting them in reality? Is the digital exchange replacing direct contact with friends?

For the age group surveyed in the Child Study, the answer is "generally no." When we compare this with the reports of 8- to 11-year-olds since 2007 on how frequently they use the Internet for chat lines, we can even see that these have become less popular. In 2007, 47% of regular Internet users reported using chat lines very often; in 2010, this was 30%; whereas in 2013, this is only 26%. This decline certainly also has to be seen in the light of the growing importance of social networks that are taking over from the classic chat line. Nonetheless, these data cannot be used to conclude that children today prefer to cultivate their social contacts on the Internet rather than in reality. Those who use Facebook very often also meet their friends more often during their free time. A total of 59% of the frequent users of social networks report meeting their friends very often. This contrasts with 55% of those who hardly ever cultivate contacts over the Internet. The same applies to those who use chat lines very often. They more frequently report meeting children they are friends with (60%) compared to children with little experience of chat lines (53%). Hence, the Internet seems to be more of a supplement that offers the children further possibilities of keeping in touch with others in addition to personal contacts rather than being something that competes with meeting friends in the real world.

Although we are unable to determine an unequivocal reason for this development, we can still see that spending leisure time together with friends is currently less popular than in the years before. It remains to be seen how this will develop further. Nonetheless, we can already see that the reduced frequency of direct social contacts in leisure time has not yet led to any social deprivation. The numbers of friends prove to be stable since 2007 (Fig. 6.2).

6.3 Fairness, Being Appreciated, and Satisfaction with the Circle of Friends

When children have friends, they want to feel good in their company, to be treated fairly, and to be appreciated. Therefore, to gain a closer look at children's friendships, we also asked how fair they consider their circle of friends to be (see Chap. 2) and whether their friends value their opinion, that is, the opinion of the child being surveyed (Chap. 7).

A total of 36% of the children consider that the way they are treated in their closest peer group is very fair and 54% that it is quite fair. Hence, the children have a thoroughly positive outlook here. The circle of friends is an area of childhood experience that is generally perceived to be fair. This part of the social environment offers the great advantage of being variable within certain limits so that each child can contribute to shaping it alone. Children do not need to make friends with peers whom they perceive to be unfair or dominant, and they can distance themselves from friends when they do not like the way that they behave. The perception of fairness also grows with increasing age and autonomy. Among 6- to 7-year-olds, 34% see the interaction among their friends as being very fair and 51% as quite fair. In the middle age group, this rises to 36% and 55%, whereas among the 10- to 11-year-olds, 37% consider behavior to be very fair and 56% as quite fair.

When asked how far friends value their opinions, 51% are convinced that they place "generally more" value on them. A further 35% consider that they are appreciated at least to some extent here ("sometimes one, sometimes the other"). This shows that the children's perceptions continue to grow in a positive direction. Whereas 43% reported "generally more" value in 2007, this was 42% in 2010 (45% of 8- to 11-year-olds), whereas in 2013 it is now 51% who feel so appreciated (53% of 8- to 11-year-olds). Here as well, we see an age effect in that older children more frequently have the impression that their friends value their opinions. Whereas 47% of 6- to 7-year-olds believe that their opinion is of generally more value, the figure rises to 49% in the 8- to 9-year-olds and 57% in the oldest group.

Being appreciated and treating each other fairly are important preconditions for satisfaction with social relations. According to the children's reports, both are to be found among the majority of the circles of friends in 6- to 11-year-olds. Are they accordingly also satisfied with their closest, intimate peer group?

Table 6.3 Significant relations between satisfaction with circle of friends and personal and social variables[a]

Children in Germany aged 6–11 years

% (per cell)	Negative to neutral	Positive	Very positive
All children	6	32	62
Social origin			
Lower class	**11**[b]	**44**[b]	45
Lower middle class	11	28	61
Middle class	7	28	65
Upper middle class	4	**36**[b]	60
Upper class	5		70
Gender			
Girls	**5**[b]	33	62
Boys	8	30	62
Circle of friends			
Small	**11**[b]	35	54
Medium	7	33	60
Large	**4**[b]	**27**[b]	69
Migration background			
Yes	**11**[b]	30	59
No	8	32	60

This seems to be the case for most children with 62% rating their own satisfaction very positively on the 5-point scale. Hence, as with the other appraisals of satisfaction, the level here is very high in general. In the following, we shall take a look at the factors influencing this satisfaction (Table 6.3).

The social class of origin impacts significantly on this aspect of childhood satisfaction as well. Compared to middle-class children, lower class children significantly more frequently rate their circle of friends as being negative to neutral (11%) or positive (44%). At only 45% very positive ratings, they are well below the corresponding average of 62% in all the children surveyed. Hence, having a low social status and the general constraints accompanying this status also influences the quality of social contacts with peers. Instead of peers serving a compensatory function in which the support of other children offsets deficits in one's own sphere, what we can see here is the emergence of another area in which socially disadvantaged children are worse off than their peers. This also has to be viewed together with the aforementioned finding that children from the lower social classes have fewer friends than their better situated peers. As Table 6.3 shows, the size of the circle of friends also impacts on satisfaction. It is interesting to see that a particularly large proportion of upper class children also rate their circle of friends only as "positive" and not as "very positive." It is not possible to derive any unequivocal reason for this from the data. Gender also proves to have a significant effect on satisfaction with the closest peer group. Girls less frequently rate this as being negative to neutral than their male peers. In contrast, children with a migration background significantly more frequently rate their circle of friends as being negative to neutral compared to their native German peers. However, age and leisure type have no impact on the children's ratings.

References

Gauze, C., Bukowski, W. M., Aquan Assee, J., & Sippola, L. K. (1996). Interactions between family environment and friendship and associations with self perceived well-being during adolescence. *Child Development, 67*, 2201–2216.

Gifford-Smith, M. E., & Brownell, C. A. (2002). Childhood peer relationships: Social acceptance, friendships, and peer networks. *Journal of School Psychology, 41*, 235–284.

Parker, J. G., & Gottman, J. M. (1989). Social and emotional development in a relational context; Friendship interaction from early childhood to adolescence. In Berndt, T. J. & Ladd, G. W. (Hrsg.), *Peer relationships in child development*. Zitiert nach: Oerter, R., & Montada, L. (1998) *Entwicklungspsychologie. Ein Lehrbuch*. Weinheim: Beltz.

Prazen, A., Wolfinger, N. H., Cahill, C., & Kowaleski-Jones, L. (2011). Joint physical custody and neighborhood friendships in middle childhood. *Sociological Inquiry, 81*(2), 247–259.

Pupeter, M., & Schneekloth, U. (2010). Die Gleichaltrigen: Gemeinsame – getrennte Welten?. In World Vision Deutschland. (Hrsg.), *Kinder in Deutschland 2010. 2. World Vision Kinderstudie* (S. 141–160). Frankfurt a. M.: Fischer.

Salvas, M.-C., Vitaro, F., Brendgen, M., Lacourse, E., Boivin, M., & Tremblay, R. E. (2011). Interplay between friends' aggression and friendship quality in the development of child aggression during the early school years. *Social Development, 20*(4), 645–663.

Chapter 7
Participation and the Children's Own Opinion

Monika Pupeter and Ulrich Schneekloth

This chapter looks at how children think they are perceived in their own frame of reference; that is, in *their own* society. In which parts of their lives can children shape things themselves, how far do they consider themselves and their opinions to be valued, and which limits to their freedom do they perceive?

Theoretically, we draw once again on the Capability Approach presented in detail in the Second World Vision Child Study (Andresen et al. 2010). Basically, this approach aims to describe the conditions for living a good life and to present these coherently. An important benchmark is the question of justice. One key demand is that individuals should be enabled to make their own decisions about how they wish to shape their lives. This requires not only the necessary resources but also the individual competencies that enable individuals to act in a self-determined way and to do what they consider to be appropriate. As we also showed in the last Child Study, the foundations for this are already laid in childhood. One central aspect is "having one's own opinion valued and taken seriously" in the way that children perceive this in the areas of life that are relevant to them, that is, in their family, at school, in their circle of friends, and during leisure time (Schneekloth and Pupeter 2010). In which areas do children experience being taken seriously? When are they asked for their opinion? Where are they allowed to participate in decision making? How do they perceive freedoms? These are the questions that we asked the children directly. We shall take a closer look at their answers here.

In the first section, we want to report on the children's possibilities of participation in everyday life. Although we shall focus on how far they can exert an influence in the home, we shall supplement this by referring to the findings on participation at school presented in detail in Chap. 4. In the second section, we shall deal with how children perceive the value placed on their own opinions; in other words, how far

M. Pupeter (✉) • U. Schneekloth
Kantar Public, München, Germany
e-mail: monika.pupeter@kantarpublic.com; ulrich.schneekloth@kantarpublic.com

S. Andresen et al. (eds.), *Well-being, Poverty and Justice from a Child's Perspective*, Children's Well-Being: Indicators and Research 17,
DOI 10.1007/978-3-319-57574-2_7

they think that their opinion counts in everyday life. Finally, in the third section, we shall look at how the children themselves judge the freedoms granted to them in their everyday lives.

7.1 Which Aspects of Their Everyday Lives Can Children Determine Themselves?

For all people, and therefore for children as well, it is important not only to have but also to perceive that one has action scopes and possibilities of shaping one's world. Participating in decision making as an independent individual promotes expectations of self-efficacy in children and helps them to practice negotiation processes and learn how to deal with differences in opinion. Being able to make one's own contribution to decision-making processes and to say what one thinks, that is, to be involved in what is happening, is something we described in Chap. 2 when considering the desire for "procedural justice" or "interaction justice." Children want to be treated as equals and thereby to be treated fairly—and not just by adults but also in comparison to adults. This is particularly the case when this concerns matters that relate to them personally and on which they then demand recognition of their own rights.

When aged 6–11 years, children are in middle childhood and continually expanding their range of action as they mature. They are beginning to separate themselves from the intimate family circle. Six-year-olds are still looked after closely by their parents, but they already go to school, even when many of them are still accompanied by adults on their way there. Older children, in contrast, travel to school by themselves, sometimes even by bus and by train, and they not only may but also increasingly have to deal with many things by themselves. The image of the way to school provides a fitting illustration of the process of separation from the parental home. Ideally, the growth in the demands placed on children is accompanied by an increasing trust in their own abilities to cope with what is new in their world.

7.1.1 Participation and Making Their Own Decisions in Everyday Life: In the First Instance, a Question of Age

We shall start by looking at the possibilities of participation in decision making at home, that is, in the primary domain of children. Which things can children decide for themselves in their everyday lives? When are they asked what they think, or how can they assert themselves in everyday life at home? Do the children's reports reveal an age effect? We wanted the children to name the areas in their everyday lives in which they have more possibilities of deciding for themselves or codetermining what they do. It was important for us to address things in everyday lives that should affect as far as possible all children regardless of their individual dispositions, preferences, or interests. Therefore, we selected the following eight aspects[1]:

Can you decide for yourself:

- Which friends do you meet?
- What clothes do you wear?
- What do you spend your pocket money on?
- What to eat at home?
- How many friends can you bring home with you?
- What do you do in your free time?
- When do you do your homework?
- What does your family do in its free time (e.g., at the weekend)?

A large majority of children can decide for themselves which friends they meet (88%) and what they do in their free time (85%). Hence, even at home, more than four-fifths of children see themselves as relevant "decision makers". Likewise, the majority report that they themselves can generally say what clothes they want to wear (79%), that they codetermine what the family does in its free time (75%), and that they themselves also generally decide what to spend their pocket money on (72%). Only roughly every second child, and thus a much smaller proportion, reports that they can decide what is to eat at home (53%) or also how many friends they can bring home with them (48%). No more than 35% of the children can generally decide when they want to do their homework (Fig. 7.1).

As to be expected, relevant differences depend on the children's age (Table 7.1). The largest—relatively speaking—possibilities of codetermination are found in the 10- to 11-year-olds. Almost every child (more than 90%) in this age group can determine what to do in her free time and can largely decide what to wear. Eighty percent can decide what to do with their pocket money. Interestingly, at 81%, significantly more children in this age group report possibilities of codetermining what the family does in its free time. Significantly more older children report, though on a lower level at 54%, that they can generally decide for themselves how many children they bring home with them, and 46% can decide for themselves when to do their homework.

Results are similar though on a somewhat lower level for the 8- to 9-year-olds. They also report more possibilities of codetermination than the 6- to 7-year-olds. This holds true for the circle of friends and for their own leisure-time choices. Although there are slight differences between 8- to 9-year-olds and 10- to 11- year-olds here, they do not attain statistical significance. The same applies to what they do with their pocket money. Here as well, the differences between 8- to 9-year-olds

[1] Specifically, we asked children: "If you think about your everyday life, which are the situations in which your opinion counts. Can you decide for yourself: . . . which friends you meet? Generally yes, Generally no, Don't know/No answer." Compared to 2010, four more domains were included, so that the question in 2013 contained seven items. A further question on possibilities of codetermining family activities during leisure time was added to the 2010 and 2013 surveys.

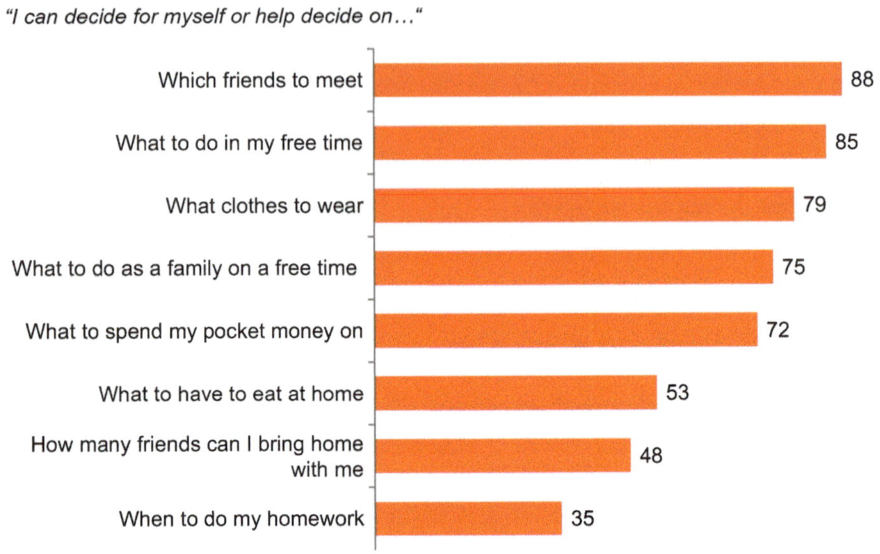

Fig. 7.1 Where can children make their own decisions in everyday life
Children in Germany aged 6–11 years (%)

Table 7.1 Which aspects of everyday life can children determine for themselves?
Children in Germany aged 6–11 years

Generally yes, columns in %	Girls	Boys	6–7 years	8–9 years	10–11 years
I can decide for myself or help decide on					
Which friends to meet	88	87	**81**[a]	89	92
What to do in my free time	85	85	**77**[a]	86	91
What clothes to wear	82	**75**[a]	**63**[a]	**79**[a]	**90**[a]
What to do as a family on a free time	77	**72**[a]	**66**[a]	**75**[a]	**81**[a]
What to spend my pocket money on	74	70	**60**[a]	73	80
What to have to eat at home	54	53	51	53	55
How many friends can I bring home with me	47	48	46	43	**54**[a]
When to do my homework	36	34	25	31	**46**[a]

[a]Significant differences between means ($p > .05$) are printed in bold

and 10- to 11- year-olds fail to attain significance. At 79%, significantly more 8- to 9-year-olds can decide for themselves what they want to wear than 6- to 7-year-olds, but significantly fewer 8- to 9-year-olds can decide this compared to 10- to 11- year-olds. The same applies for codetermining what the family does in its free time. Here, 75% of 8- to 9-year-olds can have their say—significantly more than among the 6- to 7-year-olds, but significantly less than among the 10- to 11- year-olds. However, there are no significant differences compared to the 6- to 7-year-olds regarding whether they can decide for themselves how many friends they bring home with them (43%) or when they do their homework (31%).

In comparison, 6- to 7-year-olds markedly less frequently report being able to decide for themselves. The majority at this age can determine whom they are friends with and what they do in their free time. However, only two out of three reported that they can decide what clothes they want to wear or codetermine what the family does in its free time. Sixty percent, and thereby significantly fewer compared to the other age groups, report being able to do largely what they want with their pocket money. However, as reported above, they do not differ from the 8- to 9-year-olds in terms of being able to decide how many friends they bring home with them and when they do their homework.

No significant age effects can be found regarding whether they can also decide for themselves what is to eat at home. Participation in decision-making over what is cooked at home seems to be less a question of the children's age in the sense of a continuous increase in autonomy, but primarily a question of what is the customary practice in a particular family and how they organize themselves. Family framing conditions in the form of the available domestic resources are naturally effective elsewhere as well, for example, regarding how many friends they can bring home with them, what the family does in its leisure time, or whether they can decide what to spend their pocket money on. Nonetheless, it is interesting to see where the child's age actually is and is not a major determining factor.

Comparing genders on the possibilities of participation and codetermination that children report in their everyday lives reveals only two significant differences: At 82%, girls report significantly more frequently being able to determine what clothes they wear compared to 75% of boys. In addition, girls feel more integrated into planning family activities at 77% compared to 72% of boys. Otherwise, the possibilities of codetermination in everyday life are fairly comparable in both genders. Regarding clothing, it can be assumed that "external appearances" continue to play a greater role for girls due to their socialization, and the importance of their self-determination in this domain will be encouraged more strongly. Regarding the codetermination of family leisure-time activities, no such clear explanation suggests itself.

Results do not reveal any clear trend over time. The replies to the questions on the choice of clothing and on pocket money reveal no significant differences compared to the last Child Study. For the item on the number of friends children can bring home with them, 48% report that they can decide this in 2013 compared to 42% in 2010. Currently, 75% report that they can codetermine what the family does in its leisure time compared to 80% in the last Child Study.

Table 7.2 Possibilities of self-determination in everyday life by social origin

Children in Germany aged 6–11 yearsGenerally yes, columns in %	Lower class	Lower middle class	Middle class	Upper middle class	Upper class
I can decide for myself or help decide on					
Which friends to meet	**76**[a]	**83**[a]	89	89	95
What to do in my free time	**69**[a]	82	86	87	92
What clothes to wear	78	74	80	78	82
What to do as a family on a free time	**49**[a]	72	77	79	81
What to spend my pocket money on	**56**[a]	69	72	74	79
What to have to eat at home	**34**[a]	54	56	54	59
How many friends can I bring home with me	**32**[a]	49	44	51	57
When to do my homework	38	32	33	33	**43**[a]

[a]Significant differences between means ($p > .05$) are printed in bold

7.1.2 *Lower Class Children Have the Lowest Possibilities of Self-Determination*

In contrast, there is once again a clear effect of social origin. Children from the lower class have the least decision-making scope in everyday life whereas children from the upper class in contrast have the most (Table 7.2).

The largest difference is found on the item addressing participation in planning family leisure time. Only 49% of lower class children consider that they can codetermine this compared to 72% from the lower middle class, 77% from the middle class, 79% from the upper middle class, and 81% from the upper class. Certainly, as with the item on pocket money, a lack of possibilities of codetermination will be particularly marked among lower class children when they do not even have the "basis" for them; in other words, when there is a general lack of family leisure-time activities and no pocket money.[2] Things are probably similar for the items on how many children they can bring home with them or whether they also decide on what the family eats. Lack of space and economic constraints on housekeeping certainly regulate the facts here.

It is symptomatic that at 92%, nearly all upper class children can decide for themselves how they spend their leisure time compared to only 69% of lower class children. Lower middle-class children also differ from upper class children at 82%, whereas the differences compared to the middle class (86%) and the upper middle class (87%) are not significant. At 76% in the lower and 83% in the lower middle, significantly fewer children in these classes are able to choose which friends they meet compared to the upper middle and upper class children. This notable finding is

[2]Results of the First World Vision Child Study indicated that lower class children less frequently get pocket money (Schneekloth and Leven 2007).

probably due predominantly to parents in the lower social classes seeing far higher risks in their children's circle of friends than parents in higher social milieus (Andresen and Galic 2015).

No relevant social class effects can be ascertained for the item on whether children can decide for themselves what clothes they will wear. Possible parental guidelines seem to be irrelevant here for children between 6 and 11 years. At 43%, upper class children most frequently perceive that they can also codetermine when to do their homework. Members of all other social classes, and therefore also explicitly the lower class, significantly less frequently report participation in decision making on this issue (between 32% and 38%).

7.1.3 *Possibilities of Self-Determination in Everyday Life: A Question Not Only of Age But Also of Social Origin and Family Practices*

The possibilities of self-determination we survey address various aspects of everyday life and refer to the action scopes of children in the living space of the family. Because they are determined decisively by family framing conditions and family practices,[3] the eight indicators in our survey can be aggregated to form an index distinguishing between three groups of children that differ sufficiently clearly in the scopes of action and decision making available to them in their everyday family lives (Fig. 7.2).[4]

At 58%, the majority of children have possibilities of self-determination in four to six domains and thereby more frequently possess decision-making scopes in everyday life ("*children with just about all possibilities of self-determination*"). Almost all these children choose their own leisure-time pursuits and circle of friends, and a majority also tends to be able to make their own choices in the other domains we survey. The exceptions here are the number of children they can take home with them and when they do their homework. Only one child in four can codetermine this.

A total of 27% of the children belong to the group with "*average possibilities of self-determination*" in everyday life. These children report that they can determine or codetermine in nearly all the domains we survey. The only exception here, if at

---

[3] The institutional space, in this case, the decisive "school living space" with its own binding rules and framing conditions, is excluded here. This is addressed separately in our study with special questions on codetermination and participation from the children's perspective (see Chap. 4).

[4] The computed index can take a range of values from 0 (codetermination in no domain) to 8 (codetermination in all eight domains). Referring to the mean and the standard deviation, we could distinguish three groups of children: those with 4–6 namings (mean plus or minus 1 standard deviation), 0–3 namings (lower than 1 standard deviation), and 7–8 namings (higher than 1 standard deviation).

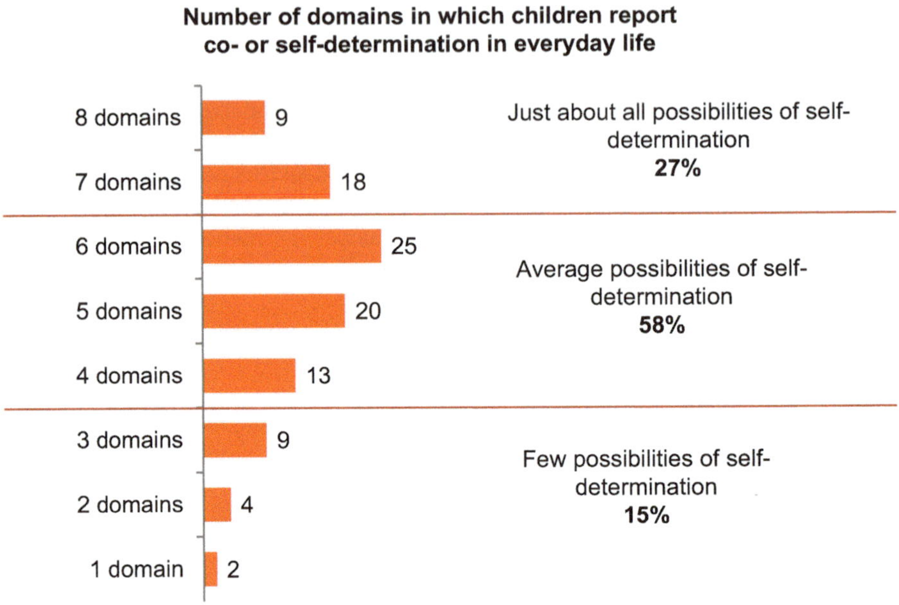

Fig. 7.2 Possibilities of self-determination in everyday life
Children in Germany aged 6–11 years (%)

all, is yet again when they do their homework. However, more than two out of three children in this group can codetermine this.

Finally, 15% of the children are in the group with "*few possibilities of self-determination*" in everyday life. Here, only just above one out of two children can determine which friends they meet, whereas in all other domains, including what they do in their leisure time, the majority report a lack of self-determination.

As reported above, the possibilities of self-determination increase as children grow older. Nonetheless, the different scopes cannot be explained by age alone. We also find variations within age groups. This becomes visible when we study which children more frequently, that is, with a greater probability, belong to one of our three groups. Analyzing the statistical relations between these features[5] confirms the effects of not only age but also other social and familial background factors (Table 7.3).

As can be expected, younger children more frequently (and older children, in contrast, less frequently) belong to the group with few possibilities of self-determination in everyday life. The older the children are, the more frequently they report being generally able to determine their everyday lives themselves. Whereas 27% of 6- to 7-year-olds report having only a few of the decision-making

[5]We tested relationships with both a multifactorial analysis of variance across our specially formed total index and an ordinal regression across the three levels "possibilities of codetermination in daily life: few, more frequent, consistent." Both approaches produced comparable findings.

Table 7.3 Significant relations between possibilities of self-determination in everyday life and personal and social variables[a]

Children in Germany aged 6–11 years

Per cell in %	Few	Average	Just about all
All children	15	58	27
Age			
6–7 years	27	**55**[b]	**18**[b]
8–9 years	13	**64**[b]	**23**[b]
10–11 years	8	**54**[b]	**38**[b]
Social origin			
Lower class	37	**50**[b]	**13**[b]
Lower middle class	19	56	25
Middle class	12	**63**[b]	25
Upper middle class	14	57	29
Upper class	8	**56**[b]	**36**[b]
Migration background			
Native German children	11	59	**30**[b]
Children with a migration background	24	**55**[b]	**21**[b]
Type of family			
One-child family	15	55	30
Two-child family	15	55	30
Three-or-more-child family	17	**64**[b]	**19**[b]
Single parent	14	60	26
Parental care and attention			
No deficit	14	57	29
Deficit in one parent	19	61	20
Care deficit	21	60	**19**[b]
Gender			
Girls	15	55	**30**[b]
Boys	15	**61**[b]	24

[a]The relationship was tested with a multivariate ordinal regression on the variable "possibilities of self-determination in everyday life"

Variables included: Age, gender, social origin, migration background, type of family, care deficit, and east vs. West Germany

[b]For ease of presentation, bivariate values are presented as percentages in the table. Notable deviations for variables that were also significant within the multivariate statistical analysis are printed in bold ($p < .05$)

scopes we surveyed in their everyday lives, this is the case for only 8% of 10- to 11-year-olds. On the other hand, there are also 55% of 6- to 7-year-olds and 54% of 10- to 11-year-olds who report more frequent possibilities of self-determination, and 18% of 6- to 7-year-olds as well as 38% of 10- to 11-year-olds who report just about all possibilities of self-determination in everyday life.

We also find a slight gender effect: At 30%, girls belong slightly more frequently than boys (at 24%) to the group with just about all possibilities of self-determination. As mentioned above, this difference can be ascertained in only two of the eight domains we survey. In these domains, we cannot rule out a possible effect of different perceptions. If we were to look at other aspects of everyday life as well, this difference might well level out. On the other hand, there are no indications that boys in this age range feel that they are granted more autonomy in everyday life and girls correspondingly less.

Independent of age, statistics once again reveal the effect of social origins: the lower the social class, the higher the proportion of children with only few possibilities of self-determination in their everyday lives. Lower class children at 37% and lower middle-class children at 19% disproportionately frequently report having few possibilities of self-determination. In contrast, 36% of upper class children disproportionately frequently report having possibilities of codetermination in just about all domains. On the one hand, the low possibilities of self-determination are, as mentioned above, due to the less favorable framing conditions typical for lower class children. If there is little space at home, then it is naturally more difficult to bring an unlimited number of friends home with you. If money is limited, then freedoms and the regulation of leisure time differ from those experienced by children in the higher social classes (see also Sect. 3.4 on how children experience poverty). On the other hand, different family practices and childrearing styles also play a role here.

Another independent factor that is not mediated by, for example, class membership is the effect of a migration background. At 30%, native German children markedly more frequently have possibilities of codetermination in just about all domains compared to 24% of children with a migration background. This result is in line with findings on different childrearing styles in native German families and families with a migration background. Not only families with roots in Islamic cultures but also *Spätaussiedler* (ethnic German immigrants from the countries of the former Soviet Union) particularly reveal a higher frequency of traditional and authoritarian childrearing styles. Especially in children in this age range, these are often combined with the demand to comply more strongly with the cultural traditions of the country of origin (Fuhrer and Uslucan 2005; Uslucan 2008).

Children with deficits in care and attention ("My mother and father do not give me enough of their time") are also more likely to have low possibilities of self-determination independent of age and social origins. They are also less likely to have possibilities of self-determination in just about all domains. It can be seen here that children who complain about a lack of parental attention are disadvantaged in many ways. Parents whose children feel that they do not look after them enough also grant their children fewer possibilities of self-determination and codetermination. This can be viewed as a restriction of the potential opportunities in these children's everyday lives.

Finally, there is an interesting relationship with the type of family. Independent from the aforementioned factors, children from families with three or more children report having somewhat fewer possibilities of self-determination in their everyday lives than children in families with only one or no siblings. Combining this with the finding in Chap. 2 that children from families with three or more children also complain somewhat more frequently about being disadvantaged in their everyday lives, there are many indications at this stage that this is not due primarily to the parental childrearing style. It is at least just as much due to the constraints imposed on families with lots of children by the lack of support for large families in everyday life in Germany.

7.1.4 Children with Low Possibilities of Self-Determination in Everyday Life Also Experience Less Codetermination at School

Relating the results on the possibilities of self-determination in everyday life to those on codetermination at school (see Chap. 4) reveals that children who are used to acting in a self-determined way in their everyday lives also experience more possibilities of codetermination at school. We asked the children about seven potential forms of codetermination at school:

- How is your classroom decorated.
- Whom are you allowed to sit next to.
- How are the desks, chairs, and tables arranged in your classroom.
- On working out the rules in your class.

And for children attending 2nd grade and above:

- Where do you all go on school outings.
- On suggesting possible topics for future class projects.
- On organizing school events.

The correlation between the possibilities of self-determination in everyday life and codetermination at school is highest in the oldest children in our survey; that is, the 10- to 11-year-olds who are generally already attending secondary school. However, those 10- to 11-year-olds with low possibilities of codetermination in everyday life report that they are often allowed to codetermine 0.9 of the 7 areas surveyed. Among children with more frequent possibilities of self-determination in everyday life, this already rises to 1.3 areas, and in children with possibilities of self-determination in just about all fields, it rises to 2.2 areas.[6] Figure 7.3 presents the means; that is, the mean number of areas in which children are often allowed to codetermine at school differentiated according to the frequency of self-determination in everyday life.

Among the 8- to 9-year-olds, that is, children generally attending 3rd or 4th grade of elementary school, those reporting low possibilities of self-determination in everyday life report less than one area in which they are able to codetermine at school. In contrast, children with more possibilities of self-determination in everyday life significantly more frequently report more areas: 1.2 codetermined areas among children with more frequent possibilities of self-determination in everyday

[6] Means would have been higher and the correlation stronger if we had added together the "often" and "sometimes" responses and thereby weighted possibilities of codetermination at school differently.

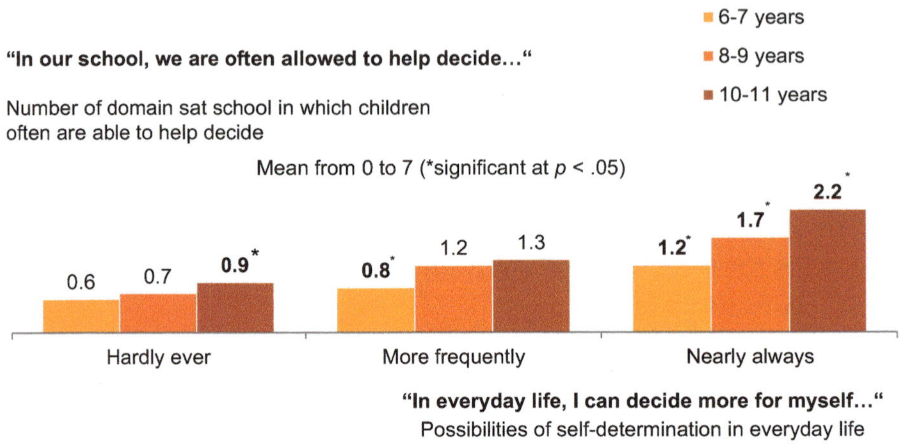

Fig. 7.3 Children with greater possibilities of self-determination in everyday life also experience a bigger decision-making scope at school
Children in Germany aged 6–11 years

life and 1.7 (thereby not significantly more) among children with possibilities of self-determination in just about all fields of everyday life. Among 6- to 7-year-olds, in contrast, with less than one reported area of codetermination at school, all differences between groups fail to attain significance.

The finding that children who have more possibilities of self-determination in everyday life also report more opportunities to codetermine at school is another decisive effect of social origins. As pointed out above, upper class children have more possibilities of self-determination not only in everyday life but also when they attend a *Gymnasium* for their secondary education. Both in the family and at school, they generally experience more possibilities of codetermination and they gain more decision-making competencies. Being able to choose and decide for oneself is an aspect of everyday life that these children take for granted, unlike children from the lower classes who markedly more frequently have no access to these opportunities for developing social competencies. In the last Child Study, we examined this aspect in more detail from the perspective of perceived self-efficacy (Schneekloth and Pupeter 2010). It is interesting to see this relationship emerge here as well.

It is also interesting to see that this correlation is already found in elementary school children. Even though somewhat weaker, it can still be confirmed statistically. We attribute this to what we call the school district principle. In Germany, elementary school children are assigned to specific elementary schools in their residential areas. Elementary schools in "posh" areas accordingly offer more possibilities of codetermination than schools in less posh areas. Viewing possibilities of codetermination as a feature of educational quality, children with a lower socioeconomic family background have less access to high-quality institutions in this sphere as well. This has also been noted critically in the German Parliament's 14th Report on Children and Youth (Deutscher Bundestag 2013). In addition, personality characteristics probably also play a role. Self-confident and "self-efficacious" children will tend to demand codetermination more than children from milieus in which hardly any possibilities of codetermination are given. Depending on the composition of the school class, this can also lead to differences along with different reactions by teachers to the topic of codetermination in the class.

7.2 Their Own Opinion

Our study also asked children whether they feel that their opinions are taken seriously: "Which of the following do you think care more about what you think and which care less?" (Table 7.4).

Six- to 11-year-olds most frequently consider that their own opinions are taken generally more seriously by their mothers (60%). Here, 27% report "sometimes one, sometimes the other"; 9% are explicitly negative with "generally less"; and 4% do not reply. Just under one-half feel they are taken seriously by their fathers (49% "generally more," 27% "sometimes one, sometimes the other," 13% "generally less," 11% no reply), and results are similar for the circle of friends (51% "generally more," 35% "sometimes one, sometimes the other", 11% "generally less", and 3% no reply).

Ratings of class teachers and, when applicable, of caregivers in institutions (day-care centers, etc.) are lower. Not even one-third of children report that their class teacher respects their opinion quite a lot (29% "generally more", 33% "sometimes one, sometimes the other", 30% "generally less", 8% no reply), and, likewise, only one-third give positive reports on the persons providing them with institutional care in the afternoons (33% "generally more", 35% "sometimes one, sometimes the other", 25% "generally less", 7% no reply).

Generally, children's evaluations of how well their opinion is valued increase as they grow older. Among the 10- to 11-year-olds, 65% report that their mothers and 52% that their fathers place generally more value on their personal opinion. Among the 8- to 9-year-olds, this applies to 59% and 49% respectively; and among the 6- to 7-year-olds, 56% and 46%. In contrast, 7% of 10- to 11-year-olds report generally less regard from their mothers and 12% (according to Table 7.4) generally less from their fathers. Among the 8- to 9-year-olds, this applies to 8% and 12% respectively; and among the 6- to 7-year-olds, 12% and 16%. Results are similar for how well their opinion is valued by their circle of friends and by their class teachers and day-care staff.

In contrast, differences in the ratings of boys and girls are less homogeneous. For example, girls somewhat more frequently give no reply when estimating the regard of their fathers whereas boy tend to rate their fathers more positively. The "sometimes one, sometimes the other" and negative answers reveal no differences. In contrast, girls rate the regard of their class teacher more positively than boys (32% vs. 25%). Correspondingly fewer girls give negative ratings than boys (28% vs. 33%).

Table 7.4 Respect for their own opinion
Children in Germany aged 6–11 years

Columns in %	All children	Girls	Boys	6–7 years	8–9 years	10–11 years
Respected by:						
Mother						
Generally more	60	60	61	56	59	65
Sometime one, sometime other	27	27	27	24	30	26
Generally less	9	8	9	12	8	7
Don't know/no reply	4	5	3	8	3	2
Father						
Generally more	49	47	52	46	49	52
Sometime one, sometime other	27	27	27	24	30	27
Generally less	13	14	13	16	12	12
Don't know/no reply	11	12	8	14	9	9
Friends						
Generally more	51	52	51	47	49	57
Sometime one, sometime other	35	35	33	36	36	32
Generally less	11	9	13	11	12	9
Don't know/no reply	3	4	3	6	3	2
Class teacher						
Generally more	29	32	25	27	28	31
Sometime one, sometime other	33	31	35	30	33	35
Generally less	30	28	33	31	31	29
Don't know/no reply	8	9	7	12	8	5
If child attends after-school care:						
Caregiver						
Generally more	33	36	30	33	30	38
Sometime one, sometime other	35	31	41	39	35	29
Generally less	25	26	23	19	29	28
Don't know/no reply	7	7	6	9	6	5

Findings seem to be similar for institutional daycare staff. Girls feel better regarded by them than boys (36% vs. 30%). On the other hand, more girls than boys give explicitly negative ratings here (26% vs. 23%).

Accordingly, the children are quite capable of taking a "critical" perspective when rating how seriously their opinion is taken. As far as the family and circle of friends are concerned, however, at 10%, only a smaller portion give explicitly negative ratings. The "sometimes one, sometimes the other" ratings that one-quarter report regarding the regard of their mothers nonetheless emphasize how sensitive children are in this age range. In comparison, answers on satisfaction with life or ratings of parental care are far more positive, but perhaps these questions are also answered without so much thought. More than 90% rate the care they receive from their parents either positively or very positively, and only a minority give neutral or even negative ratings (see Chaps. 2 und 3).

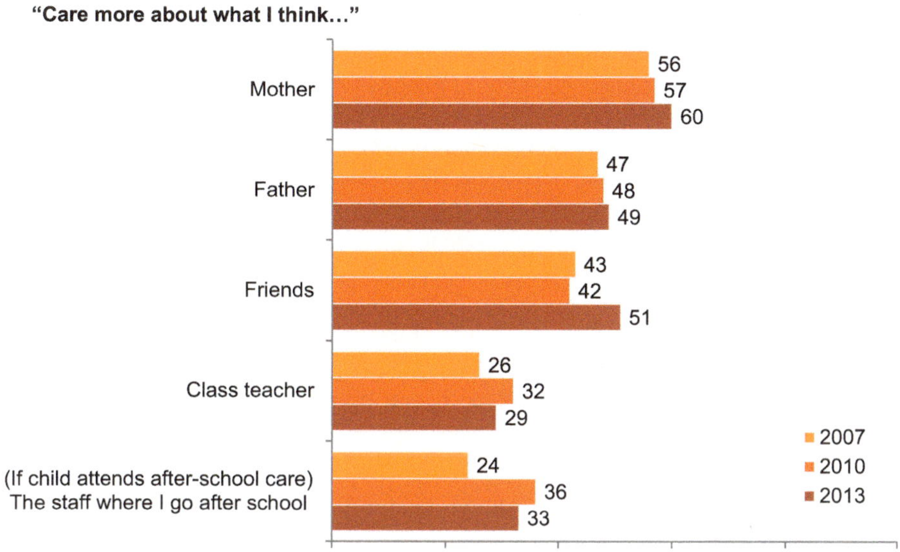

Fig. 7.4 Respect for their own opinion
Children in Germany aged 6–11 years (2007: 8 to 11 years) (%)

7.2.1 The Trend: Slightly More Regard in the Family and Circle of Friends; Ups and Downs at School and in Institutions

Viewed as a trend, the regard that children experience in the family and the circle of friends has increased slightly since our first Child Study in 2007 (Fig. 7.4). At this point, we are referring to the explicitly positive ratings ("generally more"). For mothers, the positive assessment has increased in the last two Child Studies from 56% in 2007 over 57% in 2010 to 60% in 2013. For fathers, it has risen from 47%, across 48%, to a current 49%.[7] The explicitly negative ratings fluctuate for the mothers but remain below the 10% level. In the fathers, they were 13% in 2007, 9% in 2010, and therefore slightly below the latest value of 13%. When rating the circle of friends, positive ratings have moved from 43%, across 42%, to a current 51% and thereby show the strongest increase. Negative ratings, in contrast, have remained constant at round about 10%.

In contrast, there has been a slight decline compared to the 2010 Child Study in ratings of the regard in which they are held by teachers and daycare staff. From 2007 to 2010, positive ratings rose from 26% to 32% for class teachers and from 24% to 36% for daycare staff. Currently, 29% of children give explicitly positive ratings to the esteem in which they are held by class teachers and 33% by daycare

[7] Note that the increase in reported positive regard from fathers was not large enough to attain statistical significance.

staff, when appropriate. Negative ratings for class teachers have changed from 23% in the first Child Study in 2007, across 19% in 2010, to 30% in 2013. In the daycare institutes, explicitly negative ratings have changed from 25% in 2007, across 17% in 2010, to 25% in 2013.

Regarding parents and the circle of friends, there is a clear trend toward children perceiving that their own opinion is being taken more seriously. However, regarding teachers and daycare staff, there is no recognizably stable trend, with findings fluctuating across the three waves of assessment.

Viewed in context, the degree of respect for their own opinion that children report perceiving in their mothers and fathers is determined decisively by how much time mothers or fathers dedicate to them. If children consider that their mothers spend enough time with them, then an above-average 67% give explicitly positive ratings on how well their mothers respect their opinion. If fathers devote enough time, then the proportion of children who give explicitly positive ratings on how well their fathers respect their opinion even reaches 68% (compared to an average of 49%).

More negative ratings of how seriously they are taken by their fathers or mothers are once again found more frequently among children from the lower classes. Sixteen percent of lower class children rate the regard of their mothers and even 31% that of their fathers as being explicitly negative. A notable finding is that 19% of children with a migration background compared to 10% of native German children rate the regard of their fathers negatively. There are no significant differences in ratings on the regard of their mothers. The differences in the regard of mothers versus fathers on the one hand and children with versus without a migration background on the other reveal the significance of parental childrearing styles. The children's statements can be evaluated as support for an appraisal that continues to dominate research on childrearing styles to this day: Children from less educated or socially more deprived classes tend to be reared in an authoritarian manner and this leads to differences in the regard paid to their opinion. The ratings of children with a migration background can be related to the dominance of a "traditional father role" in their families. For the rating on the regard given to one's own opinion by class teachers, it is the age of the child and the type of school that play a central role. Children attending a *Gymnasium* or also a *Realschule* somewhat more frequently consider that the class teacher takes their opinions seriously. The aforementioned gender effect with a slightly higher rating of the class teacher's regard for girls' opinions is also significant. This finding also indicates that it is not just social factors that play an important role but the individual character as well. How regard is perceived also depends on the way teachers as individuals impart the educational goals of the school.

7.2.2 Not Much Interest in Politics

Do politicians take the well-being of children into account when making their decisions? Do children feel that politicians take them seriously? We posed these questions only to children who showed some understanding of the term "politics." We first asked whether they had any interest at all in politics: "Are you interested in politics?" If necessary, we also explained "What I mean is what politicians (such as Frau Merkel) or what political parties do."

In the present Child Study, 30% did not answer this question (53% of 6- to 7-year-olds, 31% of 8- to 9-year-olds, and 11% of 10- to 11-year-olds). In 2010, this was 19% (30% of 6- to 7-year-olds, 31% of 8- to 9-year-olds, and 6% of 10- to 11-year-olds). However, we attribute this increase predominantly to method effects. In contrast to 2010, in 2013, we had already presented a series of questions on politics and social justice. The children who were unable to answer these questions (see Chap. 2) also more frequently gave no answer here either. In 2010 in contrast, 47% replied "not at all interested"—markedly more than the 37% in the 2013 Child Study (Fig. 7.5).

Otherwise, there are hardly any changes. Twenty-two percent characterize themselves as not very interested (compared to 24% in the 2010 Child Study); 9%, as interested (compared to 8%); and 2%, as very interested (same in 2010). For older children aged 8 to 11 years, we also have findings from our first Child Study in 2007. Here, 9% of 8- to 9-year-olds were interested (or even very interested) in politics. In 2010, this was 10%; and in 2013, it is also 10%. Among the 10- to 11-year-olds, the numbers were 11% in 2007, 15% in 2010, and 14% in 2013. Generally speaking, there are no relevant changes apart from the correction of the unusually low result among the 10- to 11-year-olds in 2007.

The majority of children still describe themselves as not being interested in politics. However, when we ask them to give concrete evaluations of, for example, what they think about the way certain groups are treated in Germany, most give thoroughly differentiated appraisals and also demand to be included themselves when the interests of children are at stake (see Chap. 2). This result is in line with findings on political interests in adolescents (Schneekloth 2010). Here as well, it seems to be a contemporary phenomenon that children pick up on and articulate here.

7.2.3 Skepticism Regarding Whether Politicians Bother About the Interests of Children

We asked the children who had at least some basic grasp of "politics" to rate how they felt that politicians treat children: "Do you think that politicians also pay much attention to children, that is, do they consider what they need to do so that children will have a good life?"

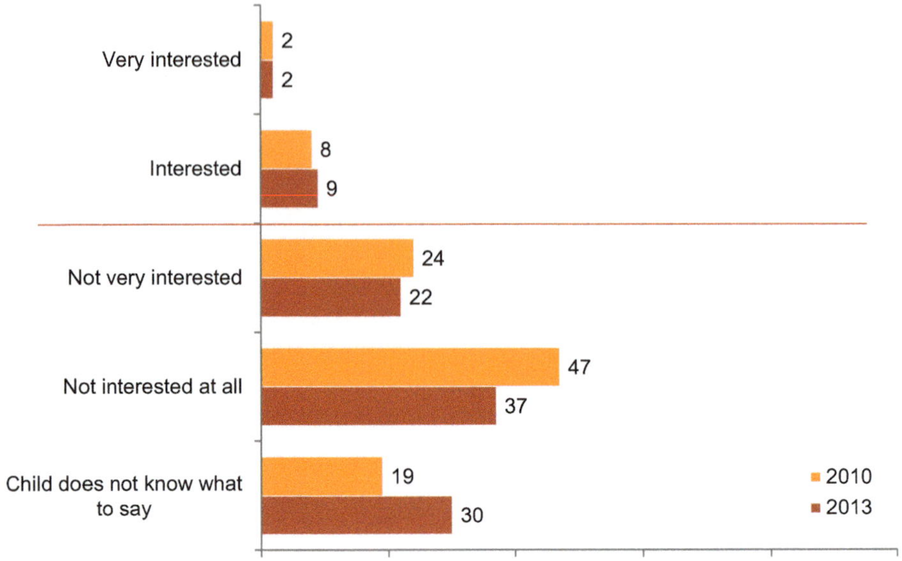

Fig. 7.5 Interest in politics
Children in Germany aged 6–11 years (%)

At 35%, the largest group of children who were given this question reply somewhat skeptically. A positive appraisal of whether politicians look after the interests of children is given by 29%, 22% are undecided, and the remaining 14% do not agree with any of the available response alternatives.

The reported appraisals depend strongly on age, even when, as here, we analyze only the responses of those who have some grasp of politics (Fig. 7.6). Among the 6- to 7-year-olds, a small relative majority of 29% answer positively; 25% rate the consideration given to them by politicians more negatively, 20% are undecided, and 26% are unable to answer the question. The opinions of 8- to 9-year-olds are balanced: 34% tend to think that politicians do not value the interests of children; 33% think they do, 21% are undecided, and 12% cannot answer the question. Among the 10- to 11-year-olds in contrast, negative appraisals dominate. The majority of 41% do not think that politicians spend much time thinking about what they should do for children, 26% appraise them positively, 23% are undecided, and 10% can give no answer. Hence skepticism about what politicians do increases with age.

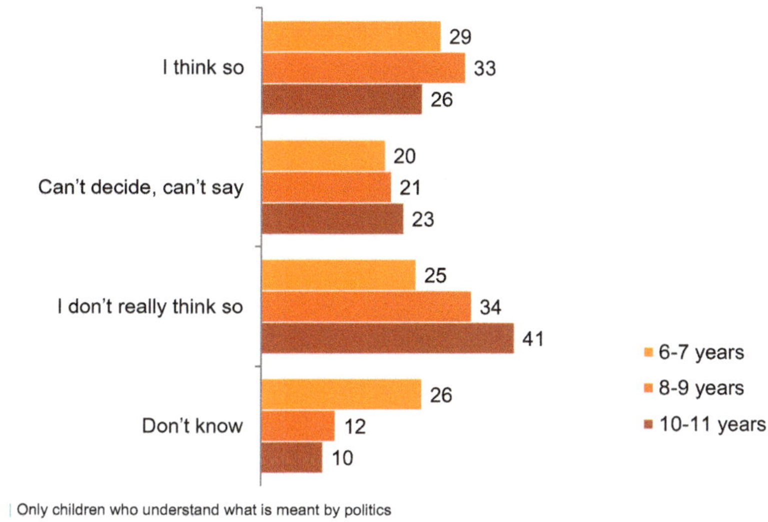

Fig. 7.6 My opinion on whether politicians also pay much attention to what they need to do so that we children can have a good life
Children in Germany aged 6–11 years (%)

7.3 General Appraisal of Freedoms in Everyday Life

When we ask the children quite generally about how they rate the freedoms their parents grant them in their everyday lives, a large majority give positive or very positive answers. At 83%, the positive rating has even increased compared to the 78% in the last Child Study in 2010 (Fig. 7.7).

This even more positive evaluation can be found in all age groups and underlines how strongly children in Germany approve of the way their parents are rearing and caring for them. Warmth, affection, and reliability, but also the willingness to dispute with the child and if necessary set limits (authoritative childrearing style, see Baumrind 1991) are appreciated by the majority of children and reflected in their answers here. Discontent is found where children gain the impression that they are not able to act in a sufficiently self-determined way in their everyday lives, or where parents lack either the time or the ability to deal with them. This particularly frequently affects 29% of lower class and 19% of lower middle-class children who give neutral to negative reports on the freedoms granted to them by their parents. In contrast, 12% of middle-class, 15% of upper middle-class, and 11% of upper class children give neutral to negative reports on this.

The importance of social origins for both satisfaction and well-being as well as for the opportunities to participate at school and during leisure time dominates the life worlds of children throughout the 2013 Child Study. We can see that children from the lower classes are disadvantaged. However, they are also disadvantaged because their families are disadvantaged and have fewer opportunities and less

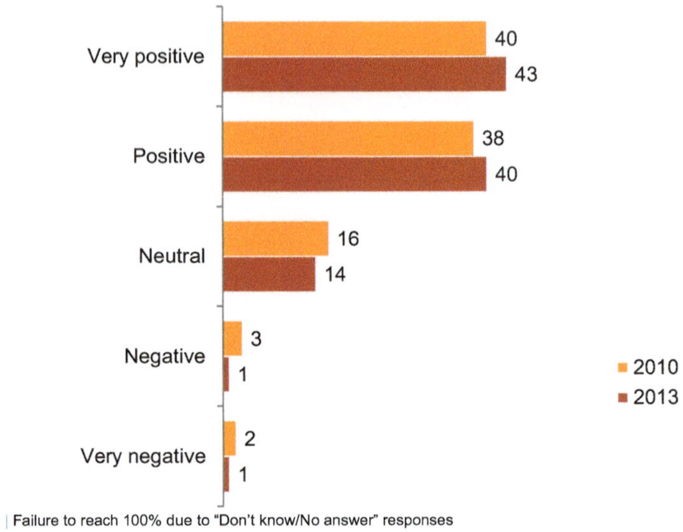

Fig. 7.7 Assessment of the amount of freedom granted by parents in daily life
Children in Germany aged 6–11 years (%)

potential to offer their children comparably good conditions and starting chances in life. It is precisely these children who also need strong families, who need to be socially well-embedded in their circles of friends, and who need to be respected in all areas of life. Children and parents need the support of "the whole village" as we have tried to portray it since our first Child Study. They do not need stigmatization and exclusion. Instead it is necessary to promote initiatives to provide concrete support in everyday life that will effectively meet the primary goal of giving children the capabilities they need in order to participate in society. The final Chap. 9 of the Child Study will go into more detail on the political challenges this embodies.

References

Andresen, S., Hurrelmann, K., & Fegter, S. (2010). Wie geht es unseren Kindern? Wohlbefinden und Lebensbedingungen der Kinder in Deutschland. In World Vision Deutschland. (Hrsg.) *Kinder in Deutschland 2010. 2. World Vision Kinderstudie* (S. 35–59). Frankfurt a. M.: Fischer.

Andresen, S., & Galic, D. (2015). Kinder. Armut. Familie. Alltagsbewältigung und Wege zu wirksamer Unterstützung. Verlag Bertelsmann Stiftung, Gütersloh

Baumrind, D. (1991). The influence of parenting style on adolescent competence and substance use. *Journal of early adolescence. Band 11, Heft 1*, S. 56–95.

Deutscher Bundestag. (2013). Der 14. Kinder- und Jugendbericht. Bericht über die Lebenssituation junger Menschen und die Leistungen und Bestrebungen der Kinder- und Jugendhilfe Iin Deutschland. Deutscher Bundestag, Drucksache 17/12200. http://dip21.bundestag.de/dip21/btd/17/122/1712200.pdf (Stand: 24.06.2013).

Fuhrer, U., & Uslucan, H.-H. (Hrsg.). (2005). *Familie, Akkulturation und Erziehung: Migration zwischen Eigen- und Fremdkultur*. Stuttgart: Kohlhammer.

Schneekloth, U. (2010). Jugend und Politik: Aktuelle Entwicklungstrends und Perspektiven. In Shell Deutschland Holding. (Hrsg.), *Jugend 2010. Eine pragmatische Generation behauptet sich* (16. Shell Jugendstudie). Frankfurt a. M.: Fischer, S. 129–164.

Schneekloth, U., & Leven, I. (2007). Familie als Zentrum: nicht für alle gleich verlässlich. In World Vision Deutschland. (Hrsg.), *Kinder in Deutschland 2007. 1. World Vision Kinderstudie* (S. 65–109). Frankfurt a. M.: Fischer.

Schneekloth, U., & Pupeter, M. (2010). Wohlbefinden, Wertschätzung, Selbstwirksamkeit: Was Kinder für ein gutes Leben brauchen. In World Vision Deutschland. (Hrsg.), *Kinder in Deutschland 2010. 2. World Vision Kinderstudie* (S. 187–221). Frankfurt a. M: Fischer.

Uslucan, H. H. (2008). Männlichkeitsbilder, Familie und Erziehung in den Communities von Zuwanderern. *Berliner Forum Gewaltprävention* (BFG Nr. 34).

Chapter 8
Challenges Facing a "Policy for Children"

Sabine Andresen, Klaus Hurrelmann, and Ulrich Schneekloth

Now that we have presented and discussed the results of this, our Third World Vision Child Study, we want to name the challenges facing a "policy for children" that we, as the research team, derive from our findings. Here, we can link up with the ideas presented in the corresponding chapter in the Second World Vision Child Study, and some of these ideas will be repeated here. However, having introduced the children's idea of justice for the first time in the present World Vision Child Study, we shall also ask how justice can serve as a benchmark for child and family policy, and what steps have to be taken to implement it. In our first step, we shall concentrate on more rights for children and present proposals regarding how to enable children to participate in those areas of life that are relevant to them. Then we shall present proposals for linking child policy together with policies for the family, education, and the common good.

S. Andresen (✉)
Department of Education, Institute of Social Pedagogy and Adult Education, Goethe University Frankfurt, Frankfurt am Main, Germany
e-mail: S.Andresen@em.uni-frankfurt.de

K. Hurrelmann
Hertie School of Governance, Berlin, Germany
e-mail: hurrelmann@hertie-school.org

U. Schneekloth
Kantar Public, München, Germany
e-mail: ulrich.schneekloth@kantarpublic.com

S. Andresen et al. (eds.), *Well-being, Poverty and Justice from a Child's Perspective*, Children's Well-Being: Indicators and Research 17,
DOI 10.1007/978-3-319-57574-2_8

8.1 Granting Children More Rights

The United Nations Convention on the Rights of the Child distinguishes the child's rights of protection, development, and participation. These rights all belong together and should ensure that children can grow up into healthy adults. In Chap. 1, we presented our justice theory approach showing how far justice depends on procedures being transparent and open to the possibility of codetermination. Nonetheless, such procedures have to be built on a legal basis that is valid and binding for all persons. This is why the formulation and ratification of basic rights are such an important step forward—precisely for those, such as children compared to adults, who possess less power because of their elementary dependence on protection and care.

8.1.1 Strictly Applying the United Nations Convention on the Rights of the Child

Germany ratified the United Nations Convention on the Rights of the Child back in 1992. The intervening years have seen discussions going far beyond Germany regarding whether and, if yes, in which areas there is a need to act and introduce reforms and which measures are needed to further support the rights of the child. One important discussion in Germany addresses whether or not the rights of the child should be formally entered into the national constitution. A frequent criticism of this is that children's rights would then have to be given primacy over parents' rights and that the two cannot be reconciled. We do not share this concern. The United Nations Convention also treats parents' rights in a sensitive way. In German law, parents' rights focus on the interests and well-being of the child and therefore expressly do not run counter to the child's rights.

Regardless of one's opinion on whether or not the rights of the child should be laid down in the constitution, it is necessary to clarify exactly what is understood by these rights, because, to some extent, we can see that different goals are being pursued in different fields of action. Precisely in light of the interests revealed by the children we surveyed, we consider this clarification to be the responsibility of politicians. Working together not only with experts but also with children, politicians need to clarify what exactly are the goals of the rights of the child, what duties they impose on which groups, and which conceivable procedures are appropriate for different age groups.

Currently, one can see different accents. These have been analyzed recently in the German parliament's 14th Report on Children and Youth (Deutscher Bundestag 2013, p. 264): The rights of the child are associated with the recognition of the legitimate interests of children and youths in light of their dependence on protection and care. Hence, the need is to establish procedures that guarantee that even the youngest children can make their voices heard and have their wishes taken into account. However, procedures designed to take the child's wishes into account have a somewhat different meaning within the family compared to public institutions. Therefore, it is necessary to clarify exactly who is required to do what in order to establish the rights of the child: be it the state, individual institutions, and/or the family. Finally, it is necessary to reach agreement on who is responsible for the rights of the child when the child herself is not in a position to stand up for them. These few comments already show that particularly from a justice perspective, there is a need to clarify how the rights of the child can be ensured and translated into sensitive but effective procedures.

8.1.2 Implementing the Right to Participation

In general, we find that attention is focused particularly on the right of participation. Participation is a central child's right, and the results reported in our Chap. 7 show how far children participate in decisions within the family. Nowadays, probably hardly anybody in a responsible position would dispute the importance of children being able to participate and being listened to. As pointed out in Chap. 1, Piaget already called for children to participate in decision making at elementary school at the earliest possible age—not least because this would cultivate their sense of justice. Nonetheless, in almost all fields, we can see how difficult it is to put this demand into practice. The Convention on the Rights of the Child also calls for their rights to be implemented in all areas of legal practice. An example of this is the German law on child and youth services. According to § 8 of Book Eight of the Social Code (SGB VIII), "depending on their level of development, children have the right to participate in all relevant decisions of public youth welfare" (AGJ 2012, p. 35, translated). This is an important and indispensable step that is supplemented by children also having the right to avail themselves of the youth services.

Such a transfer needs to be introduced in all public domains. Human rights experts such as the lawyer Hendrik Cremer (2012) are campaigning to interpret Article 12 of the Convention on the Rights of the Child as demanding that children should have the right to participate in all decisions that are relevant to their lives. In order to ascertain the best interests of the child, it is necessary to listen to what each individual child has to say in each situation, so that she or he can contribute her or his own important information, perspectives, and experience. As the results of our study show, the children themselves consider this to be appropriate and fair. By justice, they understand equal treatment; they want to be asked what they think when it comes to all decisions, and they expect matters that concern themselves to be discussed with them seriously and to be presented to them in a way they can understand. In Chap. 2, we showed how children reflect on interactional justice in their daily lives in the sense of equal treatment in personal relations; procedural justice with a view to equal rights and equal access for all; need-related justice as compensation and well-being; as well as egalitarian justice in the sense of ensuring an equal distribution.

8.1.3 Securing the Rights of the Child in the Family

Just like its two predecessors, the Third World Vision Child Study reveals how parental homes already make a major contribution to the success of participation. In their own homes, children experience being held in high regard, having the way they see things taken into consideration, and holding joint discussions on everyday issues. This is shown by our results reported in Chap. 7: Children aged 6 to 11 years decide for themselves on many aspects of everyday life such as what to spend their pocket money on, what clothes they want to put on in the morning, and which friends they have. At the same time, however, they have the backing of their parents—who protect them but finally also supervise their decisions. This provides children in many families with a protected free space in which they can develop their self-esteem and self-efficacy—a free space in which they are also able to make wrong decisions that can be corrected later.

This finding reveals how parents today make an important contribution to putting the rights of the child into practice: They transform the family into a living open discussion household. The willingness and ability of these parents should not be misunderstood as "not having the courage to rear their children properly." Involving children and getting them to participate in making decisions on topics that they can grasp does not mean giving in to them or avoiding conflicts. It is important to take one's own stance and justify it in order to take the child and the child's own outlook seriously. From the child's perspective, things are fair when everybody has to stick to the rules and receives equal treatment. What is needed is reliability and accountability rather than giving in as far as possible or ignoring problems.

Even when our study shows that a very large majority of children are very contented with the way things are in their families, from the perspective of the rights of the child, we must not forget that the family is not always a home in which people treat each other with loving respect. In all social classes, there are families in which the child's right to physical and mental integrity and the right to participation and respect have not been achieved. Recent years have seen far more public discussion and acknowledgement of neglect and the sexual abuse of children than ever before. For a long time, talking about sexual abuse was taboo—much to the detriment of the children exposed to it. Even when the dark figure of undetected crime continues to be high for these offences and we do not know precisely how widespread the problem is, one thing does seem to be clear: Most cases of sexual abuse of children take place in the proximal environment, that is, within the family. When children are faced with such abuse, they need to know that they can turn to attentive and respectful adults in their daycare centers, schools, clubs, and neighborhood; and they need to experience a climate in which they can have the courage to trust in others. A study of the sexual abuse of girls and boys in institutions carried out by the German Youth Institute (Deutsches Jugendinstitut e.V., DJI, 2011) has shown how frequently child victims turn to educators they can trust and take them into their confidence. This potential needs to be strengthened.

After a long debate over the National Child Protection Act [*Bundeskinderschutzgesetz*] in Germany, Book Eight of the Social Code (SGB VIII) now states that children and adolescents have a right to counseling independent of parental permission; however, only when counseling is necessary because of a conflict or emergency (Article 8, Paragraph 3). Precisely against the background of our knowledge that parents do not always act in the best interests of the child, this fixed right to counseling is an important and correct step. At the same time, we have to ask why this right applies only in conflict situations or emergencies. It would be more appropriate to establish a culture—without placing parents under general suspicion—in which children have a right to immediate counseling at any time and for any reason.

8.1.4 Extending the Rights of the Child in Educational Institutions

As pointed out above, the right to counseling is an important aspect of child participation wherever children are to be found. This means that those responsible in institutions, in daycare centers, in schools, boarding schools, children's homes, or sports clubs also need to think about which options and procedures they can establish to grant children comprehensive participation rights. We still see a major need for action here, because ever since our first Child Study in 2007, only about 30% of the children we survey report feeling that their opinion is respected in school and in daycare. This percentage has not changed over the years, and it is also relatively independent of a child's age. Whereas parents involve their children in decisions more and more frequently as they grow older, there are only some signs of such an approach among professionals.

From our perspective, this is a task to be tackled in professional training and further training: Respect for what children think and how they think about things is a basic precondition for participation and thus an important aspect of a professional approach to working with children. Here as well, we consider it to be important to emphasize that this attitude should not be derided as an easy way of avoiding conflict when dealing with children. Taking children seriously also means arguing with them about which is the correct path for them to take. On this basis, individual institutions can develop procedures in which the rights of the child are applied comprehensively. The *Bundesarbeitsgemeinschaft der Landesjugendämter* (2013) [National Association of Länder youth welfare offices] has recently announced that the establishment of the rights of the child is a quality feature of child daycare centers and a guideline for working with children. As well as being a feature of educational quality, it is something that institutions are obliged to implement by law. Those responsible understand the rights of the child as a central strategy for implementing child protection. This is based on the assumption of a close link between active rights such as participation and the right of protection.

All institutions—schools just as much as daycare centers or clubs—are called upon to develop a protective concept, and to do this as far as possible together with all persons involved; that is, with the children and their parents as well. Acknowledging the dark side of the family, this strategy is a response to the existing knowledge on the locations of violence and abuse (particularly of a sexual nature; see Andresen and Heitmeyer 2012). From our perspective, one element is particularly important, namely, the active participation of children themselves and their parents in developing so-called protective concepts. This is also linked to major educational processes as is also emphasized clearly in the resolution of the National Association of Länder youth welfare offices when it states:

> Children should be actively included as suggestion makers and complainants. In their daily lives at daycare centers, they should experience that their dissatisfaction will also be taken seriously and acknowledged when it is expressed in the form of crying, withdrawal, or aggressiveness. Children should receive active support in acquiring appropriate forms of making complaints within the framework of their education, whereby the participation of children is itself a precondition for effective education. (Bundesarbeitsgemeinschaft Landesjugendämter 2013, p. 4).

This call to take the dissatisfaction of children seriously, to teach them how to complain, to encourage them to do so, and to view this as a task of education represents an important step in establishing justice from the children's perspective. It is precisely the nontransparent, at times seemingly unjust behavior of adults that offends the child's idea of justice. Providing a space for these feelings and helping children to express them is an indispensable element of a progressive child policy. This has been aided by an important legal reform since 2012, because two paragraphs (§ 8b and 45) of Book Eight of the Social Code (SGB VIII) specify that institutions have to provide complaint procedures through which children and youths can express their personal concerns. Children can find themselves in situations in which they have to refer to an independent complaints office or ombudsman. Here as well, it is necessary to study how schools, in which all children spend a great deal of their time, intend to put these provisions into practice and whether they also engage in implementing children's rights more strongly than before. In the context of the school, this could certainly be linked to the theory of good teaching (Klieme et al. 2010), because this promotes three elements that are highly compatible with the rights of the child: the greatest possible own initiative in children including their cognitive activation, a good classroom climate, and a responsible and proactive class management. In Chap. 4, we have shown how important the school is for children's daily lives. Therefore, it is precisely teachers whom we wish to encourage to invest more energy than before in exploiting the potential of the school as a space in which children can experience participation and strengthen their self-efficacy (Hurrelmann and Timm 2011).

References

AGJ – Arbeitsgemeinschaft für Kinder- und Jugendhilfe. (Hrsg.). (2012). *Sozialgesetzbuch VIII auf dem Stand des Bundeskinderschutzgesetzes*. Berlin: Gesamttext und Begründungen.

Andresen, S., & Heitmeyer, W. (Hrsg.). (2012). *Zerstörerische Vorgänge. Missachtung und sexuelle Gewalt gegen Kinder und Jugendliche in Institutionen*. Weinheim und Basel: Beltz Juventa.

Bundesarbeitsgemeinschaft der Landesjugendämter. (2013). *Sicherung der Rechte von Kindern als Qualitätsmerkmal von Kindertageseinrichtungen*. http://www.bagljae.de/downloads/114_sicherung-der-rechte-von-kindern-in-kitas.pdf (Stand: 24.06.2013).

Cremer, H. (2012). Kinderrechte und der Vorrang des Kindeswohls. Die UN-Kinderrechtskonvention bietet ein weites Anwendungsfeld. *Anwaltspraxis, 4*, S. 327–329.

Deutscher Bundestag. (2013). Der 14. Kinder- und Jugendbericht. Bericht über die Lebenssituation junger Menschen und die Leistungen und Bestrebungen der Kinder- und Jugendhilfe Iin Deutschland. Deutscher Bundestag, Drucksache 17/12200. http://dip21.bundestag.de/dip21/btd/17/122/1712200.pdf (Stand: 24.06.2013).

DJI (Deutsches Jugendinstitut e.V.). (Hrsg.). (2011). *Sexuelle Gewalt gegen Kinder. Missbrauch in Institutionen, Forschungsergebnisse und Empfehlungen fur einen besseren Kinderschutz*. München: DJI.

Hurrelmann, K., & Timm, A. (2011). *Kinder, Bildung, Zukunft Drei Wege aus der Krise*. Stuttgart: Klett.

Klieme, E., Artelt, C., Hartig, J., Jude, N., Köller, O., Prenze, M., Schneider, W., & Stanat, P. (Hrsg.). (2010) *PISA 2009. Bilanz nach einem Jahrzehnt*. Münster/ New York/ München/ Berlin: Waxmann.

Appendices

Appendix 1: Methods Applied in the Third World Vision Child Study

Methodological Profile of the 2013 Child Study

The design of the Third World Vision Child Study 2013 and the methods applied are oriented toward the two earlier Child Studies of 2007 and 2010. Once again, we carried out a quantitative survey of a representative sample of 6- to 11-year-old children (in 2007, only 8- to 11-year-old children). We supplemented this standardized survey with a qualitative assessment resulting in 12 portraits of children who had been selected systematically. Within the study design, our quantitative survey served to present the living conditions and life worlds of children in all their breadth. The qualitative survey portrays selected children, thereby delivering an impression of children in their life worlds characterized by more depth and closeness to daily life.

The underlying population for the quantitative survey is children in Germany between the ages of 6 and 11 years. We surveyed 2535 children. To gather enough cases for analyses in the new German states in the east of the country, we used a disproportional sample distribution: A total of 1729 interviews were carried out in the old German states (including Berlin) and 806 in the new German states. Of course, we took this deliberate overrepresentation of children from the new German states into account when analyzing the data. We did this by using official statistics to construct a sample weighting framework and projecting the sample on to the residential population aged 6–11 years in the actual East–West relationship differentiated according to gender. We also took account of the fact that not all 6-year-olds are already attending school. Weighted in this way, the structure of the sample corresponds to the true distribution of 6- to 11-year-old school children found in official statistics.

S. Andresen et al. (eds.), *Well-being, Poverty and Justice from a Child's Perspective*, Children's Well-Being: Indicators and Research 17,
DOI 10.1007/978-3-319-57574-2

Survey Instruments

The quantitative survey is based on two different instruments: First, the interview with the children was a personal oral survey conducted by well-trained interviewers on the basis of a set standardized assessment instrument. The survey itself was computer-assisted: The respondent's answers were entered directly into the interviewer's laptop computer. The second instrument was a short written questionnaire that one parent was asked to complete preferably while the child was being interviewed. This parent questionnaire was used to gather basic sociodemographic information on the child's family background.

When developing the child questionnaire, we tried not only to ensure that the instruments were comparable with those used in the 2007 and 2010 surveys, but also to focus on one special topic in each Child Study—in this case, the idea of justice. When rating their idea of justice, the children were given visual support in the form of a 4-point smiley scale. This visual support enabled them to quickly orient themselves and perform a ranking on the given dimension. The items on satisfaction or on well-being were assessed with the 5-point smiley scale used in previous Child Studies. The children also received visual support with their qualitative ratings in other response formats (see the questionnaire in Appendix 4).

While preparing the study, we tested the suitability of our instruments as part of a cognitive pretest of children and then revised the instruments as required. In addition, when formulating items on the idea of justice, we took account of results obtained from the first qualitative interviews that had already been carried out by this time. In the subsequent pilot test in the field, several interviewers carried out 95 advance interviews with children in the target group under the same conditions as those to be used in the subsequent main survey. This also included asking the children to reply to some open unstructured questions on what they understand by the term justice.

According to the interviewers, the children responded to the Third World Vision Child Study just as willingly as they had done to the previous ones. In 87% of cases, the interviewers rated the children's willingness to answer their questions as good; and in 12%, as moderate or "sometimes one, sometimes the other." They rated the willingness to answer their questions as bad in only 21 children (< 1%). However, even in these cases, individual analyses revealed no reason to drop them from the sample. The child questionnaire is documented in Appendix 4 and the parent questionnaire in Appendix 5.

Sample

As in the first two Child Studies, the survey was based on quota sampling. Interviewers were instructed to survey a precisely defined number of school children aged 6 and above who could be classified to specific subgroups.

Quota sampling was based on the following features:

- Age groups: 6–7 years, 8–9 years, 10–11 years, differentiated according to gender
- German states and regional types of settlement pattern (*9 BIK-Siedlungsstrukturtypen*)
- Migration background: yes, no

When setting the quotas, we lowered the target for 6- and 7-year-olds by the proportion of 6-year-olds who are still not attending school (as in the previous Child Studies, we specified that 62% of the 6-year-olds should already be attending school).

Quota sampling was based on the tried and tested two-stage approach: In the first stage, interviewers were asked to report how many available target persons they had in each of the quota cells who matched the quota characteristics. These interviewer reports were collected by the operations management of TNS Infratest, the research agency responsible for carrying out the survey work.

For the Third World Vision Child Study, the number of reported target persons proved to be markedly higher than the number of interviews required. This made it possible to draw on the official statistics and gain a sample from the reported target persons that corresponded largely to our requirements. Because, as pointed out above, the sample distinguished disproportionally between the old and new German states, possible deviations in the operationalization of the interviews in terms of age groups and gender could also be balanced by using the proportional weighting procedure.

We included the following parameters from official statistics (Federal Statistical Office: population estimate, general education statistics, and special analyses all taken from the 2011 micro census) in our weighting: age groups (6–7, 8–9, and 10–11 years; 6-year-olds reduced by the estimated proportion of children not yet attending school) and gender; federal state and BIK settlement structure types; type of school (elementary, secondary, other, and special needs school); type of family (single parent: yes or no); and nationality. Generally speaking, effects on the weighted distributions tended to be small. Different East–West distributions were taken into account in all weighting variables.

Regarding the age structure in the study, it has to be noted that we set age boundaries according to the ages reported by the children. Compared to the usual practice of using year of birth in empirical social research, we found that it was far easier to get the children to just report how many years old they were.

The distribution of the sample across federal states was a relatively good fit with the target requirements, as was also the distribution according to BIK settlement structure type. Any deviations that occurred were additionally corrected by ex post weighting.

The proportion of non-German children in the sample is roughly 3%. During weighting, we also corrected this proportion to the target of roughly 6%. A further 23% of the German children in the Child Study have parents or one parent born outside of Germany. Weighting also increased this proportion to 28%, although the characteristic of migration background was not included separately in the weighting. Accordingly, the proportion of children with a migration background was 26% before and 34% after weighting.

Field Work

Data for the Third World Vision Child Study were collected between the beginning of January and the middle of February 2013. Therefore, the Third World Vision Child Study was carried out in the middle of the school year in contrast to the Second World Vision Child Study, which had been carried out at the beginning of the school year in the fall of 2009. There were 400 well-trained Infratest interviewers who each performed an average of six surveys. For 76% of the surveys, at least one further person was present. In 61% of all cases, this was the mother; in 15%, the father.

The interviewers themselves were allowed to select the specific target persons based on the given criteria in the quota sample. They could recruit these persons within their personal circle of friends and acquaintances, institutions, or typical locations in which children congregate. After gaining the parents' permission in advance (obligatory in this age range), they interviewed them in their parental homes.

The average interview lasted 37 minutes. Surveys of 6- to 7-year-old and 8- to 9-year-old target persons took only slightly longer at 37 minutes than those of 10- to 11-year-old target persons at 36 minutes. When looking at the duration in the youngest age group, it has to be considered that questions on more general topics in society were dropped if the child was unable to answer the first leading question on that topic.

As part of the Infratest controls, interviewers had to document the addresses of respondents. Infratest controlled roughly 10% of all surveyed target persons at random by asking the children's parents either directly by telephone or by post whether the interviewer had actually carried out an interview of the given length addressing the given topic. Further quality controls were applied to the completed questionnaires by checking the internal consistency of the responses. This resulted in only minor corrections. Reports that were obviously incorrect were analyzed as "no reply."

After completion of the field work and the quality controls, we were left with a valid dataset that could be subjected to a differentiated analysis with the help of the statistical software packet SPSS 19. This book presents the detailed results of these analyses.

Appendix 1.1 Methodology Profile for the 2013 Child Study

Population	Children living and attending school in Germany aged 6–11 years (2007: 8–11 years)
Sample	Household survey. Quota sample controlled for:
	Age and gender
	Type of school (elementary, *Hauptschule*, *Realschule*, *Gymnasium*, other schools, special needs school)
	Migration background
	Federal State and type of settlement structure (BIK-Type),
Case numbers	*n* = 2,535 child interviews (disproportionate allocation),
	n = 1,729 in West German states (including Berlin) und *n* = 806 in East German states
Assessment method	Individual oral child interview (CAPI: Computer Assisted Personal Interviews)
	Written parent questionnaire (self-report). German- and Turkish-language versions
Time period	Beginning of January to mid-February 2013
Weighting	Official statistics (*Bevölkerungsfortschreibung* 2011 and*Mikrozensus* 2011)

Appendix 1.2 Sample statistics

Case numbers	Actual numbers		Target numbers	
	Girls	Boys	Girls	Boys
Old German States[a]				
6-year-olds	82	84	83	91
7-year-olds	139	114	146	150
8-year-olds	164	147	144	151
9-year-olds	153	165	145	155
10-year-olds	172	182	150	160
11-year-olds	148	179	159	166
Total	858	871	827	873
New German States[a]				
6-year-olds	39	32	46	50
7-year-olds	57	70	71	73
8-year-olds	87	66	70	75
9-year-olds	56	69	68	72
10-year-olds	73	74	67	71
11-year-olds	97	86	69	70
Total	409	397	391	411

[a]Disproportionate allocation: West including Berlin, East not including Berlin

Appendix 2: Documentation of the Social Origins Index

The Social Origins Index applied in the World Vision Child Study is a combination of the parents' educational background and the material resources available to the household. Information on both aspects is taken from the Parent Survey. This is supplemented by the children's estimates on the number of books in the home and the parents' reports on the housing type. Depending on the replies, each individual variable is assigned a different number of points.

Social Origins Index: Component Variables and the Number of Points Assigned to Them

(Highest) Secondary school qualification of mother or father	
Hauptschule (basic secondary: 8th–9th grade)	2
Realschule/mittlere Reife (intermediate secondary: 10th grade)	4
Fachhochschulreife (university of applied sciences entrance qualification)	6
Abitur (university entrance qualification)	6
No secondary school qualification	2
Roughly how many books are there in your home?	
Very few (up to 10 books)	0
About one small shelf (11–24 books)	1
About one bookcase (25–100 books)	2
About two bookcases (101–200 books)	2
Three or more bookcases (more than 200 books)	3
Housing type	
Rented	1
Own property	2
How well do you manage your household with the amount of money available to you and your family every month?	
Very well	3
Well	2
Moderately	2
Poorly	1
Very poorly	0

Figure Appendix 2.1

The points awarded on the variables are added together to form a summary index. If information on both parents is available for the variable "educational background," the higher of the two qualifications is entered. The summary index can range from 3 to 14 points.

The Social Origins Index is formed by dividing the summary index into five groups. Each group then corresponds to one level on the Social Origins Index. This takes the following ranking:

Social Origins Index: Distribution of Summary Points

Lower class	3–6 points
Lower middle class	7–8 points
Middle class	9–10 points
Upper middle class	11–12 points
Upper class	13–14 points

Figure Appendix 2.2

Appendix 2.1 Social class Index: Variables included and their scores

(Highest) secondary school education of mother or father	
Hauptschule (8th–9th grade)	2
Realschule/Mittlere Reife (10th grade)	4
Fachhochschulreife	6
Abitur	6
I have no secondary school qualifications	2
Roughly how many books are there in your home?	
Only a few (up to 10 books)	0
About one shelf (11–24 books)	1
About one bookshelf (25–100 books)	2
About two bookshelves (101–200 books)	2
Three or more bookshelves (more than 200 books)	3
Type of housing	
Rented	1
Own property	2
In your own household, how well do you get by on the amount of money available to you and your family each month?	
Very well	3
Quite well	2
Just about okay	2
Less well	1
Not well at all	0

Appendix 2.2 Social class Index: Classification of sum index

Lower class	3–6 points
Lower middle class	7–8 points
Middle class	9–10 points
Upper middle class	11–12 points
Upper class	13–14 points

Appendix 3: Pretest – Unstructured Responses

Appendix 3.1 Unstructured Responses on the Topic of Justice

Basis: Children aged 6–11 years in Germany (Pretest: *n* = 95)
Categories:
1 = Equal treatment
2 = Equal rights/Equal access
3 = Equal status, well-being
4 = Equal distribution
9 = Don't know/No reply

What do you understand by the term justice?	Age	1 = Girl 2 = Boy	Category
That we can sometimes do what we want to do, that everybody has enough to eat and toys, that nobody has to go hungry. That all people are treated equally regardless of where they come from, what they look like, or whether they have a lot of money or only a little.	10	1	1, 2, 3,
When my mum sometimes allows me to go out, and she lets me play with my friends, and that it's not just my little brother who is allowed to play the learning games that I am not allowed to play with so much.	9	2	1, 2, 4
That you don't make distinctions.	11	2	1, 2
Everybody has the same rights.	9	1	1, 2
That everybody is treated in the same way and everybody has the same opportunities.	10	2	1, 2
That all people are treated equally!	11	2	1, 2
All people are on the same wavelength regardless of whether they are rich or poor.	10	1	1, 2

That everybody is free to say what they think, that there is religious freedom.	10	1	1, 2
Everybody has the same rights.	10	1	1, 2
That everybody has equal rights.	11	1	1, 2
That people are allowed to say what they want, that people don't get into trouble straight away if they do something wrong, that my children are all allowed to play together regardless of whether they come from somewhere else or are poor.	6	1	1, 2
All people should be treated equally regardles s of whether their skin color is white, yellow, or black.	10	2	1, 2
Treating the unequal unequally; the equal, equally.	9	2	1, 2
It's unjust to steal from the poor.	6	1	1, 3
By just, I understand that you help people not to hurt themselves.	10	1	1, 3
That you help other people and that you try to get as much as the others as well.	8	2	1, 4
That we are treated equally.	7	1	1
When you are treated with respect.	11	1	1
It is just, for example, when you are allowed to play outside with your friends.	9	1	1
Being allowed to play outside; not nagging very much.	8	2	1
When everybody is treated equally; that is, when nobody gets preferential treatment.	11	2	1
Having freedom.	11	2	1
Justice is when everybody is treated equally.	6	2	1
That you get what is your right when you can decide.	9	1	1
Then it should be that everybody is allowed the same things.	7	2	1
That everybody is treated equally well.	7	2	1
That you are equally nice to everybody.	7	2	1
That you are equally nice to everybody and don't give special preference to anybody.	9	1	1
That you don't cheat and there are no quarrels.	8	2	1
Everybody has the same rights and duties.	9	2	1
When everybody who puts their hand up at school gets their turn.	9	2	1
That you are polite to each other and help others.	9	1	1
That you have to treat everybody equally.	7	1	1
Justice, that all are treated equally.	11	1	1

Everybody should be nice to everybody else and adults should be as fair to others as they are to themselves.	8	1	1
No rows in the family, with friends, at school, that nobody gets beaten, that people are also not rude to foreigners.	11	1	1
That everybody treats each other nicely, nobody quarrels, and everybody is good.	6	1	1
When you get punished for doing something you are not allowed to do, and you don't do it again.	8	2	1
I can participate in decisions.	8	2	1
That everybody is equally allowed to do the things they want to do.	7	2	1
That you get punished if you do something bad!	9	2	1
For me, justice means when no distinctions are made, everybody gets the same, everyone is treated in the same way—be it financially or also in their careers.	11	1	2, 3, 4
That nobody is excluded and that everybody gets as much as everybody else.	10	1	2, 3, 4
That all people, whether rich or poor, get the same things, are able to travel, get toys, and have enough to eat.	6	2	2, 3, 4
When all children can go to school and have food to eat.	7	2	2, 3
When everybody has food to eat and is allowed to say what they want.	11	2	2, 3
Everybody is treated the same way and has enough to eat.	9	1	2, 3
That everybody has enough to eat, everybody can live in freedom, everybody can go to school, there is no poverty, and that there are not so many rich people who do not share.	11	2	2, 3
That you share with each other and don't just leave anybody out.	7	1	2, 3
Everyone has the same amount of money, the same rights, and they are all treated equally well.	11	2	2, 4
When my sister gets the same as I get and when all people are treated equally.	9	1	2, 4
That it's fair to take turns with something if there is only one available.	10	2	2
When everybody can do the same.	11	1	2
That all the people in the world, regardless of their skin color, are treated equally and children can go to school.	8	1	2

That all people are treated equally regardless of whether they are poor or rich or have another skin color.	9	1	2
When you treat someone well who is disabled or poor; when you help people who is injured or sick, that's justice for me.	10	2	2
It is just when you are rewarded for something you do, or I am given something and my brothers and sisters also get something.	7	1	3
When everybody gets what they want.	6	1	3
That everybody gets everything they need.	10	2	3
When everybody gets what they want and doesn't get what they don't want.	8	1	3
That you share something.	7	1	3
Everybody has a home, nobody has to sleep outside, everybody has something to eat.	10	1	3
When everybody has a job, a home, enough to eat, and still has money left over to afford something nice.	6	1	3
When everybody has a good livelihood, doesn't have to go hungry, and has their own home.	11	2	3
The poor get poorer all the time; the rich get richer all the time. A lot of people don't have much to eat and have to go hungry. Not enough help is given. A lot of people own nothing.	8	1	3
That you give something to other people and share with them.	6	1	3
That there are so many friends.	8	2	3
When the children in Africa have to go hungry and the children in Germany throw food away.	10	1	3
Peace.	10	1	3
Justice is when I am eating sweets with my friend and my friend gets more. That is unjust. It would be better to share things exactly.	6	1	4
When playing in a group game at school, it was unjust because there were four children in one group and only three in the other group.	6	1	4
Justice is when you have three lollipops and there are four people. Then you don't go and get lollipops but candies instead.	9	1	4
When you get the same as my brother.	9	2	4
I get the same as my friends.	6	2	4
When everybody has the same amount.	10	2	
Everybody gets the same.	7	1	4

Justice is when all children get the same present when Father Christmas comes.	8	1	4
That children of the same age also get the same amount of pocket money.	9	2	4
I don't know at the moment.	8	2	9
No statement that can be evaluated.	8	1	9
No concrete answer.	9	1	9
I can't say.	10	2	9
No answer.	10	2	9
No idea.	9	2	9
No answer.	7	1	9
I can't say exactly.	10	2	9
Don't know.	7	1	9
I don't know.	6	1	9
I don't know.	6	2	9
I don't know any answer.	9	2	9
Child does not know any direct answer.	11	1	9
At the age of 6 years, Luis still can't assign any meaning to the term "justice."	6	2	9
No answer.	10	1	9
No answer.	6	2	9
No clear classification.			

Appendix 3.1 Unstructured responses on the topic of justice

Children in Germany aged 6–11 years (Pretest $n = 95$)
Categories:
1 = Equal treatment
2 = Equal rights/Equal access
3 = Equal status, well-being
4 = Equal distribution
9 = Don't know/No reply

Unstructured Response: What do you understand by the term justice?	Age	1 = Girl 2 = Boy	Category
That we can sometimes do what we want to do; that everybody has enough to eat and toys; that nobody has to be hungry. That all people are treated equally regardless of where they come from, what they look like, or whether they have a lot of money or only a little.	10	1	1, 2, 3
When my mum sometimes allows me to go out and she lets me play with my friends, and that it's not just that my little brother is allowed to play the learning games that I am not allowed to play with so much.	9	2	1, 2 ,4
That you don't make distinctions.	11	2	1, 2
Everybody has the same rights.	9	1	1, 2

(continued)

Unstructured Response: What do you understand by the term justice?	Age	1 = Girl 2 = Boy	Category
That everybody is treated in the same way and everybody has the same opportunities.	10	2	1, 2
That all people are treated equally!	11	2	1,2
All people are on the same wavelength regardless of whether they are rich or poor.	10	1	1, 2
That everybody is free to say what they think, that there is religious freedom.	10	1	1, 2
Everybody has the same rights.	10	1	1, 2
That everybody has equal rights.	11	1	1, 2
That people are allowed to say what they want, that people don't get into trouble straight away if they do something wrong, that my children are all allowed to play together regardless of whether they come from somewhere else or are poor.	6	1	1, 2
All people should be treated equally regardless of whether their skin color is white, yellow, or black.	10	2	1, 2
Treating the unequal unequally; the equal, equally	9	2	1, 2[1]
It's unjust to steal from the poor.	6	1	1, 3
By just, I understand that you help people not to hurt themselves.	10	1	1, 3
That you help other people and that you try to get as much as the others.	8	2	1, 4
That we are treated equally.	7	1	1
When you are treated with respect.	11	1	1
It is just for example, when you are allowed to play outside with your friends.	9	1	1
Being allowed to play outside; not nagging very much.	8	2	1
When everybody is treated equally; that is, when nobody gets preferential treatment.	11	2	1
Having freedom.	11	2	1
Justice is when everybody is treated equally.	6	2	1
That you get what is your right when you can decide.	9	1	1
It should be so that everybody is allowed the same things.	7	2	1
That everybody is treated equally well.	7	2	1
That you are equally nice to everybody.	7	2	1
That you are equally nice to everybody and don't give special preference to anybody.	9	1	1
That you don't cheat and there are not quarrels.	8	2	1
Everybody has the same rights and duties.	9	2	1
When everybody who puts their hand up at school gets their turn. . .	9	2	1
That you are polite to each other and help others.	9	1	1
That you have to treat everybody equally.	7	1	1
Justice, that all are treated equally.	11	1	1

(continued)

Unstructured Response: What do you understand by the term justice?	Age	1 = Girl 2 = Boy	Category
Everybody should be nice to everybody and adults should be as just to others as they are to themselves.	8	1	1
No rows in the family, with friends, at school, that nobody gets beaten, that people are also not rude to foreigners.	11	1	1
That everybody treats each other nicely, nobody quarrels, and everybody is good.	6	1	1
When you get punished for doing something you are not allowed to do, and you don't do it again.	8	2	1
I can participate in decision making.	8	2	1
That everybody is equally allowed to do the things they want to do, and not that some are allowed to and others are not.	7	2	1
That you get punished if you do something bad!	9	2	1
For me, justice means when no distinctions are made, everybody gets the same, everyone is treated in the same way—be it financially or also in their careers.	11	1	2, 3, 4
That nobody is excluded and that everybody gets as much as everybody else.	10	1	2, 3, 4
That all people, whether rich or poor, get the same things, are able to travel, get toys, and have enough to eat.	6	2	2, 3, 4
When all children can go to school and have food to eat.	7	2	2, 3
When everybody has food to eat and is allowed to say what they want.	11	2	2, 3
Everybody is treated the same way and has enough to eat.	9	1	2, 3
That everybody has enough to eat, everybody can live in freedom, everybody can go to school, there is no poverty, and that there are not so many rich people who do not share.	11	2	2, 3
That you share with each other and don't leave anybody out.	7	1	2, 3
Everyone has the same amount of money, the same rights, and they are all treated equally well.	11	2	2, 4
When my sister gets the same as I get and when all people are treated equally.	9	1	2, 4
That it's fair to take turns with something if there is only one available.	10	2	2
When everybody can do the same.	11	1	2
That all the people in the world, regardless of their skin color, are treated equally and children can go to school.	8	1	2
That all people are treated equally regardless of whether they are poor or rich or have another skin color.	9	1	2
When you treat someone well who is handicapped or poor; when you help people who are injured or sick, that's justice for me.	10	2	2
It is just when you are rewarded for something you do, or I am given something and my brothers and sisters also get something.	7	1	3
When everybody gets what they want.	6	1	3

(continued)

Unstructured Response: What do you understand by the term justice?	Age	1 = Girl 2 = Boy	Category
That everybody gets everything they need.	10	2	3
When everybody gets what they want and doesn't get what they don't want.	8	1	3
That you share something.	7	1	3
Everybody has a home, nobody has to sleep outside, and everybody has something to eat.	10	1	3
When everybody has a job, a home, enough to eat, and still has money left over to afford something nice.	6	1	3
When everybody has a good livelihood, doesn't have to go hungry, and has their own home.	11	2	3
The poor get poorer all the time; the rich get richer all the time. A lot of people don't have much to eat and have to go hungry. Not enough help is given. A lot of people own nothing.	8	1	3
That you give something to other people and share with them.	6	1	3
That there are so many friends.	8	2	3
When the children in Africa have to be hungry and the children in Germany throw food away.	10	1	3
Peace.	10	1	3
When I am eating sweets with my friend and my friend gets more, that is unjust. It would be better to share things exactly.	6	1	4
When playing in a group game at school, it was unjust because there were four children in one group 3 and only three in the other group.	6	1	4
Justice is when you have three lollipops and there are four people. Then you don't go and get lollipops but candies instead.	9	1	4
When you get the same as my brother.	9	2	4
I get the same as my friends.	6	2	4
When everybody has the same amount.	10	2	
Everybody gets the same.	7	1	4
Justice is when all children get the same present when Father Christmas comes.	8	1	4
That children of the same age also get the same amount of pocket money.	9	2	4
I don't know at the moment.	8	2	9
No statement that can be evaluated.	8	1	9
No concrete answer.	9	1	9
I can't say.	10	2	9
No answer.	10	2	9
No idea.	9	2	9
No answer.	7	1	9
I can't say exactly.	10	2	9
Don't know.	7	1	9
I don't know.	6	1	9

(continued)

Unstructured Response: What do you understand by the term justice?	Age	1 = Girl 2 = Boy	Category
I don't know.	6	2	9
I don't know any answer.	9	2	9
Child does not know any direct answer.	11	1	9
At the age of 6 years, Luis still can't assign any meaning to the term "justice."	6	2	9
No answer.	10	1	9
No answer.	6	2	9
[1]No clear classification.			

Appendix 4: Survey Instrument: Child Questionnaire (CAPI)

Thank you for agreeing to take part in our study. I am now going to ask you a few questions that either tell me about you personally or let me know what you think about things.

Interviewer: Please enter:

1a. **Your name is?**

Child's first name.

1b. **Child is**

Male
Female

Sociodemographics and family.

2. **First of all, I'd like to know how old you are.**

Child's age (*2013: 6–11 years*).

3. **How many people live in your home? Add everybody together and please count yourself as well.**

Interviewer: Make sure that the child counts her or himself as well

Household size ________
Does not apply, I live in a children's home (wrong target group; end of survey)

4. **And who are all the people you live with in your home? Look at this list, and tell me which of these persons live with you.**

(Question text for 6-, 7-, and 8-year-olds) And who are they? I am going to read out this list, and I want you to tell me if that person lives together with you in your home.

Interviewer: Present List 4, read it out loud, and go through it together with the child.

□ Myself
□ My father
□ My mother
□ My stepfather/My mother's partner
□ My stepmother/My father's partner
□ My brother or brothers (*Interviewer: also stepsiblings*)
□ My sister or sisters
□ My grandfather
□ My grandmother
□ Other relatives (uncle or aunt, cousins, …)
□ Other people my parents know

5. *(If no siblings are named in Question 4)*

Do you have any brothers and sisters; perhaps ones who are not living together with you?

□ Yes
□ No, I do not have any brothers or sisters

6. *(If siblings are mentioned in Question 4 or 5)*

And exactly how many younger or older brothers and sisters do you have?
Interviewer: Also classify twins appropriately.
This means ALL siblings: those living in the family home AND those NOT (no longer) living in the family home

_______ Younger brother(s) none
_______ Younger sister(s) none
_______ Older brother(s) none
_______ Older sister(s) none

7. **Were your parents born in Germany, or does one or both of your parents come from another country?**

□ Parents were born in Germany
□ One parent comes from another country
□ Both parents come from another country

8. *(If one or both parents were born in another country; otherwise proceed to Question 9)*

What language do you speak mostly at home?

□ Mostly German
□ Mostly the language of my parents (my non-German parent)

9. **Do you think that your** *(if the child reports living with a father who has a new partner in Question 4, add "real")* **mother gives you enough of her time?**

□ Yes
□ Sometimes yes, sometimes no
□ No
□ Doesn't apply, mother not present

10. *(If the child reports living with a stepmother or the father's new partner in Question 4)*

And do you think that your stepmother or your father's new partner gives you enough of her time?

□ Yes
□ Sometimes yes, sometimes no
□ No

11. *How about your (if the child reports living with a mother who has a new partner in Question 4, add "real")* father? Does he give you enough of his time?

□ Yes
□ Sometimes yes, sometimes no
□ No
□ Doesn't apply, no father present

12. *(If the child reports living with a stepfather or the mother's new partner in Question 4)*

And your stepfather or your mother's new partner, does he give you enough of his time?

□ Yes
□ Sometimes yes, sometimes no
□ No

13. **Generally speaking, how happy are you about the way your parents look after you? Look at the faces on this list and show me which one fits best. You can just point with your finger or you can tell me which letter fits.**

Interviewer: Show the Smiley scale (5-point smiley scale at end of booklet). Let younger children point to the faces and then classify them.

A B C D E

14. **Now for something different. Do you pray at home?**

□ No
□ Hardly ever
□ Sometimes
□ Very often

15. **Do you regularly attend religious services at a church or mosque?**

Interviewer: This also means prayer rooms or other places of worship such as synagogues—regardless of which religion.

□ Yes, every week
□ Yes, once or twice a month
□ Less often
□ Never or hardly ever

16. **Roughly how many books are there in your home? We have prepared the following answers for you.**

(For 6-, 7-, and 8-year-olds in addition) **I shall read them out loud. (For all children) Just tell me which is the right amount or point it out to me with your finger.**

Interviewer: Present List 16, read the response categories out loud, and use your finger to point out which answer you mean. If necessary, repeat the procedure twice.
Interviewer: This item assesses the number of books in the home and not just the child's own books.

1 2 3 4 5

Only a few (up to 10 books)

About one shelf (11–24 books)

About one bookcase (25–100 books)

About two bookcases (101–200 books)

Three or more bookcases (more than 200 books)

17. **Do you have a room of your own?**

Interviewer: If the child shares her or his room with other children (e.g., brother, sister, cousin), enter 2 "Yes, together with my brother(s) or sister(s)"

□ Yes, just for me
□ Yes, together with my brother(s) or sister(s)
□ No, I do not have my own room

18. *(If the child reports having her or his own room or a room with siblings in Question 17)*

In your room, do you have

(a) Yes (b) No

_______Your own writing desk?
_______A radio?
_______A CD player or MP3 player?
_______Your own television?
_______Your own DVD player or Blue Ray?
_______Your own computer (or laptop)?
_______A game console/PlayStation for video games?
_______A portable Gameboy (PSP/Nintendo)?

19. **I am going to read out some sentences. Tell me which of them is more like the way things are in your home and which is less like the way things are in your home.**

(a) More like things are (b) Less like things are (c) Don't know *(don't read last choice out loud)*

_______In our home, we normally eat breakfast before I go to school.
_______We are often short of money in our family.
_______I generally have at least one warm meal every day.
_______We have enough money for everything we need.

Only continue with further questions when child answers "More like things are" to Question 19–2 or "Less like things are" to Question 19–4

_______Because there is not enough money in my family, I can hardly ever go to movies or swimming pool.
_______Sometimes we can't afford to buy things for school such as exercise books or pens.
_______I can't join a club or learn to play a musical instrument, because my family cannot afford to pay for it.
_______We hardly ever have children's birthday parties because they cost too much.
_______I often have to wear clothes that are out of fashion.
_______From time to time, we get food for free, for example, from the "*Tafel*" (a stall where people can get free food handouts).
_______Sometimes I am cold in winter because I do not have any warm clothes.
_______Because there is not enough money in our family, I sometimes earn some extra money myself.
_______Within the last year, my parents have had to borrow money from my own savings.
_______Every year we take at least a one-week vacation away from home.

20. **How satisfied are you in general with the amount of freedom your parents give you in your daily life; in other words, what they let you do and what they don't let you do? Please just tell me which face in the list fits best or tell me which letter fits.**

Interviewer: Show the Smiley scale at the end of the booklet. Let younger children point to the faces and then protocol them.

A B C D E

Justice

21. **I shall now read out some sentences. Please tell me whether you find them to be very fair, quite fair, rather unfair, or very unfair.**

Interviewer: Give children the list for Question 21. Let younger children point to the faces and then protocol them.

Read out the response categories once, and then as needed.

Very fair Quite fair Rather unfair Very unfair

_______Some families have very little money; others have a great deal. Do you think that is very fair, quite fair, rather unfair, or very unfair?
_______A group of children at the daycare center want to go on a trip together. It has been decided that rich parents should pay more money for the trip than

poor parents. Do you think that is very fair, quite fair, rather unfair, or very unfair?

_______Mostly it's adults—and not the children themselves—who decide where and when to build a children's playground. This is because they say that they are the ones who know best about such things. Do you think that is very fair, quite fair, rather unfair, or very unfair?

_______What would you think if non-German children had to speak only German not just in class but also in the school breaks. Do you think that is very fair, quite fair, rather unfair, or very unfair?

22. **And how fair do you think things are in general?**

Interviewer: Give children the list. Let younger children point to the smiley faces and then protocol them.

Read out the response categories once, and then as needed.

A B C D E

_______In your family, are things very fair, quite fair, rather unfair, or very unfair?

_______And in your school? Are things there very fair, quite fair, rather unfair, or very unfair?

_______And with your friends? (*pause, and when no response*) Are things very fair, quite fair, rather unfair, or very unfair?

_______And when you think about Germany as a whole? (*pause, and when no response*) Are things very fair, quite fair, rather unfair, or very unfair?

For 6- to 7-year-olds who reply to Question 22.4 with "Don't know/No answer," skip Question 22.5

_______And what about the whole world? (*pause, and when no response*) Are things very fair, quite fair, rather unfair, or very unfair?

23. *For 6- to 7-year-olds who reply to Question 22.4 or Question 22.5 with "Don't know/No, answer," skip Question 23*

What do you think: Is the way people treat the following groups in Germany very fair, quite fair, rather unfair, or very unfair?

Interviewer: Give children the list. Let younger children point to the smiley faces and then protocol them.

Read out the *response categories once, and then as needed.*

A B C D E

_______Children or adolescents

_______Old people

_______Foreigners

_______The handicapped
_______Poor people

24. **And how about you yourself? Do you feel treated unfairly for any of the following reasons?**

Interviewer: Give children the list for Question 24

(a) Often (b) Sometimes (c) Hardly ever (Does not apply)

_______Because of your age
_______Because you are a boy/girl (*depending on answer to Question 1. b*)
_______Because of your external appearance (that is, what you look like)
_______Because your parents don't have much money
_______Because your mother or your father do not come from Germany (*if child reports that either one or both parents were not born in Germany in Question 7*)

School/Institutions

25. **Now let's turn to school. What grade are you in?**

□ _____ grade (1st–7th grade)
□ I haven't started school yet

26. **How do you like school? Please point to the smiley that fits or tell me which letter fits.**

Interviewer: Show the Smiley scale. Let younger children point to the faces and then protocol them.

A B C D E

27. **What would you say? Are you**

□ Not a good student at all
□ Not a very good student
□ An average student
□ A good student
□ A very good student

28. **Do you go to a half-day school that normally ends at midday, or do you go to an all-day school with regular lessons and other activities in the afternoon?**

Interviewer: The latter does not mean a daycare center, lunchtime childcare, or other nonschool care provision.

- ☐ Half-day school *(Continue with Question 30)*
- ☐ All-day school *(Continue with Question 29)*
- ☐ Don't know/Other *(Filter: If child reports "Don't know" or makes no report, proceed to Questions 29 and 31)*

29. **Would you rather go to a school that ended at midday?**

- ☐ Yes
- ☐ No

30. **In your school, are you allowed to help decide:**

Interviewer: Give child the list for Question 30 and read out the response categories

(a) Often (b) Sometimes (c) Hardly ever

_______How your classroom is decorated?
_______Whom you are allowed to sit next to?
_______How the desks, chairs, and tables are arranged in your classroom?
_______ *(Filter: Skip Grade 1*) Where you will all go on school outings (e.g., by being given a list of different places to choose from)?
_______ *(Filter: Skip Grade 1*) On suggesting possible topics for future class projects?
_______On working out the rules in your class, that is, how everybody treats each other in the class?
_______ *(Filter: Skip Grade 1*) On organizing school events (e.g., what should be included in the program)?

31. *(If Question 28 = half-day school)*

After school, do you regularly go to one of the following care centers?

Interviewer: At least twice a week. Multiple answers possible. If child reports several institutions, give the one the child attends most frequently on weekdays

- ☐ Midday care at the school
- ☐ An after-school care center
- ☐ Some other kind of afternoon care center or group
- ☐ No, none of them/I don't go to any center *(Proceed to Question 33)*

32. *(If child reports 1, 2, or 3 in Question 31)*

How do you like it there (daycare or afternoon care)? Simply point to the right Smiley or tell me which letter.
Interviewer: Show the Smiley scale. Let younger children point to the faces and then protocol them. If child reports several institutions, give the one the child attends most frequently on weekdays

A B C D E

33. Do you have private lessons to help you keep up with your school work?

□ No
□ Yes, once a week
□ Yes, more than once a week

34. *(If child reports up to 4th grade on Question 25)*

Which type of secondary school would you like to go to later?
Interviewer: If there is uncertainty regarding the type of school (e.g., when the child wishes to attend a comprehensive school covering the entire three-track system), classify according to the type of school-leaving certificate.

□ Basic secondary school (*Hauptschule – Hauptschulabschluss*)
□ Intermediate secondary school (*Realschule – Realschulabschluss*)
□ Upper secondary school (*Gymnasium – Abitur*)
□ Don't know/Don't care

35. *(If child reports 5th grade or higher on Question 25)*

Which type of school-leaving certificate would you like to attain?

□ Basic secondary school leaving certificate (*Hauptschulabschluss*)
□ Intermediate secondary school leaving certificate (*Realschulabschluss*)
□ University entrance qualification (*Abitur*)
□ Don't know/Don't care

Leisure Time, Media Consumption, and Friendships

Now let's turn to your free time and your friends

36. **I shall read you a list of things children do in their free time, and I want you to tell me which ones you never do or hardly ever do, which ones you do sometimes, and which ones you do a lot of the time.**

Interviewer: Give the child List 36 and read the response categories out loud.

(a) Hardly ever (b) Sometimes (c) Very often

_______Sports (swimming, playing soccer, etc.)
_______Riding a bike, inline skating, or skateboarding
_______Theater group, dance, or ballet
_______Watching television
_______Meeting friends
_______Playing with my toys at home
_______Playing a musical instrument, making music
_______PlayStation, Nintendo, Wii, computer games
_______Reading books or magazines *(Text for 6- to 7-year-olds: "Looking at")*
_______Handicrafts, painting, or drawing
_______Making things with tools
_______Listening to music
_______Building things with Lego™ or playing with Playmobil™
_______Doing things together with my family (going on excursions)
_______Engaging with nature or animals
_______Playing outside on the street
_______Listening to audio plays or stories.

37. **Generally speaking, how happy are you with what you do in your free time?**

Interviewer: Show the 5-point Smiley scale at the end of the booklet. Let younger children point to the faces and then protocol them.

A B C D E

38a. *(Text: for 8- to 11-year-olds as reported in Question 2)*

How often do you spend some time reading a book (except when doing homework)?

38b. *(Text: for 6- to 7-***year***-olds as reported in Question 2)*

How often do you spend some time looking at a book (except when doing homework)?

Interviewer: Some time means at least one quarter of an hour.

□ Hardly ever
□ Not very often
□ Once a week
□ Several times a week
□ Every day

39. *(Skip question if child reports "hardly ever" watching television in Question 36)*

And how long do you normally watch television or DVDs every day?
Interviewer: This question addresses regular television viewing on weekdays.

□ At the most, half an hour
□ Half an hour to one hour
□ One to two hours
□ Two to three hours
□ Three hours and more
□ I hardly ever watch television *(Proceed to Question 40)*

40. *(Skip question if child reports "hardly ever" playing computer games in Question 36)*

And how about computer games, Gameboy, PlayStation, and the like? How often do you play with them?

□ Not very often
□ At the most, one hour a week
□ Several times a week *(Proceed to Question 41)*
□ Every day *(Proceed to Question 41)*
□ I hardly ever play computer games

41. *(Answers 3 or 4 on Question 40)* **And roughly how many hours do you play with them each day** *(on Question 40 = 4)***/on these days** *(on Question 40 = 3)***?**

Interviewer: Please ask *for the exact amount of time: Half an hour is 0.5 h and a quarter of an hour is 0.25 h.*

□ No more than half an hour
□ Up to one hour
□ *For more than one hour, give exact number of hours:* Number of hours___. ___ *(1.25–24 h)*

42. **Do you have your own mobile phone?**

□ Yes
□ No, I do not have my own mobile phone

43. **Do you have access to the Internet (that is, can you go online with a computer)?** *(Filter: Proceed to Question 47 if child reports "No answer/Don't know"*

□ No *(Proceed to Question 47)*
□ Yes *(Proceed to Question 44)*

44. *(If Question 43 = yes)* **Do you use the Internet regularly every week?** *(Filter: Proceed to Question 47 if child reports "No answer/Don't know").*

□ Yes
□ No, only occasionally, or never *(Proceed to Question 47)*

45. *(If Question 44 = yes)* **And for roughly how long do you use the Internet each week?**

□ Not more than half an hour
□ Up to 1 hour
□ Up to 2 hours
□ Up to 3 hours
□ Up to 4 hours
□ Up to 5 hours
□ More than 5 hours *(Follow-up question: 5 to 10 hours, 10 to 20 hours, or 20 hours and more)*

46. *(If child reports "Up to 1 hour" and above on Question 45)*

What do you do most of the time on the Internet?
Interviewer: Present list. Name the response categories again for each question. For younger children, read them out loud while using your finger to point out which answer you mean.

(a) Hardly ever (b) Sometimes (c) Very often

_______Send e-mails
_______Search for something in particular
_______Use Facebook (or other social networks such as Local List)
_______Chat, that is, talk to others on the Internet
_______Just surf to see what I can find
_______Play computer games
_______Look at or download videos
_______Download music
_______Twitter

47. **Now, make a rough guess: Round about how many friends do you have?**

- □ One
- □ 2–3
- □ 4–5
- □ 6–9
- □ 10 or more
- □ None at all *(Proceed to Question 49)*

48. *Skip if child reports "None at all" in Question 47; still pose question if child reports "No answer/Don't know"*

And how many really good friends do you have?

- □ 1
- □ 2
- □ 3
- □ 4
- □ 5
- □ 6–9
- □ 10 or more
- □ None at all

Check*: Number reported in Question 48 should not be higher than that reported in Question 47*

49. **Do you find it easier or more difficult to make friends?**

- □ Easier
- □ More difficult

50. *If child reports between "1" and "10 or more" in Question 47* **or** *between "1" and "10 or more" in Question 48. Skip if child reports "None at all" in Question 48*

How frequently do you meet your friends/friend?
Interviewer: Present the list and read out the response categories

(a) Just about every day (b) Several times a week (c) Hardly ever/ Never

_______At school?

________During midday care or after-school care? *(Filter, only if indicated in answer to Question 31)*
________Outside (outside, playground, school yard)?
________At your home?
________At your friend's house?
________At a club?
________*(Filter, when child reports "yes" in Question 44)* Online?

51. **And how happy are you with your circle of friends?**

Interviewer: Show the Smiley scale (5-point smiley scale at end of booklet). Let younger children point to the faces and then protocol them.

A B C D E

52. **People can be more or less happy in the place where they live. Which of the following sentences is more or less true for you?**

(a) More true (b) Less true

________In the place where I live, there is very little public transport such as buses or trams.
________Our neighbors are always complaining because they think we are too loud.
________I have enough friends to play with living in my neighborhood.
________There is too much traffic in the street where I live.
________I am afraid of aggressive youths and adults in my neighborhood.
________At any time, I have a playground or an open field to play in within walking distance.

53. **Now just a few more questions about you yourself: How happy are you with your bodyweight? Do you think that you are**

- □ Much too thin
- □ A bit too thin
- □ Just the right weight
- □ A bit too fat
- □ Much too fat

Own Opinion and Codetermination in Daily Life

54. **If you think about your everyday life, which are the situations in which your opinion counts: Can you decide for yourself**

(a) Generally yes (b) Generally no

_______Which friends you meet?
_______What clothes you wear?
_______What you spend your pocket money on?
_______What's to eat at home?
_______How many friends you can bring home with you?
_______What you do in your free time?
_______When you do your homework?

55. **And are you allowed to help decide what your family does in its free time (e.g., at the weekend)?**

□ Generally yes
□ Generally no

56. **Which of the following people do you think care more about what you think and which care less?**

Interviewer: Please do not read "Sometimes one, sometimes the other" out loud. Only offer it as a response category when *the child is hesitant.*

(a) Generally more (b) Generally less (c) Sometimes, one, sometimes the other

_______Your mother (does she tend to care more about what you think or less?)
_______Your father.
_______Your friends.
_______Your class teacher.
_______ *(If child reports attending some sort of after-school care in Question 31)* The staff at the place you go to after school.

57. **Do the following things worry you?**

Interviewer: Give the child the list. Name the response categories again for each question. For younger children, read them out loud while using your finger to point out which answer you mean.

(a) Hardly ever (b) Sometimes (c) Very often

_______Poor grades and that I won't be able to keep up with the others at school
_______That my parents will become unemployed or not be able to find any work
_______That somebody might bully or hit me
_______That environmental pollution is increasing
_______That there are more and more people who are poor in Germany
_______That a war might suddenly break out in Germany
_______That more and more foreigners are coming to Germany all the time

58. **Are you interested in politics? Would you say that you are**

Interviewer: If the child does not understand what is meant by politics, then please explain as follows:
"What I mean is what *politicians (such as Frau Merkel) or what political parties do."*

- □ Not interested at all
- □ Not very interested
- □ Interested
- □ Very interested
- □ Child does not know what to say; doesn't know how to handle the term politics *(Proceed to Question 60)*

59. *Filter: Skip when answer to Question 58 = 5)*

Do you think that politicians also pay much attention to children; that is, do they consider what they need to do so that children will have a good life?

- □ I think so
- □ I don't really think so
- □ Can't decide, can't say

60. **And, finally, how happy are you with your life in general?**

Interviewer: Show the Smiley scale (5-point smiley scale at end of booklet). Let younger children point to the faces and then classify them.

A B C D E

Thank you for taking part and answering my questions!

To be completed by the interviewer.

61. **How willing was the child to answer the questions?**

- □ Very willing
- □ Moderately willing
- □ Unwilling
- □ Sometimes one, sometimes the other

62. **Were other persons present during the interview?**

- □ No
- □ Yes

63. *(If Question 62 = yes)* **Which persons were present?**

Interviewer*: Multiple answers possible!*

□ The mother
□ The father
□ Grandparents
□ Siblings
□ Other relatives
□ Other children
□ Other adults

64. *(If Question 62 = yes)* **Did anybody intervene during the course of the interview (e.g., by reformulating questions, giving hints, or influencing the direction of answers)?**

□ Yes, very frequently
□ Yes, occasionally
□ No, generally not
□ No, not at all

Appendix 5: Survey Instrument: Parent Questionnaire

Dear Parents,

Thank you very much for granting permission for your child to participate in the Third World Vision Child Study and allowing us to ask our questions. In the following questionnaire, we would like to obtain some background information on you and your family.

Naturally, your answers will be dealt with completely anonymously and they will not be passed on or made available to any third persons.

Attention interviewer: Please enter in advance

Name of the child being surveyed:

Please answer the following:

P 01 I am

The child's mother

The child's father

P 02 I am

Married

Not married, but raising the child together with my partner

A single parent

P 03a My present age is
years.

P 03b If you are married or living with your partner

The present age of my partner is

years.

P 04a My (highest) secondary school education is
Hauptschule (8th–9th grade)
Realschule/Mittlere Reife (10th grade)
Fachhochschulreife
Abitur
I have no secondary school qualifications
I am still attending secondary school

P 04b If you are married or living with your partner
My partner's (highest) secondary school education is
Hauptschule (8th–9th grade)
Realschule/mittlere Reife (10th grade)
Fachhochschulreife
Abitur
My partner has no secondary school qualifications
My partner is still attending secondary school

P 05a I am currently
Employed full-time (35 h a week or more)
Employed part-time (between 15 and 35 h a week)
Marginally employed (less than 15 h a week)
Unemployed
Taking parental leave or some other form of leave
In training
Studying or still attending secondary school
A housewife or househusband or for some other reason not employed

P 05b If you are married or living with your partner
My partner is currently
Employed full-time (35 h a week or more)
Employed part-time (between 15 and 35 h a week)

Marginally employed (less than 15 h a week)
Unemployed
Taking parental leave or some other form of leave
In training
Studying or still attending secondary school
A housewife or househusband or for some other reason not employed

P 06a (when employed) I am employed as a
Manual worker
Clerical worker
Public official
Freelance university graduate (e.g., lawyer, physician, …)
Self-employed

P 06b If you are married or living with your partner and your partner is employed
My partner is employed as a
Manual worker
Clerical worker
Public official
Freelance university graduate (e.g., lawyer, physician, …)
Self-employed

P 07a Have you been unemployed for a period of 3 months or more during the past 2 years?
Yes
No
Does not apply, I am not gainfully employed and I have not sought employment

P 07b If you are married or living with your partner
Has your partner been unemployed for a period of 3 months or more during the past 2 years?
Yes
No
Does not apply, my partner is not gainfully employed and has not sought employment

P 07c If you are employed: Would you prefer to work more hours or fewer hours?
Work more
Work less
Things are fine the way they are

P 07d If you are NOT employed: Would you like to be employed?
Yes, full-time
Yes, part-time
No, things are fine the way they are

P 08a I was born in
Germany

Turkey
Greece
Italy
Former Yugoslavia
Former Soviet Union
Another West European country
Another East European country
An Arabic country
An African country
Another country

P 08b If you are married or living with your partner
My partner was born in
Germany
Turkey
Greece
Italy
Former Yugoslavia
Former Soviet Union
Another West European country
Another East European country
An Arabic country
An African country
Another country

P 09a My current nationality is
German
Turkish
Greek
Italian
Former Yugoslavian
Former Soviet Union
Another West European country
Another East European country
An Arabic country
An African country
Another country

P 09b If you are married or living with your partner
My partner's current nationality is
German
Turkish
Greek
Italian

Former Yugoslavian
Former Soviet Union
Another West European country
Another East European country
An Arabic country.
African
Another country

P 10a My religion
Catholic
Protestant
Other Christian religion
Islam
Other non-Christian religion
No religious affiliation

P 10b If you are married or living with your partner
My partner's religion
Catholic
Protestant
Other Christian religion
Islam
Other non-Christian religion
No religious affiliation

P 11 What is your child's nationality?
German
Non-German
My child has dual nationality

P 12 What type of school is your child currently attending?
Elementary school
Hauptschule
Realschule
Gymnasium
School with several tracks (orientation stage [*Orientierungsstufe*], comprehensive, ...)
Special needs school

P 13 Does your child spend some time outside the family or school in, for example, a club such as a sports club, a social group, a music group, a church group, a nature or animal protection group, or the like?
Sports club (soccer, swimming, horse riding, tennis, ...)
Music group/Music school
Dance club/Ballet
Painting/drawing group
Theater or movie group

Church group
Girl guides/Boy scouts
Nature or animal protection society
Organized group in a child or youth club
Trachtenverein [society for traditional costumes]/*Brauchtumspflege* [cultural folklore group]
Other group or club (please specify) ______________________
No, my child does not belong to any organized group or a club

P 14 And when your child was younger, did she or he attend a day nursery?
No, my child did not attend a day nursery (Proceed to Question P 15)
Yes, my child did attend a day nursery (Proceed to Question P 14a)

P 14a How old was your child when she or he first attended a day nursery?
Age when my child first attended a day nursery:
Less than one year old
One year old
Two years old
More than two years old

P 15 Did your child attend a *Kindergarten* or preschool?
No, my child did not attend a *Kindergarten* or preschool (Proceed to Question P 16)
Yes, my child did attend a *Kindergarten* or preschool (Proceed to Question P 15a)

P 15a How old was your child when she or he first attended a *Kindergarten* or preschool?
Age when my child first attended a *Kindergarten* or preschool
Less than three years old
Three years old
Four years old
Five years old
More than five years old

P 16 We live in a
Single family house (terraced house or detached)
In a smaller building containing several apartments (up to 12 apartments)
In a larger building or block (more than 12 apartments)

P 17 Type of housing
Rented
Own property

P 18 In your own household, how well do you get by on the amount of money available to you and your family each month?
Very well
Quite well
Just about okay
Less well

Not well at all

P 19 Nowadays, there is a lot of talk about reconciling work and family life. How well does this work for you? How well do you manage to reconcile work and family life in your family?
Very well
Quite well
Just about okay
Less well
Not well at all

Thank you for your time and your cooperation!

Appendix 6: Case Scenarios

Circus Story

Next month, a famous circus will be coming to town. The children in a school class would really like to go to the circus and see the show. Although the class has its own savings account with money to pay for excursions, there is not enough money to pay for tickets for everybody to go to the circus. The class is discussing what they can do. The children come up with the idea of holding a garage sale. All the children should bring things they no longer need from home so that they can be put on sale.

On the day of the garage sale, all the children bring things to be sold. Only Jana and Emil come with empty hands. Anton and Luise, in contrast, have brought a particularly large number of things. What do you think: Should all the children be able to go to the circus?

After the question has been discussed in detail, the next question probes deeper:

At the circus, the class has reserved a complete block of seats. One-half of the children can sit in the front row; the other one-half have to sit behind them. How should the children decide who gets to sit in the front row? Why?

If the children fail to grasp the dilemma themselves, the questioner poses follow-up questions and asks whether the children would judge the following two versions differently:

Version A: Jana didn't manage to bring anything because she was ill and Emil simply didn't have anything at home that he could bring.

Version B: Jana and Emil couldn't be bothered/had something else they wanted to do on the day they should have spent some time looking for things to bring.

Flute Story

Three children—Anne, Bob, and Carla—are quarrelling over who should get a flute to play with. Imagine you have to decide which child should get the flute. Anne claims the flute because she is the only one of the three who knows how to play it. Bob points out that he is the only one of the three who has no other toys to play with because he is poor. Carla, in contrast, claims the flute because she is the one who spent several months working hard to make it. Which child should get the flute and why should that child get it?

Money for School Grades

Lukas and Philipp are twins. Now that the school marks the children's work and gives them grades, their parents have decided to give them a reward of two Euros for every Grade 1 (Excellent) and one Euro for every Grade 2 (Good). They get no money for a Grade 3 (Fair). Philipp is happy, because even when he doesn't bother to do any revision on the day before the test, he still always manages to get a 1 or a 2. Things are different for Lukas. He also wants to get good grades and he tries very hard. Sometimes, he even starts learning and revising hard a couple of days before the test. Nonetheless, he often manages to get only a 3 and sometimes occasionally a 2.

Lukas goes to his parents and tells them that he finds the arrangement unfair because he hardly ever gets a reward—even though he works much harder than Philipp! What do you think?

Provocation and Punishment

Jakob and Carsten don't like each other very much, so they mostly just avoid each other. During a break in the schoolyard, Carsten suddenly starts to call Jakob names. Jakob tries not to listen, but Carsten doesn't stop. He provokes Jakob more and more. Eventually, Jakob gets very angry and gives Carsten a hard push. Carsten falls down and grazes his knee. The teacher sees this and steps in immediately. Jakob is kept in after school and given extra work to do as a punishment. What do you think of that?

Majority Versus Minority

A class goes on regular school trips. The children get to vote where the class will go on each trip. Every time there is a vote, 12 children vote for the swimming pool and 8 children vote for the zoo. The class has already gone swimming twice. On the third time, the children who want to go to the zoo protest. They think that it is not fair when they have to go the swimming pool again on their school trip. What do you think?

After the question has been discussed in detail, the next question follows:

Udo is the only child who has always wanted to go to the museum. Hardly any of the other children want this. Should the class nonetheless take one trip to the museum?

Participation

A small town has a playground where the younger children like to go and play. The town mayor believes that there are still not enough places in the town where youths can meet each other. He wants to organize a meeting with the citizens of the town and discuss whether the playground should be replaced by a youth center. All the adult residents of the town are invited to an evening meeting at the town hall. They should vote whether to keep the playground or to build a youth center instead. The children are not invited to attend the meeting. What do you think of that?

References

AGJ – Arbeitsgemeinschaft für Kinder- und Jugendhilfe. (Hrsg.). (2012). *Sozialgesetzbuch VIII auf dem Stand des Bundeskinderschutzgesetzes*. Berlin: Gesamttext und Begründungen.

Allbus: Datenreport. (2011). *Ein Sozialbericht für die Bundesrepublik Deutschland.* Bonn: Bundeszentrale für politische Bildung.

Allensbacher Institut für Demoskopie. (2013). Was ist gerecht? Gerechtigkeitsbegriff und -wahrnehmung der Bürger. Allensbacher Archiv, IfD-Umfrage 11001, Allensbach.

Andresen, S., & Heitmeyer, W. (Hrsg.). (2012). *Zerstörerische Vorgänge. Missachtung und sexuelle Gewalt gegen Kinder und Jugendliche in Institutionen.* Weinheim und Basel: Beltz Juventa.

Andresen, S., & Hurrelmann, K. (2007). Was bedeutet es, heute ein Kind zu sein? Die World Vision Kinderstudie als Beitrag zur Kinder- und Kindheitsforschung. In World Vision Deutschland. (Hrsg.) *Kinder in Deutschland 2007. 1. World Vision Kinderstudie* (S. 35–64). Frankfurt a. M.: Fischer.

Andresen, S., Hurrelmann, K., & Fegter, S. (2010). Wie geht es unseren Kindern? Wohlbefinden und Lebensbedingungen der Kinder in Deutschland. In World Vision Deutschland. (Hrsg.) *Kinder in Deutschland 2010. 2. World Vision Kinderstudie* (S. 35–59). Frankfurt a. M.: Fischer.

Andresen, S., Hurrelmann, K., & Schneekloth, U. (2012). Care and freedom. Theoretical and empirical aspects of children's well-being. *Child Indicators Research, 5*, 437–448.

Andresen, S., Mailand, S., Milanovic, D., & Blume, J. (2013). Erfahrungen und Erleben von Armut aus der Sicht von Kindern: »Ich würde meiner Familie was schenken und dafür sorgen, dass sie nicht so viel in Schwierigkeiten sind.« Unsere Jugend 65. Jg. (S. 123–129).

Autorengruppe Bildungsberichterstattung. (2012). *Bildung in Deutschland 2012.* Ein indikatorengestützter Bericht mit einer Analyse zu Perspektiven des Bildungswesens im demografischen Wandel. Bielefeld: W. Bertelsmann Verlag.

AWO-ISS. (2012). *Lebenssituation und Zukunftschancen von (armen) Kindern und Jugendlichen.* AWO-Verlag.

Bacher, J., Winkelhofer, U., & Teubner, M. (2007). Partizipation von Kindern in der Grundschule. In Alt, C. (Hrsg.), *Kinderleben – Start in die Grundschule* (Band 3: Ergebnisse aus der zweiten Welle, S. 137–163). Wiesbaden: Verlag für Sozialwissenschaften.

Baumert, J., Stanat, P., & Watermann, R. (Hrsg.). (2006). *Herkunftsbedingte Disparitäten im Bildungswesen.* Wiesbaden: Verlag für Sozialwissenschaften.

Baumrind, D. (1991). The influence of parenting style on adolescent competence and substance use. *Journal of early adolescence. Band 11, Heft 1*, S. 56–95.

Bertelsmann Ländermonitor Frühkindliche Bildungssysteme (o. J.) (2013) Tabelle 6, Tabelle 7, Tabelle 8 (Stand ab 2007). http://www.laendermonitor.de/downloads-presse/index.nc.html?no_cache=1 (Stand: 19.06.2013).

S. Andresen et al. (eds.), *Well-being, Poverty and Justice from a Child's Perspective*, Children's Well-Being: Indicators and Research 17,
DOI 10.1007/978-3-319-57574-2

BMAS (Bundesministerium für Arbeit und Soziales). (2013a). *Lebenslagen in Deutschland.* Der vierte Armuts- und Reichtumsbericht der Bundesregierung. (Endfassung: 06.03.2013). Verfügbar unter. http://www.bmas.de/.

BMAS (Bundesministerium für Arbeit und Soziales). (2013b). *Das Bildungspaket.* Das ist drin im Bildungspaket. Verfügbar unter. www.bildungspaket.bmas.de.

BMFSFJ. (2005). 12. Kinder- und Jugendbericht. Berlin: BT. Drs. 15/6014.

BMFSFJ. (2006). *Familie zwischen Flexibilität und Verlässlichkeit. Perspektiven für eine lebenslaufbezogene Familienpolitik.* 7. Familienbericht. Berlin: BT. Drs. 16/1360.

Bos, W., Klieme, E., & Köller, O. (Hrsg.). (2010). *Schulische Lerngelegenheiten und Kompetenzentwicklung.* Münster: Waxmann.

Bradshaw, J., Martorano, B., Natali, L., & de Neubourg, C. (2013) *Children's subjective well-being in rich countries* (Working Paper). UNICEF Office of Research, Florence.

Bremm, N. (2013). Schulen mit ganztägigem Angebot. Vorbereitung einer Typologie. *Diskurs Kindheits- und Jugendforschung* 12, S. 23–38.

Bundesarbeitsgemeinschaft der Landesjugendämter. (2013). *Sicherung der Rechte von Kindern als Qualitätsmerkmal von Kindertageseinrichtungen.* http://www.bagljae.de/downloads/114_sicherung-der-rechte-von-kindern-in-kitas.pdf (Stand: 24.06.2013).

Coleman, J. (1988). Social capital and the creating of human capital. *American Journal of Sociology, 94*, 95–120.

Cremer, H. (2012). Kinderrechte und der Vorrang des Kindeswohls. Die UN-Kinderrechtskonvention bietet ein weites Anwendungsfeld. *Anwaltspraxis, 4*, S. 327–329.

Dalbert, C. (1983). Die Gerechte-Welt-Skala (GWS). In Preiser, S. (Hrsg.), *Soziales Handeln im Kindes- und Jugendalter* (Dokumentation von Forschungs- und Diagnoseinstrumenten). Weinheim: Beltz, S. 139.

Dalbert, C., Montada, L., & Schmitt, M. (1987). Glaube an eine gerechte Welt als Motiv: Validierungskorrelate zweier Skalen. *Psychologische Beiträge, 29*, S. 596–615.

Deutscher Bundestag. (2013). Der 14. Kinder- und Jugendbericht. Bericht über die Lebenssituation junger Menschen und die Leistungen und Bestrebungen der Kinder- und Jugendhilfe Iin Deutschland. Deutscher Bundestag, Drucksache 17/12200. http://dip21.bundestag.de/dip21/btd/17/122/1712200.pdf (Stand: 24.06.2013).

DJI (Deutsches Jugendinstitut e.V.). (Hrsg.). (2011). *Sexuelle Gewalt gegen Kinder. Missbrauch in Institutionen, Forschungsergebnisse und Empfehlungen für einen besseren Kinderschutz.* München: DJI.

Essau, C. A. (2003). *Angst bei Kindern und Jugendlichen.* Stuttgart: UTB.

Fattore, T., Mason, J., & Watson, E. (2012): Locating the child centrally as subject in research: Towards a child interpretation of well-being. *Child Indicators Research, 5*(3), S. 423–435.

Fegter, S., & Richter, M. (2013). The capability approach as a framework for research on children's well-being. In A. Ben-Arieh, F. Casas, I. Frones, & J. Korbin (Eds.), *Handbook of child well-being: theory, indicators, measures and policies.* Dordrecht/Heidelberg/ London/New York: Springer. Chapter No. 151.

Fehr, E., Bernhard, H., & Rockenbach, B. (2008). Egalitarianism in young children. In *Nature* (Vol. 454, pp. 1079–1083).

Fischer, N., Holtappels, H. G., Rauschenbach, T., Stecher, L., & Zürchner, I. (Hrsg.). (2011). *Ganztagsschule; Entwicklung, Qualität, Wirkungen.* Weinheim: Beltz Juventa.

Fuhrer, U., & Uslucan, H.-H. (Hrsg.). (2005). *Familie, Akkulturation und Erziehung: Migration zwischen Eigen- und Fremdkultur.* Stuttgart: Kohlhammer.

Gauze, C., Bukowski, W. M., Aquan Assee, J., & Sippola, L. K. (1996). Interactions between family environment and friendship and associations with self perceived well-being during adolescence. *Child Development, 67*, 2201–2216.

Gifford-Smith, M. E., & Brownell, C. A. (2002). Childhood peer relationships: Social acceptance, friendships, and peer networks. *Journal of School Psychology, 41*, 235–284.

Glatzer, W. (2009). Gefühlte (Un)Gerechtigkeit. *Aus Politik und Zeitgeschichte, 47*/2009, S. 15–20.

Hadjar, A., & Becker, R. (Hrsg.). (2006). *Die Bildungsexpansion*. Wiesbaden: Verlag für Sozialwissenschaften.

Hamann, K., Warneken, F., Greenberg, J. R., & Tomasello, M. (2011). Collaboration encourages equal sharing in children but not chimpanzees. *Nature*. doi: 10.1038/nature10278. http://wkprc.eva.mpg.de/pdf/2011/Hamann_Warneken_Greenberg_Tomasello_2011.pdf (Stand: 20.08.2013).

HBSC-Team Deutschland. (2011). Studie Health Behaviour in School-aged Children – Faktenblatt »Lebenszufriedenheit von Kindern und Jugendlichen". Bielefeld: WHO Collaborating Centre for Child and Adolescent Health Promotion.

Hernandez, D. J., & Marotz, K. G. (2012). Disparities in child well-being across income groups: Trends in the U.S. from 1985 to 2008. *Child Indicators Research*, *5*(1) S. 93–121.

Hinsch, W. (2002). *Gerechtfertigte Ungleichheiten: Grundsätze sozialer Gerechtigkeit*. Berlin: Walter de Gruyter.

Holst, E., & Seifert, H. (2012). Arbeitszeitpolitische Kontroversen im Spiegel der Arbeitszeitwünsche. *WSI-Mitteilungen*, *2*/2012, S. 141–149.

Hopf, W. (2010). *Freiheit-Leistung-Ungleichheit. Bildung und soziale Herkunft in Deutschland*. Weinheim: Beltz.

Hunner-Kreisel, C., & Stephan, M. (Hrsg.). (2013). *Neue Zeiten, neue Räume: Kindheit und Familie im Kontext von (Trans-)Migration und sozialem Wandel*. Wiesbaden: Verlag für Sozialwissenschaften.

Hurrelmann, K., & Schultz, T. (Hrsg.). (2012). *Jungen als Bildungsverlierer*. Weinheim: Beltz Juventa.

Hurrelmann, K., & Timm, A. (2011). *Kinder, Bildung, Zukunft Drei Wege aus der Krise*. Stuttgart: Klett.

Hurrelmann, K., Quenzel, G., & Rathmann, K. (2011). Bildungspolitik als Bestandteil moderner Wohlfahrtspolitik. *Zeitschrift für Soziologie der Erziehung und Sozialisation, 31*, S. 313–328.

Ittel, A., & Scheithauer, H. (2007). Geschlecht als »Stärke« oder »Risiko«? Überlegungen zur geschlechterspezifischen Resilienz. In Opp, G., & Fingerle, M. (Hrsg.). *Was Kinder stärkt. Erziehung zwischen Risiko und Resilienz* (S. 98–115). München/Basel: Reinhardt.

Jampert, K., Zehnbauer, A., Sens, A., Leuckefeld, K., & Laier, M. (Hrsg.). (2009). *Kinder-Sprache stärken. Aufwachsen mit mehreren Sprachen. Praxismaterial*. Weimar/Berlin: Das Netz.

Klieme, E., Artelt, C., Hartig, J., Jude, N., Köller, O., Prenze, M., Schneider, W., & Stanat, P. (Hrsg.). (2010) *PISA 2009. Bilanz nach einem Jahrzehnt*. Münster/ New York/ München/ Berlin: Waxmann.

KMK Sekretariat. (2012). *Allgemein bildende Schulen in Ganztagsform in Ländern der Bundesrepublik Deutschland*. Bonn und Berlin: KMK.

Kohlberg, L. (1964). The development of moral character and ideology. In M. L. Hoffmann (Ed.), *Review of child development research*. New York: Wiley.

Kohlberg, L. (1974). *Zur kognitiven Entwicklung des Kindes*. Frankfurt: Suhrkamp.

LBS-Kinderbarometer. (2011). *Stimmungen, Trends und Meinungen von Kindern aus Deutschland*. Recklinghausen: RDN Verlag.

Leven, I., & Schneekloth, U. (2007). Die Freizeit. Anregen lassen oder fernsehen. In World Vision Deutschland. (Hrsg.), *Kinder in Deutschland 2007. 1. World Vision Kinderstudie* (S. 165–200). Frankfurt a. M.: Fischer.

Leven, I., & Schneekloth, U. (2010). Die Schule: Frühe Vergabe von Lebenschancen. In World Vision Deutschland. (Hrsg.), *Kinder in Deutschland 2010* (S. 161–185). Frankfurt a. M.: Fischer.

Liebig, S., & Lengfeld, H. (Hrsg.). (2002). *Interdisziplinäre Gerechtigkeitsforschung. Zur Verknüpfung empirischer und normativer Perspektiven*. Hamburg: Campus.

Liebig, S., & May, M. (2009). Dimensionen sozialer Gerechtigkeit. *Aus Politik und Zeitgeschichte, 47*/2009, S. 3–8.

Luthar, S. S. (1999). *Poverty and children's adjustment*. Thousand Oaks: Sage.

Maaz, K., Baumert, J., Gresch, C., & McElvany, N. (Hrsg.). (2010) *Der Übergang von der Grundschule in die weiterführenden Schulen*. Berlin und Bonn: BMBF.

Medienpädagogischer Forschungsverbund Südwest. (Hrsg.). (2012). *FIM-Studie (2011): Familie, Interaktion & Medien*. Untersuchung zur Kommunikation und Mediennutzung in Familien. Stuttgart: Medienpädagogischer Forschungsverbund Südwest: LFK.

Meiland, S., Andresen, S., Milanovic, D., & Blume, J. (2013a) Denkst du, die Kinder sind hier arm? Sichtweisen und Erfahrungen von Kindern in prekären Lebenslagen. In Fisher, D., Gathen, J., Höhmann, K., Klaffke, T., Rademacker, H. (Hrsg.). *Friedrich Jahresheft XXXI 2013, Schule und Armut* (S. 16–18). Oldenburg: Friedrich Verlag.

Meiland, S., Andresen, S., Milanovic, D., & Blume, J. (2013b). *Erfahrungen und Erleben von Armut aus der Sicht von Kindern: »Ich würde meiner Familie was schenken und dafür sorgen, dass sie nicht so viel in Schwierigkeiten sind.«* Unsere Jugend 65. Jg. (S. 123–129).

Minkkinen, J. (2013). The structural model of child well-being. *Child Indicators Research, 6*(3), 547–558.

Morschitzky, H. (2009). *Angststörungen. Diagnostik, Konzepte, Theorie, Selbsthilfe* (4. Auflage). Heidelberg: Springer.

Oerter, R., & Montada, L. (Hrsg.). (2002). *Entwicklungspsychologie* (5. vollständig überarbeitete Auflage). Weinheim: Beltz.

O'Hare, W. P., & Gutierrez, F. (2012). The use of domains in constructing a comprehensive composite index of child well-being. *Child Indicators Research, 5*, 609–629.

Olk, T., & Roth, R. (2007). *Mehr Partizipation wagen*. Gütersloh: Bertelsmann Stiftung.

Parker, J. G., & Gottman, J. M. (1989). Social and emotional development in a relational context; Friendship interaction from early childhood to adolescence. In Berndt, T. J. & Ladd, G. W. (Hrsg.), *Peer relationships in child development*. Zitiert nach: Oerter, R., & Montada, L. (1998) *Entwicklungspsychologie. Ein Lehrbuch*. Weinheim: Beltz.

Piaget, J. (1932/1983). *Das moralische Urteil beim Kinde*. Stuttgart: Klett.

Piaget, J. (1937/1975). *Der Aufbau der Wirklichkeit beim Kinde*. Stuttgart: Klett.

Piaget, J. (1999). *Über Pädagogik*. Beltz: Weinheim.

Prazen, A., Wolfinger, N. H., Cahill, C., & Kowaleski-Jones, L. (2011). Joint physical custody and neighborhood friendships in middle childhood. *Sociological Inquiry, 81*(2), 247–259.

Pupeter, M., & Schneekloth, U. (2010). Die Gleichaltrigen: Gemeinsame – getrennte Welten?. In World Vision Deutschland. (Hrsg.), *Kinder in Deutschland 2010. 2. World Vision Kinderstudie* (S. 141–160). Frankfurt a. M.: Fischer.

Quenzel, G., & Hurrelmann, K. (Hrsg.). (2010). *Bildungsverlierer*. Wiesbaden: Verlag für Sozialwissenschaften.

Rawls, J. (1971). *A theory of justice*. Harvard University Press.

Robert Bosch Stiftung. (2012). *Starke Kinder – starke Familie. Wohlbefinden von Kindern in Städten und Gemeinden*. Stuttgart: Robert Bosch Stiftung.

Salvas, M.-C., Vitaro, F., Brendgen, M., Lacourse, E., Boivin, M., & Tremblay, R. E. (2011). Interplay between friends' aggression and friendship quality in the development of child aggression during the early school years. *Social Development, 20*(4), 645–663.

Schneekloth, U. (2010). Jugend und Politik: Aktuelle Entwicklungstrends und Perspektiven. In Shell Deutschland Holding. (Hrsg.), *Jugend 2010. Eine pragmatische Generation behauptet sich* (16. Shell Jugendstudie). Frankfurt a. M.: Fischer, S. 129–164.

Schneekloth, U., & Leven, I. (2007). Familie als Zentrum: nicht für alle gleich verlässlich. In World Vision Deutschland. (Hrsg.), *Kinder in Deutschland 2007. 1. World Vision Kinderstudie* (S. 65–109). Frankfurt a. M.: Fischer.

Schneekloth, U., & Pupeter, M. (2010a). Familie als Zentrum: Bunt und vielfältig, aber nicht für alle Kinder gleich verlässlich. In World Vision Deutschland. (Hrsg.), *Kinder in Deutschland 2010. 2. World Vision Kinderstudie* (S. 61–94). Frankfurt a. M.: Fischer.

Schneekloth, U., & Pupeter, M. (2010b). Wohlbefinden, Wertschätzung, Selbstwirksamkeit: Was Kinder für ein gutes Leben brauchen. In World Vision Deutschland. (Hrsg.), *Kinder in Deutschland 2010. 2. World Vision Kinderstudie* (S. 187–221). Frankfurt a. M: Fischer.

Schneewind, K. A. (2008). Sozialisation in der Familie. In Hurrelmann, K., Grundmann, M., & Walper, S. (Hrsg.), *Handbuch Sozialisationsforschung* (7. vollst. überarbeitete Auflage, S. 256–273). Weinheim: Beltz.

Schroeder, D., Picot, S., & Andresen, S. (2010). Die qualitative Studie: 12 Porträts von Kinderpersönlichkeiten. In World Vision Deutschland. (Hrsg.), *Kinder in Deutschland 2010. 2. World Vision Kinderstudie* (S. 223–240). Frankfurt a. M.: Fischer.

Sen, A. (2010). *Die Idee der Gerechtigkeit*. München: C. H. Beck Verlag.

Sikorski, U., & Kuchler, B. (2011). Wer muss worauf verzichten? Einschätzungen zur Wohn- und Lebenssituation der privaten Haushalte. *Wirtschaft und Statistik, 5*/2011, S. 484–492.

Stange, W., Meinhold-Henschel, S., & Schack, S. (2009). Mitwirkung (er)leben. *Handbuch zur Durchführung von Beteiligungsprojekten mit Kindern und Jugendlichen*. Gütersloh: Bertelsmann Stiftung.

Statistisches Bundesamt. (2009). *Bevölkerung und Erwerbstätigkeit-Einbürgerung 2008* (Fachserie 1 Reihe 2.1). Wiesbaden.

Statistisches Bundesamt. (2011a). *Bevölkerung und Erwerbstätigkeit. Bevölkerung mit Migrationshintergrund-Ergebnisse des Mikrozensus 2010* (Fachserie 1 Reihe 2.2). Wiesbaden.

Statistisches Bundesamt. (2011b). Pressemitteilung Nr. 345 vom 20. September 2011: Knapp die Hälfte der Großstadtkinder aus Familien mit Migrationshintergrund. Wiesbaden.

Stecher, L., Krüger, H. H., & Rauschenbach, T. (Hrsg.). (2011). *Ganztagsschule – neue Schule?* Wiesbaden: Verlag für Sozialwissenschaften.

Stubbe, T. (2009). *Bildungsentscheidungen und sekundäre Herkunftseffekte*. Münster: Waxmann.

Tracy, R. (2007). *Wie Kinder Sprachen lernen. Und wie wir sie dabei unterstützen können.* Tübingen: Francke.

Trautner, H. M. (1991). *Lehrbuch der Entwicklungspsychologie* (Bd. 2: Theorien und Befunde). Göttingen: Hogrefe.

UNICEF. (2012). *Measuring child poverty*. New league tables of child poverty in the world's rich countries. Report Card 10, Innocenti Research Centre, online unter. www.unicef-irc.org/publications/pdf/rc10_eng.pdf (Stand: 14.07.2013).

UNICEF. (2013a). The state of the world's children 2013: Children with disabilities. online: http://www.unicef.org/sowc2013/files/SWCR2013_ENG_Lo_res_24_Apr_2013.pdf (Stand: 14.07.2013).

UNICEF. (2013b). *Child well-being in rich countries. A comparative overview* (Innocenti Report Card 11 (UNICEF)).

Uslucan, H. H. (2008). Männlichkeitsbilder, Familie und Erziehung in den Communities von Zuwanderern. *Berliner Forum Gewaltprävention* (BFG Nr. 34).

Woodward, L. J., & Fergusson, D. M. (2001). Life course of young people with anxiety disorders in adolescence. *Journal of the American Academy of Child and Adolescent Psychiatry, 40*, 1086–1093.

Zander, M. (2013). Resilienz – Gender – Prekäre Lebenslagen. Wie kann eine gendersensible Resilienzförderung aussehen? *Betrifft Mädchen, 3*/2013.

Index

S. Andresen et al. (eds.), *Well-being, Poverty and Justice from a Child's Perspective*, Children's Well-Being: Indicators and Research 17,
DOI 10.1007/978-3-319-57574-2